KAWASAKI

80·450cc SINGLES·1966-1977

SERVICE · REPAIR · PERFORMANCE

ERIC JORGENSEN
Editor

JEFF ROBINSON
Publisher

CLYMER PUBLICATIONS

World's largest publisher of books devoted exclusively to
automobiles and motorcycles.

12860 MUSCATINE STREET · P.O. BOX 20 · ARLETA, CALIFORNIA 91331

FIRST EDITION
First Printing November, 1971

SECOND EDITION
Revised to include 1972 models
Published April, 1972

THIRD EDITION
Revised to include 1973 models
Published September, 1973

FOURTH EDITION
Revised to include 1974 models
Published June, 1974

FIFTH EDITION
Revised to include 1975-1976 models
Published June, 1976

SIXTH EDITION
Revised by David Sales to include 1977 models
First Printing April, 1977
Second Printing September, 1977
Third Printing September, 1978
Fourth Printing April, 1979
Fifth Printing September, 1979
Sixth Printing April, 1980

Printed in U.S.A.

ISBN: 0-89287-152-0

MOTORCYCLE INDUSTRY COUNCIL

Technical assistance by Sullivan's Cycle Sales, Simi Valley, California

•

Cover photo by Steve French, Looking Glass Photography, Willows, California

Chapter One
General Information

1

Chapter Two
Periodic Maintenance

2

Chapter Three
Engine, Transmission, and Clutch

3

Chapter Four
Electrical System

4

Chapter Five
Carburetion

5

Chapter Six
Frame, Suspension, and Steering

6

Chapter Seven
Troubleshooting

7

Chapter Eight
Performance Improvement

8

Appendix
Specifications

9

Index

10

CONTENTS

QUICK REFERENCE DATA VII

CHAPTER ONE

GENERAL INFORMATION 1

Service hints
Tools
Expendable supplies

Mechanic's tips
Safety first

CHAPTER TWO

PERIODIC MAINTENANCE 8

Engine tune-up
Clutch adjustment
Electrical equipment
Drive chain
Brakes

Wheels and tires
Fork oil
Steering head bearings
Swinging arm

CHAPTER THREE

ENGINE, TRANSMISSION, AND CLUTCH 24

Rotary valve engines
Piston port engines
Engine lubrication
Preparation for engine
    disassembly
Engine removal
Cylinder and cylinder head
Piston, piston pin and
    piston rings
Left crankcase cover
Flywheel magneto and
    starter-generator

Engine sprocket
Right crankcase cover
Primary drive gear
Clutch
Rotary valve
Gearshift mechanism
Crankcase
Kickstarter
Crankshaft
Transmission
Drain pump

CHAPTER FOUR

ELECTRICAL SYSTEM 93

Flywheel magneto
Magneto troubleshooting
Starter-generator
Starter-generator troubleshooting
Rectifier
High voltage cable

Capacitor discharge ignition
    system operation
Solid state voltage regulator
Lights
Horn
Main switch
Battery

CHAPTER FIVE

CARBURETION 112

Operation
Overhaul
Adjustment

Components
Miscellaneous carburetor problems

CHAPTER SIX

FRAME, SUSPENSION, AND STEERING 131

Handlebars
Wheels and tires
Brakes
Front forks
Steering system
Shock absorbers
Fenders

Swinging arm
Rear sprocket
Fuel and oil tanks
Seat
Stands and footrests
Exhaust pipe and muffler
Drive chain

CHAPTER SEVEN

TROUBLESHOOTING 163

Operating requirements
Starting difficulties
Poor idling
Misfiring
Flat spots
Power loss
Overheating
Backfiring

Engine noises
Piston seizure
Excessive vibration
Clutch slip or drag
Poor handling
Brake problems
Lighting problems
Troubleshooting guide

CHAPTER EIGHT

PERFORMANCE IMPROVEMENT 168

What do you want?
Restoration
Specifications
Weight reduction
Lighting
Wheels, brakes, and hubs
Axles
Tubes and tires
Gearing
Chain tensioner
Frame
Suspension and handling
  improvement
Rear suspension
Steering and front suspension
Transmission
Clutch
Exhaust system

Ignition system
Battery
Ignition coil
Spark plugs
Electronic ignition systems
Fuel system
Carburetor
Air cleaner
Engine lubrication
Cylinder head
Rotary valve
Connecting rods
Piston
Piston rings
Cylinder
Summary
Performance parts and service
  suppliers

APPENDIX

SPECIFICATIONS 198

INDEX 209

QUICK REFERENCE DATA

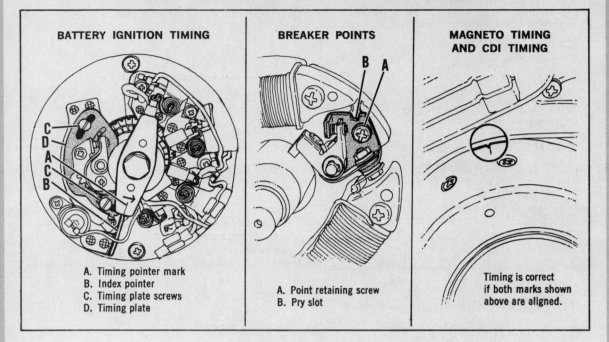

BATTERY IGNITION TIMING

A. Timing pointer mark
B. Index pointer
C. Timing plate screws
D. Timing plate

BREAKER POINTS

A. Point retaining screw
B. Pry slot

MAGNETO TIMING AND CDI TIMING

Timing is correct if both marks shown above are aligned.

IGNITION SPECIFICATIONS

Breaker point gap	0.012-0.016 in. (0.30-0.40mm)
Spark plug gap	0.024 in. (0.6mm)

IGNITION TIMING

Model	mm	(inches)	Degrees	Model	mm	(inches)	Degrees
J1, G1L	1.58	(0.062)	19°	KX125	1.91	(0.075)	20° @ 6,000
G1M	2.30	(0.090)	23°	F2	2.09	(0.082)	20°
GA1, GA2, G3SS,	1.96	(0.077)	20°	F3	2.75	(0.108)	23°
G3TR, MC1,				F7	2.94	(0.116)	23° @ 6,000
G4, G5				KE175	2.69	(0.106)	22° @ 4,000
G31M	2.51	(0.099)	23°	F21M, F4	3.09	(0.121)	23°
KE100, KH100,	1.96	(0.077)	20°	KT250	3.25	(0.128)	23° @ 4,000
KV100				KX250	2.90	(0.114)	22° @ 6,000
C1D	1.97	(0.078)	20°	F81M	2.34	(0.092)	19°
C2SS	1.78	(0.070)	19°	F5, F9	3.41	(0.134)	23° @ 6,000
B1L	1.93	(0.076)	20°	F8	2.59	(0.101)	20°
B1M	2.33	(0.092)	22°	KX400	3.20	(0.125)	23° @ 6,000
F6	2.94	(0.116)	23°	KX450	4.48	(0.176)	25° @ 5,000
KD125, KS125,	2.52	(0.099)	23°				
KE125							

ADJUSTMENTS

Clutch cable free play	See Chapter Three
Starter and throttle cables free play	0.2-0.3 in. (5.0-7.5mm)
Drive chain free play	¾-1 in. (20-25mm)
Front brake cable free play	Approximately 1 in. (25mm)
Rear brake pedal free play	1.0-1.4 in. (25-35mm)

RECOMMENDED FUEL AND LUBRICANTS

Engine oil	A good quality 2-cycle engine oil
Transmission oil	SAE 10W/30 or 10W/40 motor oil
Front forks	SAE 5W/20 motor oil or ATF (automatic transmission fluid)
Drive chain	SAE 90 oil or special chain lubricant
Fuel	85-95 (Research) octane

SPARK PLUG APPLICATION

Model	NGK	ND
GA1, GA2	B-7HZ	W24F
G3SS, G4TR, G5	B-8HC	W25FC
C1D, B1L	B-7H	W225T1
F5, F9	B-10H	W31FS
B1M, F21M, G1L, G1M, G31M	B-8HN	W25FN
F4, F81M, F7	B-9HCS	W27FC
F8, F3, KS125, F6, KD125, G3TR, G5	B-8HCS	W25FC
C2SS, F2, MC1, KV100, G4, G4TR,2 KT250	B-7HS	W22FS
KX125, KX250, KX400	B-9EV	W27ESG
KX450, KE175	B-9HS	W27FS
KH100, KE100, KE125	B-8HS	W24FS

BATTERY APPLICATION

Battery	Model
6N2-2A-3	F5, F8, F9, early G4TR
6N4-2A-3	Early G3SS and G3TR; GA1, GA2, J1, G1L, C2SS
6N4-2A-5	G5, F6, F7; later G3SS and G3TR, and G4TR; MC1
6N4B-2A-2	F9 A, B, C
12N12-3B	B1L, F2, F3
12N10-4B	C1D

TIRE PRESSURE

Tire Size	Tire Pressure Pounds per Square Inch Front	Rear
3.00-16	23	28
2.50-18	23	28
2.75-18	23	28
3.00-18	23	28
3.25-18	23	28
3.25-18	14*	14*
3.50-18	23	28
4.00-18	23	28
3.00-19	23	28
3.00-21	14*	14*

*Motocross racing

IDLE SPEED

Model	Idle rpm
J1, G1L, G series	900-1,100
KE, KH, KV100	900-1,100
KD, KE, KS125	1,300
F2, F3, F4, F6	900-1,100
C1D, C2SS	900-1,100
B1 series	900-1,100
F5, F7, F8, F9	1,000-1,300
KE175	1,300

FORK OIL QUANTITY

Model	Ounces	(cc)
J1, G1 Series	4.6	(135)
M Series	3.0	(90)
GA, G3 Series	4.4	(130)
G4TR, G5	5.7	(170)
F21M	5.7	(170)
KE, KH, KV100	5.7	(170)
F21M	5.7	(170)
KD, KE, KS125	5.0	(150)
KX125	4.0	(120)
KE175	5.0	(150)
G31M-A, F7	3.9	(115)
C1D, F2, B1 Series	5.9	(175)
C2SS (early)	4.0	(120)
C2SS (late), F6	5.9	(175)
F3	6.0	(180)
F4	6.6	(195)
F5, F8, F9, F81M	5.9	(175)
KT250	5.7	(170)
KX250	6.8	(200)
KX400, KX450	6.0	(180)

TIGHTENING TORQUES

Cylinder head	
8mm nuts	15 ft.-lb. (2.0 mkg)
10mm nuts	25 ft.-lb. (3.5 mkg)
Flywheel nut	
F5, F7, F8, F9	72 ft.-lb. (10 mkg)
All other models	36 ft.-lb. (5 mkg)
Primary pinion gear nut	36 ft.-lb. (5 mkg)
Spark plug	18.5-21 ft.-lb. (2.5-3.0 mkg)

KAWASAKI
80-450cc SINGLES · 1966-1977
SERVICE · REPAIR · PERFORMANCE

CHAPTER ONE

GENERAL INFORMATION

This book was written to provide service guidance to owners of Kawasaki motorcycles. Its contents cover all popular single-cylinder models since 1966.

SERVICE HINTS

Most of the service procedures described in this book are straightforward, and can be performed by anyone who is reasonably handy with tools. It is suggested, however, that you consider your own capabilities carefully before you attempt any operation which involves major disassembly of the engine.

Crankshaft disassembly, for example, requires the use of a press. It would be wiser to have that operation performed by a shop equipped for such work, rather than to try it with makeshift equipment. Other procedures require precision measurements. Unless you have the skills and equipment to make these measurements, call on a competent service outlet.

You will find that repairs will go much faster and easier if your machine is clean before you begin work. There are special cleaners for washing the engine and related parts. You just brush or spray on the cleaning solution, let it stand, and rinse it away with a garden hose. Clean all oily or greasy parts with cleaning solvent as you

remove them. *Never use gasoline as a cleaning agent.* Gasoline presents an extreme fire hazard. Be sure to work in a well ventilated area when you use cleaning solvent. Keep a fire extinguisher handy, just in case.

Special tools are required for some service procedures. These tools may be purchased at Kawasaki dealers. If you are on good terms with the dealer's service department, you may be able to use his.

Much of the labor charge for repairs made by dealers is for removal and disassembly of other parts to reach the defective one. It is frequently possible for you to do all of this yourself, then take the affected subassembly, such as the crankshaft mentioned earlier, into the dealer for repair.

Once you decide to tackle the job yourself, read the entire section in this manual which pertains to the job. Study the illustrations and the text until you have a good idea of what is involved. If special tools are required, make arrangements to get them before you start the job. It is frustrating to get partly into a job and find that you are unable to complete it.

TOOLS

Every motorcyclist should carry a small tool kit with him, to help make minor roadside adjustments and repairs. A suggested kit, available at most dealers, is shown in **Figure 1**.

For more extensive servicing, an assortment of ordinary hand tools is required. As a minimum, have the following available. Note that all threaded fasteners are metric sizes.

1. Combination wrenches
2. Socket wrenches
3. Assorted screwdrivers
4. Assorted pliers
5. Spark plug gauge
6. Spark plug wrench
7. Small hammer
8. Plastic mallet
9. Parts cleaning brush

A few special tools may also be required. The first 4 can be considered essential.

1. *Flywheel puller* (**Figure 2**). Bikes with magnetos require that the flywheel be removed to gain access to the breaker points. This tool costs around $6, and it is available at most motorcycle shops or by mail order from accessory dealers. Be sure to specify the model of your machine when ordering. There is no satisfactory substitute for this tool; but there have been many unhappy owners who bought expensive new crankshafts and flywheels after trying makeshift flywheel removal methods.

2. *Ignition gauge* (**Figure 3**). This tool combines round wire spark plug gap gauges with narrow breaker point feeler gauges. Most bikes with magnetos require that point gap be adjusted through a narrow slot in the flywheel. Standard feeler gauges will not fit through this slot, making point gap adjustment difficult or impossible. This tool costs about $3 at auto accessory stores.

3. *Timing tester* (**Figure 4**). This unit signals the instant when breaker points just open. On

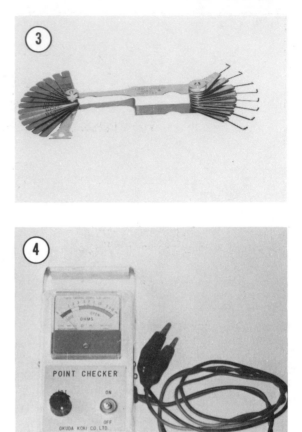

models with magnetos, this point is sometimes difficult to determine with a test light or ohmmeter, because the breaker points are shunted by a low-resistance coil.

4. *Hydrometer* (**Figure 5**). This tool measures charge of the battery, and tells much about battery condition. Available at any auto parts store and through most mail order outlets, a typical hydrometer costs less than $3.

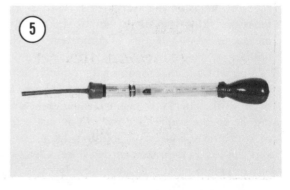

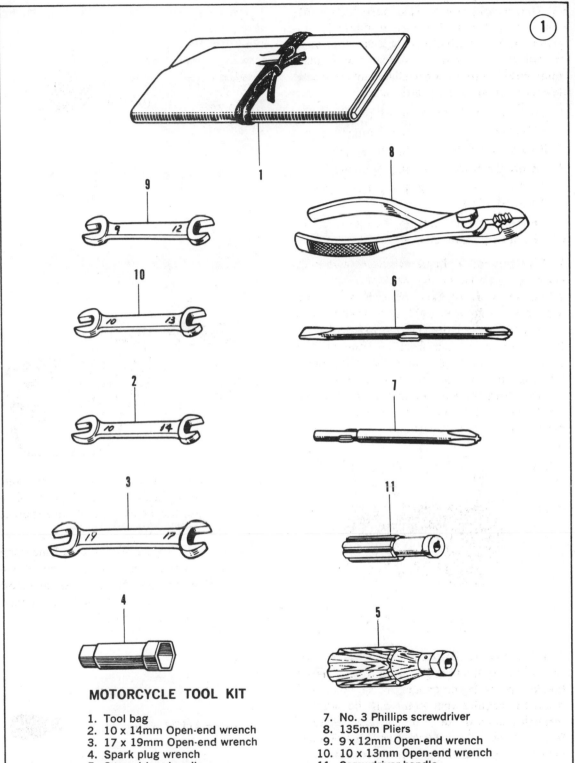

MOTORCYCLE TOOL KIT

1. Tool bag
2. 10 x 14mm Open-end wrench
3. 17 x 19mm Open-end wrench
4. Spark plug wrench
5. Screwdriver handle
6. No. 2 Phillips and slotted
   screwdriver
7. No. 3 Phillips screwdriver
8. 135mm Pliers
9. 9 x 12mm Open-end wrench
10. 10 x 13mm Open-end wrench
11. Screwdriver handle

5. *Multimeter, or VOM* (**Figure 6**). This instrument is invaluable for electrical system troubleshooting and service. A few of its functions may be duplicated by locally fabricated substitutes, but for the serious hobbyist, it's a must. Its uses are described in the applicable sections of this book. Prices start at around $10 at electronics hobbyists stores and mail order outlets.

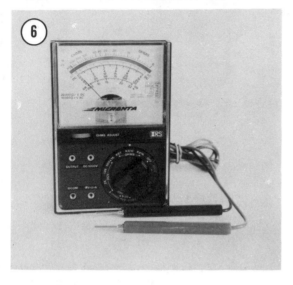

6. *Compression gauge* (**Figure 7**). An engine with low compression cannot be properly tuned and will not develop full power. The compression gauge shown has a flexible stem, which enables it to reach cylinders where there is little clearance between the cylinder head and frame. Inexpensive gauges start at around $3, and are available at auto accessory stores or by mail order.

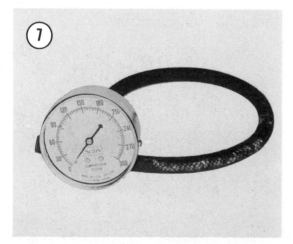

7. *Impact driver* (**Figure 8**). This tool might have been designed with the motorcyclist in mind. It makes removal of engine cover screws easy, and eliminates damaged screw slots. Good ones run about $12 at larger hardware stores.

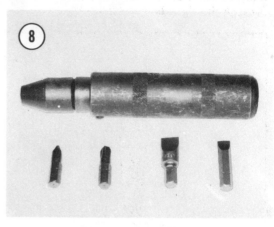

EXPENDABLE SUPPLIES

Certain expendable supplies are also required. These include grease, oil, gasket cement, wiping rags, cleaning solvent, and distilled water. Cleaning solvent is available at many service stations. Distilled water, required for battery service, is available at every supermarket. It is sold for use in steam irons, and is quite inexpensive.

MECHANIC'S TIPS

Removing Frozen Nuts and Screws

When a fastener rusts and cannot be removed, several methods may be used to loosen it. First apply penetrating oil liberally. Rap the fastener several times with a small hammer; don't hit it hard enough to cause damage.

For frozen screws, apply oil as described, then insert a screwdriver in the slot and rap the top of the screwdriver with a hammer. This loosens the rust so the screw can be removed in the normal way. If the screw head is too chewed up to use a screwdriver, grip the head with vise-type pliers and turn the screw out.

For a frozen bolt or nut, apply penetrating oil, then rap it with a hammer. Turn off with the proper size wrench. If the points are rounded off, grip with vise-type pliers as described for screws.

Stripped Threads

Occasionally, threads are stripped through carelessness or impact damage. Often the threads can be cleaned up by running a tap (for internal threads) or die (for external threads) through the threads. See **Figure 9**.

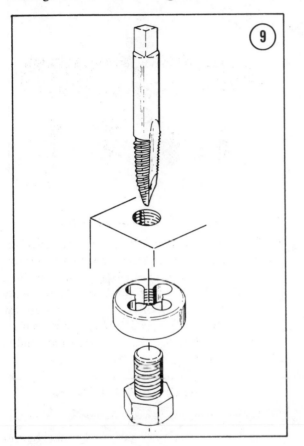

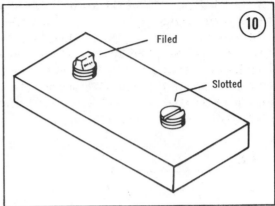

Broken Screw or Bolt

When the head breaks off a screw or bolt, several methods are available for removing the remaining portion.

If a large portion of the remainder projects out, try gripping it with vise-type pliers. If the projection portion is too small, try filing it to fit a wrench or cut a slot in it to fit a screwdriver. See **Figure 10**.

If the head breaks off flush, as it usually does, remove it with a screw extractor. Refer to **Figure 11**. Center-punch the broken part, then drill a hole into it. Drill sizes are marked on the tool. Tap the extractor into the broken part, then back it out with a wrench.

Removing Damaged Screws

WARNING
When removing screws by this method, always wear suitable eye protection.

CAUTION
Use clean rags to cover bearings or any other parts which might be harmed by metal chips produced during this procedure.

Figure 12 illustrates damaged screws typical of those on many bikes. Such screws may usually be removed easily by drilling. Select a bit with a diameter larger than that of the damaged screw, but smaller than its head, then drill into the screw head (**Figure 13**) until the head separates from the screw. The remainder of the screw may then be turned out easily. **Figure 14** illustrates one screw head removed in this manner. The other has been drilled to just the point where the head is separating from the screw body. Note that there is no damage to the plate which these screws retain.

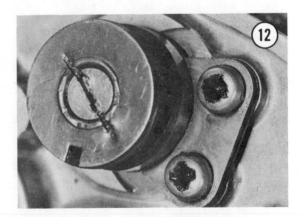

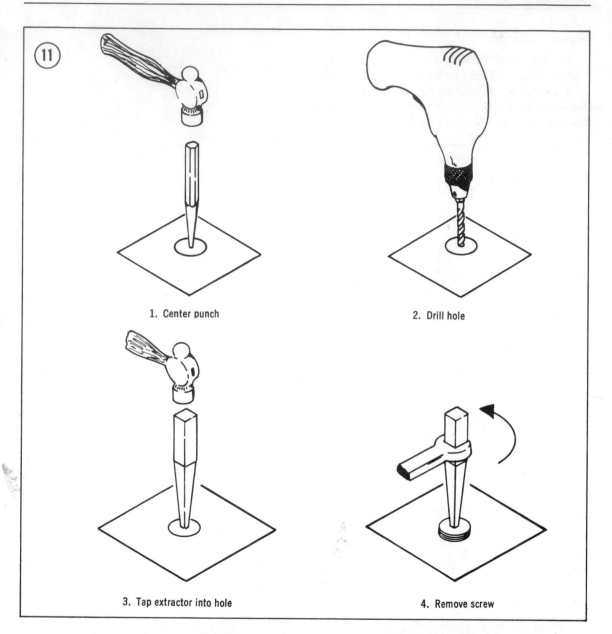

1. Center punch

2. Drill hole

3. Tap extractor into hole

4. Remove screw

SAFETY FIRST

Professional mechanics can work for years without sustaining serious injury. If you observe a few rules of common sense and safety, you can also enjoy many safe hours servicing your own machine. You can also hurt yourself or damage the bike if you ignore these rules:

1. Never use gasoline as a cleaning solvent.

2. Never smoke or use a torch near flammable liquids, such as cleaning solvent in open containers.

3. Never smoke or use a torch in an area where batteries are charging. Highly explosive hydrogen gas is formed during the charging process.

4. If welding or brazing is required on the machine, remove the fuel tank to a safe distance, at least 50 feet away.

5. Be sure to use proper size wrenches for nut turning.

6. If a nut is tight, think for a moment what would happen to your hand should the wrench slip. Be guided accordingly.

7. Keep your work area clean and uncluttered.

8. Wear safety goggles in all operations involving drilling, grinding, or use of a chisel.

9. Never use worn tools.

10. Keep a fire extinguisher handy. Be sure that it is rated for gasoline and electrical fires.

CHAPTER TWO

PERIODIC MAINTENANCE

To gain the utmost in safety, performance, and useful life from your motorcycle, it is necessary to make periodic inspections and adjustments. It frequently happens that minor problems found during such inspections are simple and inexpensive to correct at the time, but could lead to major failures later. This chapter describes such services.

Table 1 is a suggested maintenance schedule.

Table 1   MAINTENANCE SCHEDULE

Maintenance Item	Mile		
	Initial 500	1,000	2,000
Change oil	X	X	
Engine tune-up	X		X
Adjust clutch	X		X
Clean exhaust system			X
Adjust brakes	X	X	
Inspect and adjust chain	X		X
Check spokes	X	X	
Tighten all fastenings	X		X
Check battery	X	X	
Check electrical equipment	X	X	

ENGINE TUNE-UP

The number of definitions of the term "tune-up" is probably equal to the number of people defining it. For purposes of this book, we will define a tune-up as a general adjustment and/or maintenance of all service items to ensure continued peak operating efficiency of a motorcycle engine.

As part of a proper tune-up, some service procedures are essential. The following paragraphs discuss details of these procedures. Service operations should be performed in the order specified. Unless otherwise specified, the engine should be thoroughly cool before starting any tune-up service.

Spark Plug

As the first step in any tune-up, remove and examine the spark plug, because spark plug condition can tell much about engine condition and carburetor adjustment.

To remove the spark plug, first clean the area around its base to prevent dirt or other foreign material from entering the cylinder. Then unscrew the spark plug, using a suitable deep socket. If difficulty is encountered removing a spark plug, apply penetrating oil to its base and allow some 20 minutes for the oil to work in. It may also be helpful to rap the cylinder head lightly with a rubber or plastic mallet; this procedure sets up vibrations which help the penetrating oil to work in. Be careful not to break any cooling fins when tapping the cylinder head.

Figure 1 illustrates various conditions which might be encountered upon plug removal.

Normal condition—If plugs have a light tan or gray colored deposit and no abnormal gap wear or erosion, this indicates good engine, carburetion, and ignition condition. The plug is of the proper heat range, and may be serviced and returned to use.

Carbon fouled—Soft, dry sooty deposits are evidence of incomplete combustion and can usually be attributed to rich carburetion. The condition is also sometimes caused by weak ignition, retarded timing, or low compression. Such a plug may usually be cleaned and returned to service, but the condition which causes fouling should be corrected.

Oil fouled—This plug exhibits a black insulator tip, damp oily film over the firing end, and a carbon layer over the entire nose. Electrodes will not be worn. Common causes for this condition are listed below:

    a. Improper fuel/oil mixture

    b. Wrong type of oil

    c. Idle speed too low

    d. Idle mixture too rich

    e. Clogged air filter

    f. Weak ignition

    g. Excessive idling

    h. Oil pump out of adjustment

    i. Wrong spark plugs (too cold)

Oil-fouled spark plugs may be cleaned in a pinch, but it is better to replace them. It is important to correct the cause of fouling before the engine is returned to service.

Gap bridging—Plugs with this condition exhibit gaps shorted out by combustion chamber deposits fused between electrodes. Any of the following may be the cause.

    a. Improper fuel/oil mixture

    b. Clogged exhaust

    c. Oil pump misadjusted

Be sure to locate and correct the cause of this spark plug condition. Such plugs must be replaced with new ones.

Overheated—Overheated spark plugs exhibit burned electrodes. The insulator tip will be light gray or even chalk white. The most common cause for this condition is using a spark plug of the wrong heat range (too hot). If it is known that the correct plug is used, other causes are lean fuel mixture, engine overloading or lugging, loose carburetor mounting, or timing advanced too far. Always correct the fault before putting the bike back into service. Such plugs cannot be salvaged; replace with new ones.

Worn out—Corrosive gasses formed by combustion and high voltage sparks have eroded the electrodes. Spark plugs in this condition require more voltage to fire under hard acceleration; often more than the ignition system can supply. Replace them with new plugs of the same heat range.

Preignition—If electrodes are melted, preignition is almost certainly the cause. Check for loose carburetor mounting or overadvanced ignition timing. It is also possible that a plug of the wrong heat range (too hot) is being used. Find the cause of preignition before placing the engine back into service.

Spark plugs may usually be cleaned and regapped, which will restore them to near new condition. Since the effort involved is considerable, such service may not be worth it, since new spark plugs are relatively inexpensive.

For those who wish to service used plugs, the following procedure is recommended.

1. Clean all oily deposits from the spark plug with cleaning solvent, then blow dry with compressed air. If this precaution is not taken, oily deposits will cause gumming or caking of the sandblast cleaner.

2. Place the spark plug in a sandblast cleaner and blast 3-5 seconds, then turn on air only to remove particles from the plug.

3. Repeat Step 2 as required until the plug is cleaned. Prolonged sandblasting will erode the insulator and make the plug much more susceptible to fouling.

2

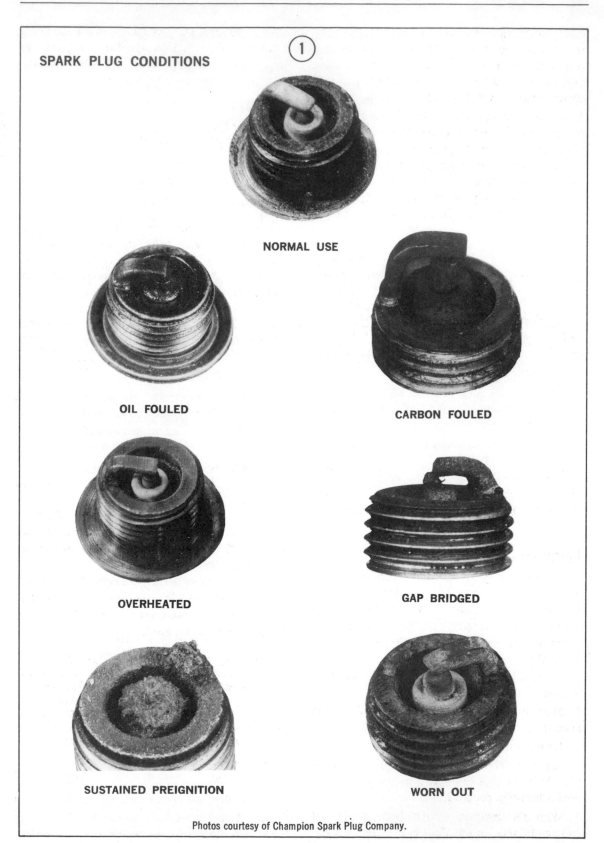

SPARK PLUG CONDITIONS

NORMAL USE

OIL FOULED

CARBON FOULED

OVERHEATED

GAP BRIDGED

SUSTAINED PREIGNITION

WORN OUT

Photos courtesy of Champion Spark Plug Company.

4. Bend the side electrode up slightly, then file the center electrode so that its edges are not rounded. The reason for this step is that less voltage is required to jump between sharp corners than between rounded edges.

5. Adjust spark plug gap to 0.024 in. (0.6mm) for all models except those with surface gap plugs. Surface gap plugs are not adjustable. Use a round wire gauge for measurement (**Figure 2**). Always adjust spark plug gap by bending the outer electrode only. A spark plug gapping tool does the best job, if one is available.

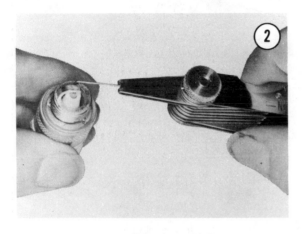

It will be easier to turn the engine over for other service operations if the spark plug is not installed until it is time to start the engine.

Compression Test

An engine requires adequate compression to develop full power. If for any reason compression is low, the engine will not develop full power. A compression test, or even better, a series of them over the life of the bike, will tell much about engine condition.

To make a compression test, proceed as follows:

1. Start the engine, then ride the bike long enough to warm it thoroughly.

2. Remove the spark plug.

3. Screw the compression gauge into the spark plug hole, or if a press-in type gauge is used, hold it firmly in position.

4. With the ignition switch OFF, crank the engine briskly with the kickstarter several times; the compression gauge indication will increase with each kick. Continue to crank the engine until the gauge shows no more increase, then record the gauge indication.

Example:
1st kick	90 psi
2nd kick	140 psi
3rd kick	160 psi
4th kick	170 psi
5th kick	170 psi

Because of differences in engine design, carbon deposits, and other factors, no definite compression readings can be specified for any one engine. Typical compression pressures are listed in **Table 2**.

Table 2   TYPICAL COMPRESSION PRESSURES

Engine size	Compression pressure PSI
100	120
125-175	100
250	120
350	150
400-450	120

A series of measurements made over a period of time may reveal an indication of trouble ahead, long before the engine exhibits serious symptoms.

Consider the following example (**Table 3**) for a typical bike. A difference of 20 percent between successive readings over a period of time is an indication of trouble.

Table 3   COMPRESSION HISTORY

Mileage	Compression Pressure PSI
New	130
2,000	125
4,000	125
6,000	120
8,000	95

Note that a one-time compression test made at 8,000 miles might be considered normal, but compared with the engine's past history, it is an indication of trouble.

It is for the reasons outlined in the foregoing paragraphs that a serious motorcycle hobbyist will want to own and use his own compression gauge, and also keep a permanent record of its findings. It should be pointed out, however, that measurements taken with different gauges are not necessarily conclusive, because of production tolerances, calibration errors, and other factors.

Carbon Removal

Two-stroke engines are particularly susceptible to carbon formation. Deposits form on the inside of the cylinder head, on top of the piston, and within the exhaust port. Combustion chamber deposits can abnormally increase compression ratio, causing overheating, preignition, and possible severe engine damage. Carbon deposits within the exhaust port, exhaust pipe, and muffler restrict engine breathing, causing loss of power.

To remove carbon from the engine, first remove the cylinder head (**Figure 3**) and cylinder (**Figure 4**). It is usually unnecessary to remove the piston. Be sure to stuff a clean rag into the crankcase opening to prevent entry of foreign material.

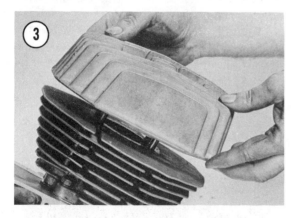

Always allow the engine to cool to avoid possible cylinder head warpage. To remove the cylinder head, proceed as follows.

1. Remove the spark plug.

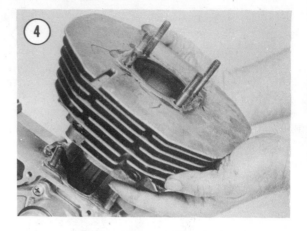

2. Following a crisscross sequence, loosen each cylinder head retaining nut ½ turn at a time until each one turns freely. This procedure minimizes chances for cylinder head warpage.

3. Lift the cylinder head from the cylinder. If it sticks, tap it lightly with a rubber mallet. Do not pry it off; doing so may cause damage to sealing surfaces.

4. Reverse the procedure to install the head. Always use a new cylinder head gasket. Torque cylinder head nuts as follows.

| 8mm nuts | 15 ft.-lb. |
| 10mm nuts | 25 ft.-lb. |

An easy method for removing cylinder head deposits is to use the rounded end of a hacksaw blade as a scraper, as shown in **Figure 5**. Be very careful not to cause any damage to the sealing surface.

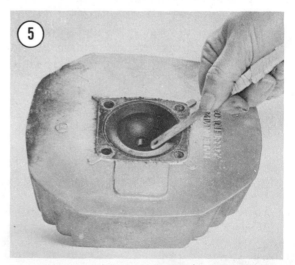

The same tool may be used for removing carbon deposits from piston heads (**Figure 6**). After removing all deposits from the piston head, clean all carbon and gum from the piston ring grooves using a ring groove cleaning tool or broken piston ring (**Figure 7**). Any deposits left in the grooves will cause the piston rings to stick, thereby causing gas blow-by and loss of power.

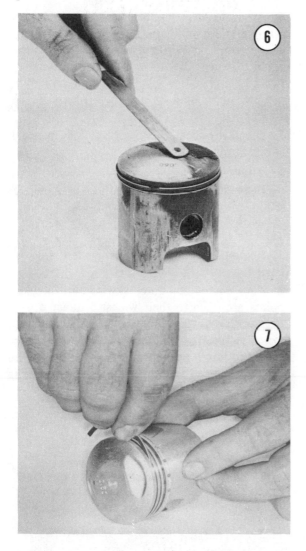

To remove piston rings, it is only necessary to spread the top ring with a thumb on each end (**Figure 8**), then remove it upward. Repeat the procedure for each remaining ring. When replacing rings, be sure that the ends of the rings engage the locating pins in the grooves (**Figure 9**).

Finally, scrape all carbon deposits from the cylinder exhaust port, as shown in **Figure 10**. A blunted screwdriver is a suitable tool for this job.

Reverse the removal procedure to install the cylinder. Be sure to lubricate the piston and cylinder liberally before installation. Note that when replacing the cylinder, it is necessary to compress each piston ring as it enters the cylinder. A ring compressor tool makes the job easier, but the rings may be compressed by hand with little difficulty.

Breaker Points

Normal use of a motorcycle causes the breaker points to burn and pit gradually. If they are not too pitted, they can be dressed with a few strokes of a clean point file. Do not use emery cloth or sandpaper, because particles can remain on the points and cause arcing and burning. If a few strokes of a file do not smooth the points completely, replace them.

Oil or dirt may get on the points, resulting in poor performance or even premature failure. Common causes for this condition are defective oil seals, improper or excessive breaker cam lubrication, or lack of care when the breaker point cover is removed.

Points should be cleaned and regapped approximately every 1,500-2,000 miles (2,000-3,000 km). To clean the points, first dress them lightly with a clean point file, then remove all residue with lacquer thinner. Close the points on a piece of clean white paper such as a business card. Continue to pull the card through the closed points until no discoloration or residue remains on the card. Finally, rotate the engine and observe the points as they open and close. If they do not meet squarely, replace them.

If poor engine performance has been traced to oil-fouled points, correct the cause before returning the motorcycle to service.

To service or replace breaker points on models with magneto ignition, proceed as follows.

1. Remove gearshift lever. Note that its clamping bolt must be removed completely before the lever can be pulled from the shaft.

2. Remove left crankcase cover. An impact driver makes it easy to loosen the cover screws without damaging them.

3. Remove flywheel retaining nut and its lockwasher.

4. Screw a flywheel puller (left-hand thread) into the flywheel to its full depth. Be sure that the puller screw is backed out fully when installing the puller. Turn the puller screw clockwise to remove the flywheel.

5. Refer to **Figure 11**. Remove both wires, then remove point retaining screw (A).

6. After the new points are installed, tighten screw (A) just enough so that the stationary contact does not slip, but not so much that the contact cannot be moved by a screwdriver twisted in pry slots (B). Move the stationary contact until both points just barely make contact.

7. Install flywheel, lockwasher, and flywheel retaining nut.

8. Adjust ignition timing.

Breaker point service on models with battery ignition is similar to that on models with magnetos, however point gap must be adjusted separately.

1. Remove ignition cover from left side of engine.

2. Turn engine counterclockwise until breaker points are open to their widest distance apart. Measure point gap (**Figure 12**), using a clean feeler gauge. If point gap is 0.012-0.016 in. (0.30-0.40mm), no adjustment is required.

3. If adjustment is required, refer to **Figure 13**. Loosen screws (A) just enough so that stationary contact (B) may be moved to adjust point gap to 0.012-0.016 in. (0.30-0.40mm). A screwdriver inserted into pry slots (C) makes adjustment easy.

4. Tighten screws (A), then recheck adjustment.

5. Adjust ignition timing.

Ignition Timing
(Models With Magnetos)

It is necessary to adjust ignition timing whenever breaker points are serviced. Proceed as follows.

1. Refer to **Figure 14**. Turn engine counterclockwise until mark (A) on flywheel aligns with index (B) on crankcase.

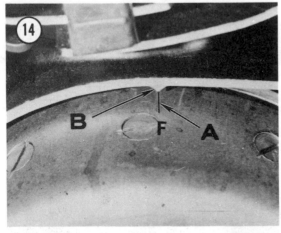

4. Check the adjustment by rotating the flywheel counterclockwise. The points must just begin to open as mark (A) on the flywheel aligns with mark (B) on the crankcase.

5. When timing is adjusted correctly, maximum point gap will be 0.012-0.016 in. (0.3-0.4mm). It is not necessary to adjust point gap separately on the models.

Note that magnetos on F8 models have slotted mounting holes for adjustment. It is necessary that the marks on the magneto base and crankcase be aligned before adjustment.

2. Connect a timing tester to the breaker point terminal and a good engine ground. Follow the manufacturer's instructions.

3. Refer to **Figure 15**. Loosen screw (C) slightly, then move stationary contact with a screwdriver inserted into pry slots (D) and (E) until the timing tester indicates that the breaker points just open. Be sure to tighten screw (C) after adjustment.

Ignition Timing (Battery Ignition)

Refer to **Figure 16**, then proceed as follows.

1. Turn engine counterclockwise until mark on timing pointer (A) aligns with index pointer (B).

2. Connect a test light, ohmmeter, timing tester to the terminal on the breaker points. Also connect to a good ground.

3. Loosen timing plate screws (C) slightly, then move timing plate (D) up or down as required,

Note: Flywheel shown removed for clarity. Adjust ignition timing with flywheel in place.

until the breaker points just open. Tighten screws (C).

4. Recheck the adjustment by turning the engine clockwise slightly, then counterclockwise slowly. The points must open just as timing pointer (A) aligns with index pointer (B).

Ignition Timing (CDI)

Because a signal pulse is generated only when the engine is running, it is not possible to time the ignition statically, as in the case with ignition systems which use breaker points. To check timing, proceed as follows.

1. Remove chaincase and magneto cover.

2. Connect a timing light (**Figure 17**).

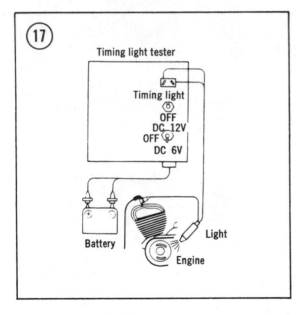

3. Start the engine and run it at 4,000 rpm.

4. Direct the timing light on the timing marks on the flywheel and crankcase, as shown in **Figure 18**. Timing is correct if both marks are aligned.

If the marks are not aligned, ignition timing must be adjusted. Refer to **Figure 19**, then proceed as follows.

1. Insert a screwdriver through the hole in the flywheel, then loosen stator screws at locations (A), (B), and (C).

2. Rotate the magneto base with a screwdriver inserted into notch (D). Counterclockwise rota-

tion retards timing; clockwise rotation advances timing.

3. Tighten screws at locations (A).

4. Reconnect the timing light and recheck timing with the light. Repeat the procedure as necessary.

Air Cleaner Service

As part of any tune-up, air cleaner elements should be cleaned or replaced, as required. A clogged air cleaner results in an overrich mixture, causing power loss and poor gas mileage. Be sure that the air cleaner element is not torn and that it fits so that no dirt can leak past its edges.

Replace air cleaner elements if they become torn, punctured, or so clogged that dirt cannot be removed.

Some models are equipped with polyurethane foam air cleaner elements. Wash such elements in solvent, dry thoroughly, then wet lightly but thoroughly with engine oil before installation. Replace the element if it is torn or punctured.

Fuel Strainer

Remove and clean the fuel strainer. Blow dry with compressed air. On models with automatic fuel cocks, be sure that there are no leaks in the signal tube from the carburetor to the fuel cock. Air leaks will result in poor fuel flow.

NOTE: Flywheel shown removed for clarity. Adjust timing with flywheel in place.

Carburetor Adjustment

Carburetor adjustment is left as the last step to be done on the engine, because it cannot be done accurately until all other adjustments are correct. The carburetor must also be adjusted with the engine thoroughly warmed, while most other adjustments either must be or are more easily done with the engine cold.

Idle speed and idle mixture are normally the only carburetor adjustments performed at the time of engine tune-up. If other adjustments seem to be required, refer to Chapter Five for details of major carburetor service. Refer to **Figure 20**.

1. Turn in idle mixture screw (A) until it seats lightly, then back it out 1¼ turns.

2. Start the engine, then ride the bike long enough to warm it thoroughly.

3. Turn idle speed adjuster (B) until the engine runs slower and begins to falter.

4. Turn idle mixture screw (A) as required to make the engine run smoothly.

5. Repeat Steps 3 and 4 to achieve the lowest stable idle speed.

6. Adjust final idle speed to that specified in **Table 4**.

Oil Pump Adjustment

Since oil pump and throttle valve operation are related, it is essential to adjust the oil pump and throttle cables so that they operate simultaneously.

1. With the engine at normal operating temperature, adjust idle speed to that specified in foregoing Table 4.

2. Refer to **Figure 21**. Loosen throttle cable locknut (a), then turn cable adjuster (A) to provide 0.2-0.3 in. play. Repeat the procedure for the starter cable. Tighten the locknuts.

Table 4   IDLE SPEED

Model	Idle rpm
J1	900-1,100
G1L	900-1,100
G series	900-1,100
KE, KH, KV100	900-1,100
KD, KE, KS125	1,300
F2, F3, F4, F6	900-1,100
C1D, C2SS	900-1,100
B1 series	900-1,100
F5, F7, F8, F9	1,000-1,300
KE175	1,300

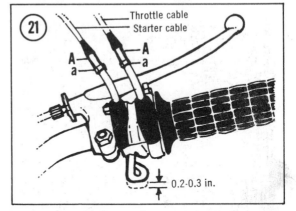

3. Refer to **Figure 22**. Remove throttle cable play by turning adjuster (A) at the top of the carburetor.

4. Refer to **Figure 23**. Loosen locknut on pump cable, then turn cable adjuster until mark on lever aligns with line on lever. Be sure to tighten cable adjuster locknut.

Battery Service

Tune-up time is also battery service time. Complete battery service information is contained in Chapter Four. Briefly, the following items should be attended to regularly.

1. Test state of charge. Recharge if at half charge (1.220 specific gravity) or less.

2. Add distilled water if required.

3. Clean battery top.

4. Clean and tighten terminals.

2

A. Adjust oil pump cable length so that mark on pump lever
   aligns with mark on lever stop.

Oil Change

Probably the single most important maintenance item which contributes to long transmission life is that of regular oil changes. Oil

becomes contaminated with products of combustion, condensation, and dirt. Some of these con-
taminants react with oil, forming acids which
attack vital components, and thereby result in
premature wear.

To change oil, first ride the bike until it is
thoroughly warm. Place a flat pan under the
engine, then remove the oil drain plug from the
bottom of the engine and allow oil to drain. It
may be helpful to rock the motorcycle from
side to side and also forward and backward to
get out as much as possible.

Replace the drain plug, then refill with fresh
engine oil which meets API specification MS
or SE. Maintain oil level between both marks
on the dipstick.

CLUTCH ADJUSTMENT

Adjust the clutch at 1,000-mile (1,500-km)
intervals, or more often if required. Complete
clutch adjustment procedures are discussed in
Chapter Three.

ELECTRICAL EQUIPMENT

Check all electrical equipment for proper operation—lights, horn, starter, etc. Refer to Chapter Four for electrical system service.

DRIVE CHAIN

Clean, lubricate, and adjust the drive chain every 1,000 miles (1,500 km). Adjust drive chain tension to provide ¾-1 in. (20-25mm) up and down play in the center of the lower chain run. Both wheels should be on the ground and a rider in the saddle when this measurement is made. Be sure to adjust the rear brake after chain tension adjustment.

BRAKES

Adjust front and rear brakes every 1,000 miles (1,500 km), or more often as needed. Remove wheels and check brake lining at 6,000-mile (9,000-km) intervals. Check and service wheel bearings at the same time.

WHEELS AND TIRES

Check wheels for bent rims and loose or missing spokes. Complete wheel inspection and service procedures are detailed in Chapter Six.

Check tires for worn treads, cuts, and proper inflation. Inflate tires to the value specified in **Table 5**.

Table 5   TIRE PRESSURE

Tire Size	Tire Pressure Pounds per Square Inch Front	Rear
3.00-16	23	28
2.50-18	23	28
2.75-18	23	28
3.00-18	23	28
3.25-18	23	28
3.25-18	14*	14*
3.50-18	23	28
4.00-18	23	28
3.00-19	23	28
3.00-21	14*	14*
*Motocross racing		

FORK OIL

Replace fork oil at 3,000-mile (4,500-km) intervals. To do so, place a pan under each fork leg, then remove the drain plug at the lower end of each fork leg (**Figure 24**). Replace with fresh fork oil through the upper fork bolts. Refill quantities are listed in **Table 6**.

Complete fork service is described in Chapter Six.

Table 6   FORK OIL QUANTITY

Model	Quart	(Milliliters)
J1, G1 Series	0.14	(135)
M Series	0.09	(90)
GA, G3 Series	0.14	(130)
G4TR, G5	0.18	(170)
F21M	0.18	(170)
KE, KH, KV100	0.18	(170)
F21M	0.18	(170)
KD, KE, KS125	0.16	(150)
KX125	0.13	(120)
KE175	0.16	(150)
G31M-A, F7	0.12	(115)
C1D, F2, B1 Series	0.18	(175)
C2SS (early)	0.13	(120)
C2SS (late), F6	0.18	(175)
F3	0.19	(180)
F4	0.21	(195)
F5, F8, F9, F81M	0.18	(175)
KT250	0.18	(170)
KX250	0.21	(200)
KX400, KX450	0.19	(180)

STEERING HEAD BEARINGS

Check steering bearings for looseness or binding. *If any exists, find out and correct the cause immediately.* Complete service instructions are in Chapter Six.

SWINGING ARM

Disassemble the swinging arm and grease its pivot shaft and bushings every 6,000 miles (9,000 km). Complete service and inspection procedures are in Chapter Six.

CHAPTER THREE

ENGINE, TRANSMISSION, AND CLUTCH

This chapter describes removal, disassembly, service, and reassembly of the engine, transmission, and clutch. It is suggested that the engine be serviced without removing it from the chassis except for overhaul of the crankshaft assembly, transmission, or bearings. Operating principles of rotary valve and piston port 2-stroke engines are also discussed in this chapter.

ROTARY VALVE ENGINES

Figures 1 through 4 illustrate the 4 phases of the operating cycle. During this discussion, assume that the crankshaft is rotating counter-clockwise. In Figure 1, as the piston travels downward, a transfer, or scavenging port (A) is opened. Exhaust gases leave the cylinder through exhaust port (B), which is opened by downward movement of piston (C). A fresh fuel/air charge, which has previously been compressed slightly, travels from crankcase (D) through transfer port (A) as the port opens.

Figure 2 illustrates the second phase. As the crankshaft rotates, the piston moves upward, closing the exhaust and transfer ports. Fresh fuel/air mixture is trapped in the cylinder and compressed by upward movement of the piston. Notice also that a low pressure area is created in the crankcase as the piston moves upward. Rotary valve (E), which is attached to the crank-

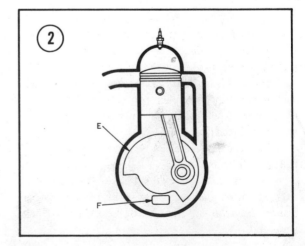

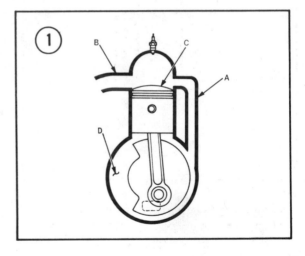

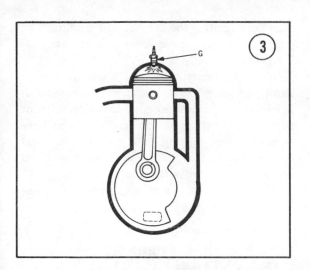

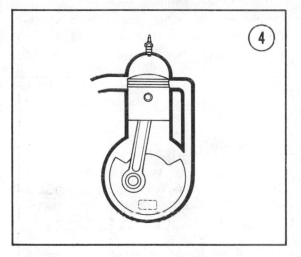

PISTON PORT ENGINES

Figures 5 through 8 illustrate operating principles of piston port engines. During this discussion, assume that the crankshaft is rotating counterclockwise. In Figure 5, as the piston travels downward, a scavenging port (A) between the crankcase and the cylinder is uncovered. Exhaust gases leave the cylinder through the exhaust port (B), which is also opened by downward movement of the piston. A fresh fuel/air charge, which has previously been compressed slightly, travels from crankcase (C) to the cylinder through scavenging port (A) as the port opens. Since the incoming charge is under pressure, it rushes into the cylinder quickly and helps to expel exhaust gases from the previous cycle.

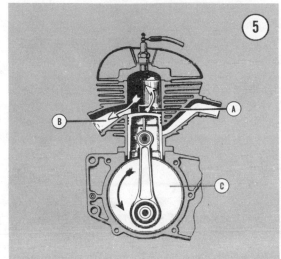

Figure 6 illustrates the next phase of the cycle. As the crankshaft continues to rotate, the piston moves upward, closing the exhaust and scavenging ports. As the piston continues upward, the air/fuel mixture in the cylinder is compressed. Notice also that a low pressure area is created in the crankcase at the same time. Further upward movement of the piston uncovers intake port (D). A fresh fuel/air charge is then drawn into the crankcase through the intake port because of the low pressure created by the upward piston movement.

The third phase is shown in Figure 7. As the piston approaches top dead center, the spark

shaft and rotates with it, opens intake port (F). The upward movement of the piston then draws a fresh fuel/air charge into the crankcase through the intake port.

The third phase is shown in Figure 3. As the piston approaches top dead center, spark plug (G) fires, igniting the air/fuel mixture. The piston is then driven downward by the expanding gases. The rotary valve also closes as the piston reaches top dead center. As the piston continues downward, the mixture trapped in the crankcase is compressed.

When the piston uncovers the exhaust port, the fourth phase begins, as shown in Figure 4. The exhaust gases leave the cylinder through the exhaust port. Further movement of the piston opens the transfer port, and the cycle is then repeated.

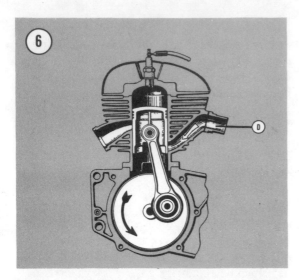

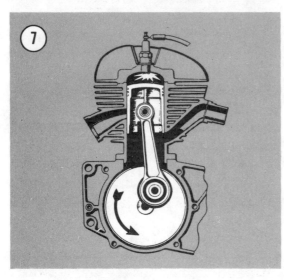

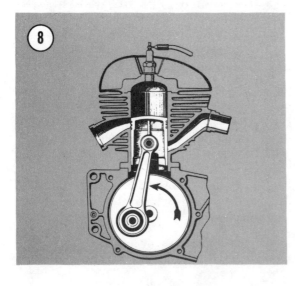

plug fires, igniting the compressed mixture. The piston is then driven downward by the expanding gases.

When the top of the piston uncovers the exhaust port, the fourth phase begins, as shown in Figure 8. The exhaust gases leave the cylinder through the exhaust port. As the piston continues downward, the intake port is closed and the mixture in the crankcase is compressed in preparation for the next cycle.

As in rotary valve engines, every downward stroke of the piston is a power stroke.

ENGINE LUBRICATION

It can be seen from the foregoing discussion that the engine cannot receive its lubrication from an oil supply in the crankcase. Oil splash in the crankcase would be carried into the cylinder with the fuel/air charge, resulting in high oil consumption and spark plug fouling. Kawasaki 2-stroke engines use one of 3 methods for engine lubrication.

Fuel and Oil Mixture

Some competition models are lubricated by oil premixed with the fuel. Sufficient oil is added to the fuel to provide adequate lubrication for the engine under the high speed and load conditions found in competition. Under low speed and load conditions, however, the engine receives more oil than is necessary, resulting in possible plug fouling. In addition, oil starvation can occur in prolonged periods during which the engine turns at high speeds with the throttle closed, as when descending a long hill. These situations don't occur during competition, but could cause problems for machines intended for street use.

Superlube System

To overcome objections to the oil/fuel mixture lubrication method, Kawasaki developed its Superlube system. This system is used on most models. A separate engine-driven oil pump (**Figure 9**) supplies oil to the engine induction tract. The output from the pump is controlled not only by engine speed, but also by throttle position, which is closely related to

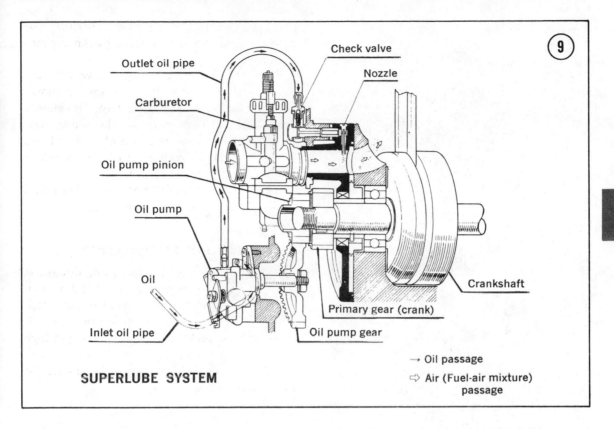

SUPERLUBE SYSTEM

→ Oil passage
⇨ Air (Fuel-air mixture) passage

engine load. The engine is thereby supplied with the proper amount of oil under all operating conditions.

Injectolube System

Injectolube, used on larger models, is similar to the Superlube system in that it supplies oil to the engine in varying quantities. The oil pump has an additional output, however, which supplies oil under pressure to the main bearings (**Figure 10**) in the engine.

Checking the Oil Pump

CAUTION
Operate the engine on a 20:1 fuel/oil mixture during the following procedure. Failure to do so may result in severe engine damage.

1. Remove the oil pump outlet tube at the check valve.

2. Start the engine and run it at 2,000 rpm.

3. Hold the end of the oil outlet tube over a suitable collecting vessel.

4. Pull the oil pump lever to the fully upward position.

5. Measure the quantity of oil pumped in 3 minutes. The proper oil volume should be as specified in **Table 1**.

Table 1   OIL PUMP OUTPUT

Model	Ounce	Milliliters
J1	0.095	2.8
G Series	0.095	2.8
M Series	0.095	2.8
KE, KH, KV100	0.095	2.8
KD, KE, KS125	0.095	2.8
KE175	0.14	4.1
C1D, C2SS	0.11	3.1
B1L, B1L-A	0.11	3.1
KT250	0.13	3.8
F6	0.14	4.1
F2, F3, F7	0.19	5.5
F4, F8	0.20	6.0
F5, F9	0.34	10.0

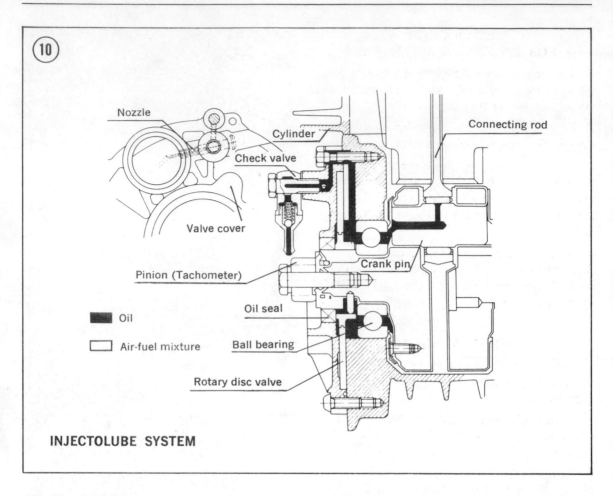

Nozzle

Cylinder

Connecting rod

Check valve

Valve cover

Crank pin

Pinion (Tachometer)

Oil seal

■ Oil

□ Air-fuel mixture

Ball bearing

Rotary disc valve

INJECTOLUBE SYSTEM

Bleeding the Oil Pump

Air will enter the oil pump whenever the pump is disconnected or the oil tank has run dry. After such an occurrence, the oil pump must be bled.

> CAUTION
> *Operate the engine on a 20:1 fuel/oil mixture during the following procedure. Failure to do so may result in severe engine damage.*

To bleed the oil pump, start the engine and run it at approximately 2,000 rpm. Pull up the control lever and operate the engine until no more air bubbles appear. If after a short time, bubbles continue to appear, check connections at the suction side of the pump, pump discharge port, and banjo connection.

Finally, remove the banjo bolt at the oil pump suction inlet and fill the tube with oil until no more bubbles appear.

Oil Pump Check Valve

The check valve (**Figure 11**) prevents oil from flowing away from the engine when it is not running, thereby preventing dry starts. Avoid disassembly of the check valve. If it is assembled carelessly, it will not operate properly. In the event of malfunction, the check valve should be replaced.

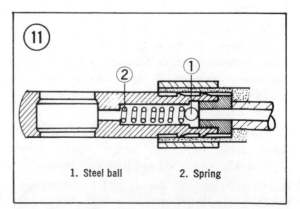

1. Steel ball   2. Spring

PREPARATION
FOR ENGINE DISASSEMBLY

1. Thoroughly clean the engine exterior of dirt, oil, and foreign material, using one of the cleaners formulated for the purpose.

2. Be sure that you have the proper tools for the job. See *General Information*, Chapter One.

3. As you remove parts from the engine, place them in trays in the order of their disassembly. Doing so will make assembly faster and easier, and will ensure correct installation of all engine parts.

4. Note that the disassembly procedures vary slightly between the different models. Be sure to read all steps carefully and follow those which apply to your engine.

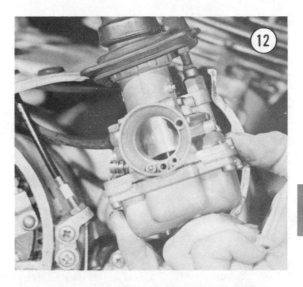

ENGINE REMOVAL

Engine removal is generally similar for all models. The following steps are set forth as a guide.

1. If the engine runs, start it and let it run for a few minutes to warm the oil. Then remove the drain plug and drain the transmission oil.

2. Remove the exhaust pipe at the cylinder, and the muffler attaching bolts. The muffler and exhaust pipe may then be removed together.

3. On all but GA series, remove the air cleaner assembly.

4. Turn the fuel petcock to OFF, then remove the fuel line at the carburetor.

5. Remove the carburetor (**Figure 12**). A hole is provided in the cover for access to its attaching screw.

6. Remove the inner wire from the oil pump control lever. Remove the banjo bolt and the inlet oil line from the oil pump. Be sure to plug the tube to prevent oil from flowing out. Remove the fitting screw and withdraw the tachometer cable.

7. Slacken the outer clutch cable, remove the inner cable from the clutch release lever (**Figure 13**), then remove the clutch cable.

8. Remove the gear change pedal, then the left crankcase cover.

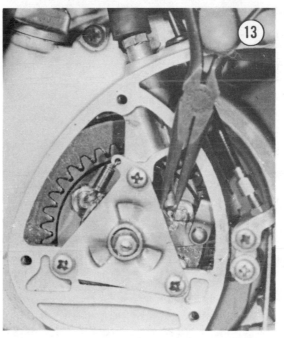

9. Remove the master link, then the drive chain. It may be necessary to rotate the rear wheel to position the master link for convenient removal. When installing the chain, be sure to position the master link clip as shown in **Figure 14**.

10. Disconnect all wiring at the flywheel magneto or generator.

11. Remove the spark plug cap.

12. Remove all engine mount bolts.

13. Straddle the machine and remove the engine from the frame.

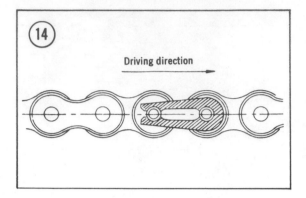

14. Reverse the removal procedure to install the engine. Be sure to check the following items before starting the engine:

   a. Oil supply

   b. Transmission oil level

   c. Clutch adjustment

   d. Oil pump and throttle cables

   e. Drive chain adjustment

   f. Engine mounting bolts

   g. Ignition timing

CYLINDER AND CYLINDER HEAD

Kawasaki engines are variously supplied with aluminum alloy and cast iron cylinders. Aluminum alloy cylinders are fitted with cast iron liners.

Cylinder Head Removal/Installation

With the engine cold, loosen each cylinder head nut a little bit at a time, in crisscross order, until all are loose. Then remove all nuts. Lift the cylinder head from the cylinder (**Figure 15**). It may be necessary to tap the head lightly with a rubber mallet to free it; if so, take care not to break any cooling fins.

Upon installation, always use a new cylinder head gasket. Torque cylinder head nuts in crisscross order to 18 ft.-lb. (2.5 mkg) for 8mm nuts, and 25 ft.-lb. (4.0 mkg) for 10mm nuts.

Removing Carbon Deposits

Carbon deposits in the combustion chamber cause increased compression ratio and may lead to preignition, overheating, and excessive fuel

consumption. To remove these deposits, scrape them off with the rounded end of a hacksaw blade, as shown in **Figure 16**. Be careful not to damage the gasket surface.

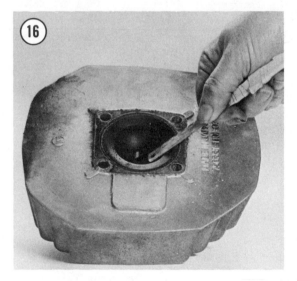

Cylinder Removal

With the cylinder head and any cylinder base nuts removed, tap the cylinder around the exhaust port with a plastic mallet, then pull it away from the crankcase (**Figure 17**). Stuff a clean rag into the crankcase opening to prevent entry of any foreign material.

Checking the Cylinder

Measure cylinder wall wear at locations (a), (b), (c), and (d) with a cylinder gauge or inside micrometer, as shown in **Figure 18**. Position the instrument parallel, and then at right angles

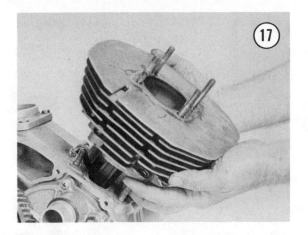

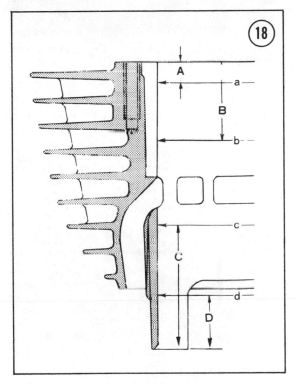

Table 2   CYLINDER DIAMETER

	Standard Dimensions	
Model	Inches	(Millimeters)
J1	1.850	(47.0)
M Series	1.850	(47.0)
G1	1.929	(49.0)
GA Series	1.850	(47.0)
G355-A, G3TR	1.850	(47.0)
G3TR-A, G4, G31M-A	1.949	(49.5)
KE, KH, KV100	1.949	(49.5)
F6	2.047	(52.0)
C1D, C2SS	2.087	(53.0)
B1, B1L, B1L-A	2.165	(55.0)
KD, KE, KS, KX125	2.205	(56.0)
KE175	2.421	(61.5)
F7	2.421	(61.5)
F2, F3	2.441	(62.0)
F8, F31M	2.667	(68.0)
KX250	2.736	(69.5)
KT250	2.756	(70.0)
F4, F21M	2.756	(70.0)
F5, F9	3.169	(80.5)
KX400	3.228	(82.0)
KX450	3.386	(86.0)

Removing Carbon Deposits

Scrape carbon deposits from around the cylinder exhaust port, as shown in **Figure 19**. The rounded end of a hacksaw blade is a suitable tool for carbon removal.

to the crankshaft at each depth. If any measurement exceeds 0.006 in. (0.15mm) over the standard valve, or if the difference between any measurements exceeds 0.002 in. (0.05mm), rebore and hone the cylinder to the next oversize, or replace the cylinder. Pistons are available in oversizes of 0.02 in. (0.50mm) and 0.04 in. (1.00mm). After boring and honing, the difference between maximum and minimum diameters must not be more than 0.0004 in. (0.01mm). Standard measurements are listed in **Table 2**.

Cylinder Installation

Be sure that each piston ring end gap is aligned with its locating pin in the ring groove. Lubricate the piston and cylinder, then insert the piston into the lower end of the cylinder. It will be necessary to compress each piston ring as it goes into the cylinder. Always use a new cylinder base gasket upon reassembly.

PISTON, PISTON PIN, AND PISTON RINGS

Remove the clip at each end of the piston pin with needle nose pliers (**Figure 20**). Press out the piston pin (**Figure 21**). A tool is available for this job, but it can be done by hand if the piston is first heated by wrapping in rags soaked in hot water. Also remove the upper end bearing (**Figure 22**).

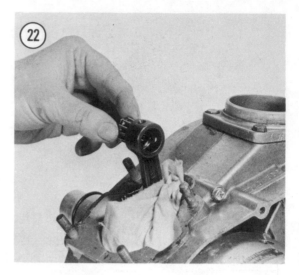

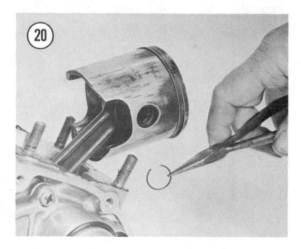

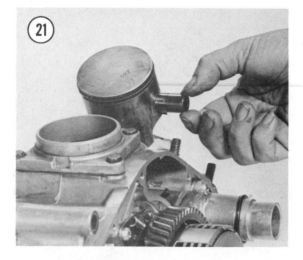

Piston Rings

Remove the piston rings by spreading the top ring with a thumb on each end, as shown in **Figure 23**. Then remove the ring from the top of the piston. Repeat this procedure for the remaining ring or rings. Expander rings used on some models may be removed easily by prying the ends with a narrow screwdriver.

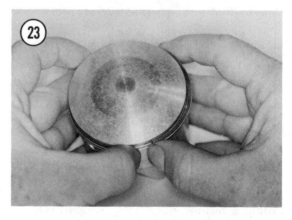

Measure each ring for wear as shown in **Figure 24**. Insert the ring 0.2 in. (5mm) into the cylinder, then measure ring gap with a feeler gauge. To ensure that the ring is squarely in the cylinder, push it into position with the head of the piston. If gap is not as specified in **Table 3**, replace the piston rings.

Scrape carbon deposits from the head of the piston (**Figure 25**). Then clean all carbon and gum from the piston ring grooves (**Figure 26**)

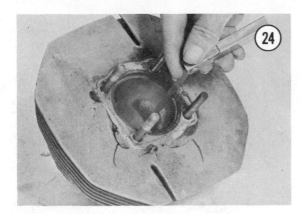

Table 3   PISTON RING GAP

Model	Inch	(Millimeter)
J1	0.008-0.012	(0.20-0.30)
M Series	0.006-0.012	(0.15-0.30)
G Series	0.006-0.022	(0.15-0.55)
KE, KH, KV100	0.006-0.014	(0.15-0.35)
C1, C2	0.008-0.012	(0.20-0.30)
B1 Series	0.008-0.012	(0.20-0.30)
F6	0.006-0.014	(0.15-0.35)
KD, KE, KS, KX125	0.006-0.014	(0.15-0.35)
KE175 (top)	0.006-0.014	(0.15-0.35)
(bottom)	0.008-0.016	(0.20-0.40)
F7, F8, F31M	0.008-0.016	(0.20-0.40)
F2, F3, F4	0.008-0.012	(0.20-0.30)
KT250	0.008-0.016	(0.20-0.40)
KX250	0.012-0.020	(0.30-0.50)
F5, F9	0.010-0.018	(0.25-0.45)
KX400	0.008-0.016	(0.20-0.40)
KX450	0.008-0.016	(0.20-0.40)

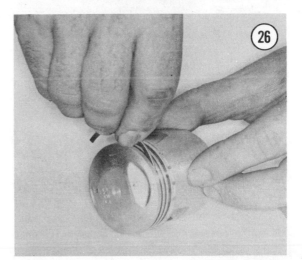

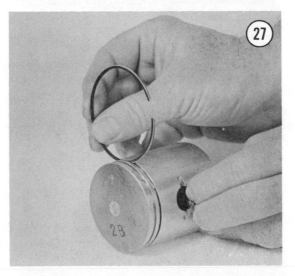

using a broken piston ring, or a ring groove cleaning tool. Any deposits left in the grooves will cause the rings to stick, leading to gas blow-by and loss of power.

To check fit of the piston ring in its groove, slip the outer surface of the ring into the groove next to the locating pin, then roll the ring completely around the piston (**Figure 27**). If any binding occurs, determine and correct the cause before proceeding.

When replacing rings, install the lower one first. Be sure that any printing on the ring is toward the top of the piston. Spread the rings carefully with your thumbs, just enough to slip them over the piston. Align end gaps with the locating pin in each ring groove.

Checking and Correcting Piston Clearance

Piston clearance is the difference between maximum piston diameter and minimum cylinder diameter. Measure outside diameter of the piston skirt (**Figure 28**) at right angles to the piston pin. The measurement should be made 0.2 in. (5mm) from the bottom of the piston. Proper piston clearances are listed in **Table 4**.

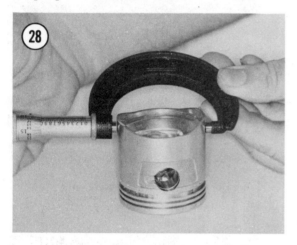

A piston showing signs of seizure will result in noise, loss of power, and damage to the cylinder wall. If such a piston is reused without correction, another seizure will develop. To correct this condition, lightly smooth the affected area with No. 400 emery paper or a fine oilstone (**Figure 29**).

Install the piston with arrow mark (**Figure 30**) pointing toward the front of the machine. This is vital because the hole for the piston pin is offset slightly to prevent piston slap.

LEFT CRANKCASE COVER

The left crankcase cover protects generator or magneto, engine sprocket, and bearings from dust and dirt. Covers on smaller models are of one-piece construction. Larger models use a 2-piece cover, consisting of an engine cover and a front chaincase cover.

Table 4   PISTON CLEARANCE

Model	Inch	(Millimeter)
J1	0.0010	(0.026)
M Series	0.0011-0.0017	(0.028-0.044)
G1L	0.001	(0.025)
G1M	0.0026-0.0037	(0.067-0.094)
GA Series	0.0026	(0.067)
G3SS	0.0026	(0.067)
G3TR	0.0014	(0.036)
G3TR-A, G4, G5	0.0018	(0.046)
G31M-A	0.0025-0.0033	(0.066-0.086)
KE, KH, KV100	0.001-0.0012	(0.025-0.031)
C1D	0.0006	(0.015)
C2SS	0.0027	(0.068)
B1L, B1L-A	0.002	(0.051)
KD, KE, KS, KX125	0.0018-0.0036	(0.03-0.06)
F6, F81M	0.0032	(0.083)
KE175	0.0015-0.0017	(0.038-0.043)
F2	0.0012	(0.030)
F3	0.0030-0.0038	(0.077-0.096)
F7	0.0025	(0.064)
KT250	0.002	(0.051)
F4, F21M	0.0024-0.0040	(0.062-0.101)
F5, F9	0.0039	(0.100)
KX250	0.005	(0.145)
KX400	0.0031-0.0039	(0.08-0.10)
KX450	0.0031-0.0039	(0.08-0.10)

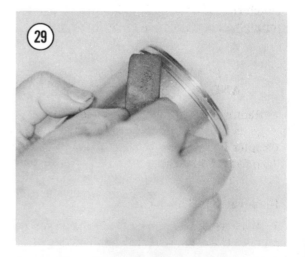

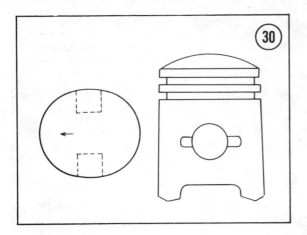

Removal (Smaller Models)

To remove the cover on these models, proceed as follows.

1. Completely remove gearshift pedal clamp bolt.

2. Pull gearshift pedal from its shaft.

3. Remove cover attaching screws, then pull cover from engine.

Removal (F Series)

1. Remove breaker contact cover on models so equipped.

2. Remove chaincase cover.

3. Remove left engine cover.

Installation (All Models)

Reverse the removal procedure to install the crankcase cover. Be sure that the gearshift shaft oil seal is in good condition. Be sure that the clutch release lever on F series models operates through an angle of about 90-100 degrees.

FLYWHEEL MAGNETO
AND STARTER-GENERATOR

Removal and installation only of these components is discussed in this chapter. Refer to Chapter Four for troubleshooting, or to Chapter Two for routine service.

Removal (Smaller Models)

1. Remove the flywheel mounting nut, then use a puller (**Figure 31**) to remove the flywheel.

NOTE: *Feed a rolled-up rag between the primary reduction gears on the other side of the engine to prevent the flywheel from turning.*

2. Remove the wiring from the neutral indicator switch.

3. Remove the screws from the magneto base, then remove the magneto base.

4. Remove the Woodruff key from the shaft.

Removal (Larger Models)

1. Remove the flywheel nut. Insert a screwdriver through one of the holes in the flywheel into the hole in the magneto base to prevent the flywheel from turning.

2. Pull the flywheel from the shaft, using a flywheel puller.

Magneto Installation (All Models)

1. Reverse the removal procedure to install the magneto.

2. Be sure to align mark (A) on the magneto base (**Figure 32**) with mark (B) on the crankcase. Failure to do so will make proper ignition timing impossible.

3. Tighten flywheel nut to 36 ft.-lb. (5 mkg) for all models but F5, F7, F8, and F9. Tighten flywheel nuts to 72 ft.-lb. (10 mkg) on those models.

Starter-Generator
Removal/Installation

1. Remove both yoke mounting screws.

2. Pull yoke from engine (**Figure 33**).

3. Using a suitable puller, remove armature (**Figure 34**).

4. Remove Woodruff key from crankshaft.

5. Reverse the removal procedure to install the starter-generator. It is much easier to install the yoke if all brushes are held up by their springs (**Figure 35**) until the mounting screws are in place. Don't forget to snap brush springs back into position.

ENGINE SPROCKET

Removal

1. Use a blunted chisel to straighten the tab on the lockwasher.

2. Loosen the mounting and remove sprocket (**Figure 36**).

Inspection

Inspect sprocket teeth for wear. Excessive wear results in shortened drive chain life. Re-

place the sprocket if it is worn. **Figure 37** compares worn and serviceable sprockets.

Installation

Reverse the removal procedure to install the sprocket. Be sure to insert the tang on the lockwasher into the hole in the sprocket, and also be sure that one edge of the lockwasher is bent up against the sprocket nut.

RIGHT CRANKCASE COVER

Removal (Smaller Models)

1. Remove the kickstarter pinch bolt, then slide the kickstarter pedal from the shaft.

2. Remove the carburetor cover.

3. Remove the carburetor and the clutch cable from the clutch release mechanism (**Figure 38**).

4. Remove the oil pump cover, then remove the oil pump cable and oil inlet tube. Plug the tube to prevent loss of oil.

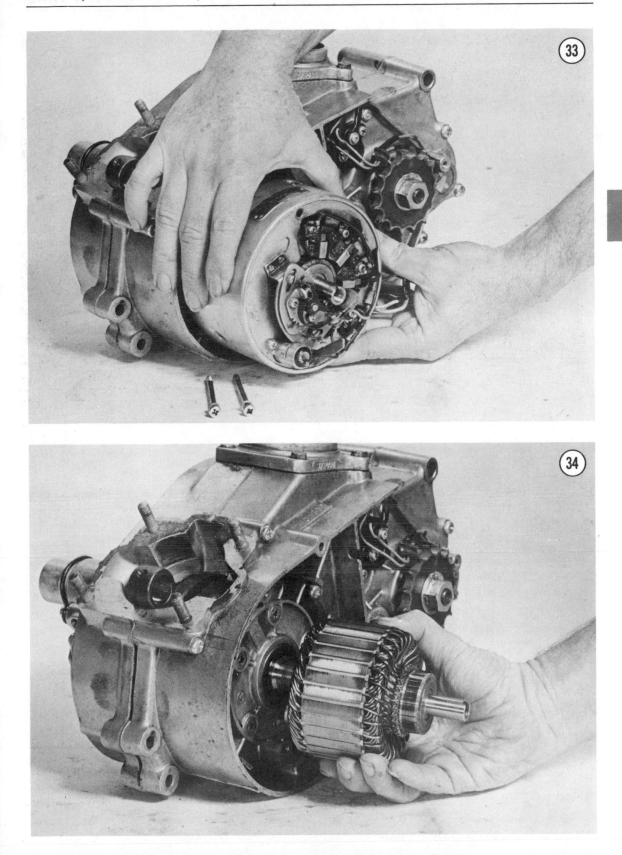

1. Brush in position for installation   2. Brush in normal position

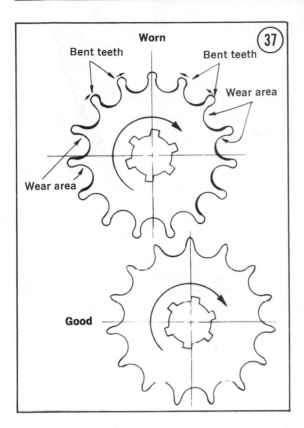

5. Remove the screws which attach the crankcase cover, and pull the cover away from the engine. It is not necessary to remove the oil pump, the clutch release mechanism, or the oil outlet tube.

Removal (Larger Models)

Right crankcase cover removal is similar, except that the clutch release mechanism is located on the other side of the engine, on the front chaincase cover.

Inspection

1. Make certain that the oil drain tube under the carburetor is not clogged.

2. Check the oil seal around the kickstarter shaft. Replace it if it is damaged or shows evidence of leakage.

3. Inspect the gasket. Replace it if damaged.

Installation

Reverse the removal procedure to install the cover. Take particular care that the O-rings on

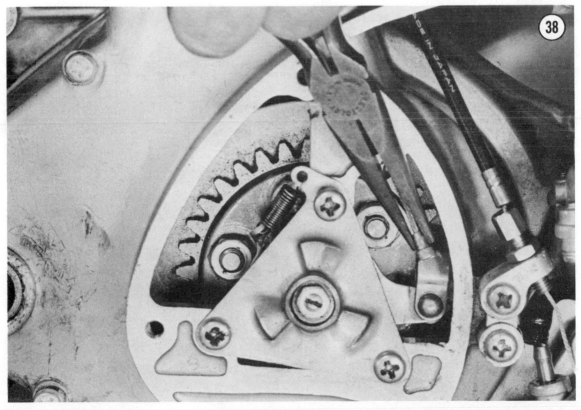

the valve cover and check valves are installed correctly (**Figure 39**). Also be sure that the clutch holder assembly and oil pump gear are correctly positioned. Rotate the flywheel, if necessary, to mesh the oil pump gears.

PRIMARY DRIVE GEAR

Removal (Smaller Models)

1. Use a blunted chisel to straighten the tab on the lockwasher.

2. Prevent crankshaft from turning by feeding a rolled-up rag between both primary reduction gears.

3. Remove the primary drive gear nut, then pull off the gear (**Figure 40**). Remove Woodruff key.

Removal (Larger Models)

1. Use a blunted chisel to straighten the lockwasher on the oil pump pinion.

2. Prevent the crankshaft from turning, then remove the oil pump pinion nut.

3. Remove the lockwasher and primary drive gear from the crankshaft.

4. Remove the Woodruff key.

Inspection

Check the gear teeth for wear or damage. Slight roughness may be smoothed with an oilstone. Replace the gear if damage cannot be dressed.

Installation

Reverse the removal procedure to install the gear. Torque the primary gear or oil pump gear nut to 36 ft.-lb. (5 mkg). Be sure to bend the tab on the lockwasher tightly against one flat on the nut. On models F5, F8, and F9, punch the lockwasher into the small hole on the pinion, as shown in **Figure 41**.

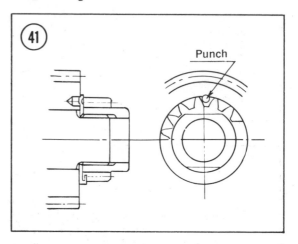

CLUTCH

Operation (Type 1 Clutch)

Figures 42 and 43 are exploded and sectional views of the clutch and clutch release mechanism used principally on F series. As the rider operates the clutch lever, the clutch cable pulls release lever (3), causing it to rotate in release housing (5). As the release lever rotates, helical splines force the lever to move away from the release housing. As the release lever moves, short (6) and long (7) pushrods move with it, and disengage the clutch. Screw (2) and locknut (1) are used to adjust the clutch.

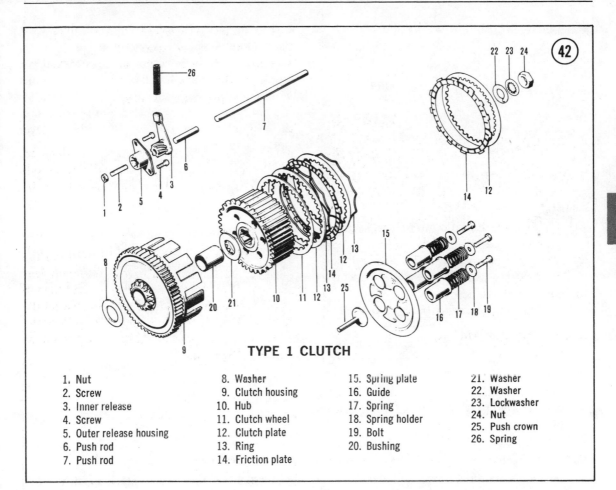

TYPE 1 CLUTCH

1. Nut
2. Screw
3. Inner release
4. Screw
5. Outer release housing
6. Push rod
7. Push rod

8. Washer
9. Clutch housing
10. Hub
11. Clutch wheel
12. Clutch plate
13. Ring
14. Friction plate

15. Spring plate
16. Guide
17. Spring
18. Spring holder
19. Bolt
20. Bushing

21. Washer
22. Washer
23. Lockwasher
24. Nut
25. Push crown
26. Spring

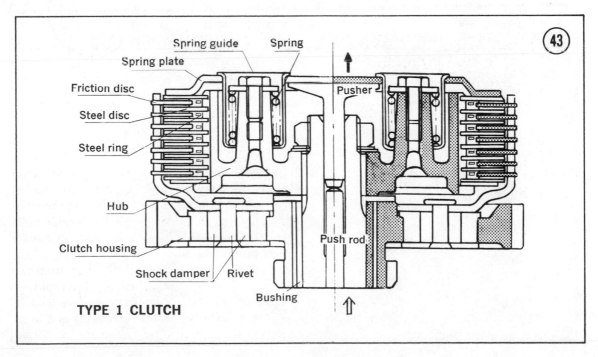

TYPE 1 CLUTCH

Release Mechanism (Type 1 Clutch)

To remove the clutch release mechanism on these models, proceed as follows.

1. Remove the front chain cover. On F6 and F7 models, it is necessary to remove the breaker plate cover.

2. Remove the clutch cable from the clutch release lever.

3. Remove the retaining screws from the clutch release housing. Remove the clutch release housing from the chain cover.

4. Pull short pushrod out through oil seal.

Check the assembled parts for wear or play by moving the release lever. Replace both parts if any large scratches or cracks are evident, as these impair clutch action.

Assemble the release lever and release housing, then install the clutch release housing into the front chaincase cover. Consider the operating angle of the clutch release lever, as it is pulled by the clutch cable. This angle should be about 90-100 degrees. Tighten the mounting screws evenly to prevent warpage of the release housing.

Operation (Types 2 and 3 Clutches)

Figures 44 and 45 are exploded and sectional views of type 2 clutches. Type 3 clutches, shown in **Figure 46**, are similar.

The clutch release mechanism on types 2 and 3 clutches is similar to that of type 1, except that it is mounted on the right side of the engine. Because this release mechanism is on the same side of the engine as the clutch, the 2 pushrods are not required. A short steel pin in the center of the splined portion of the release lever operates the clutch.

Removal, inspection, and installation procedures are similar to those for type 1 clutches.

Operation (Type 4 Clutch)

Figure 47 is an exploded view of this clutch. **Figure 48** is a sectional view of its release mechanism. The steel balls in release ball assembly (20) normally rest in depressions in clutch release plate (19). As the rider operates the clutch lever on the handlebar, the clutch cable pulls the arm on the clutch release plate, causing it to rotate. As the clutch release plate rotates, the balls are forced out of the depression. The balls then force the release plate and cam plate (5) apart. Roller (18) then moves pusher (14) to release the clutch.

Release Mechanism

To remove the release mechanism, refer to **Figure 49**. Remove the retaining screws, then take off the assembly. Inspect all parts carefully,

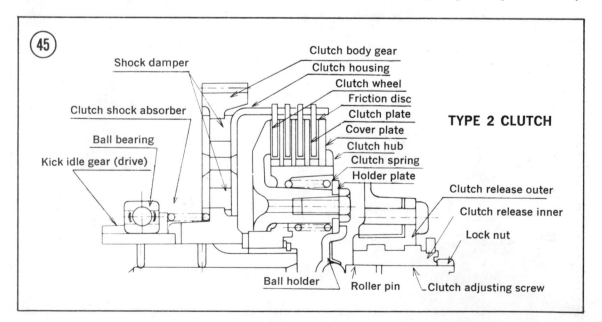

(45) Shock damper — Clutch body gear — Clutch housing — Clutch wheel — Friction disc — Clutch plate — Cover plate — Clutch hub — Clutch spring — Holder plate — Clutch shock absorber — Ball bearing — Kick idle gear (drive) — Clutch release outer — Clutch release inner — Lock nut — Ball holder — Roller pin — Clutch adjusting screw — **TYPE 2 CLUTCH**

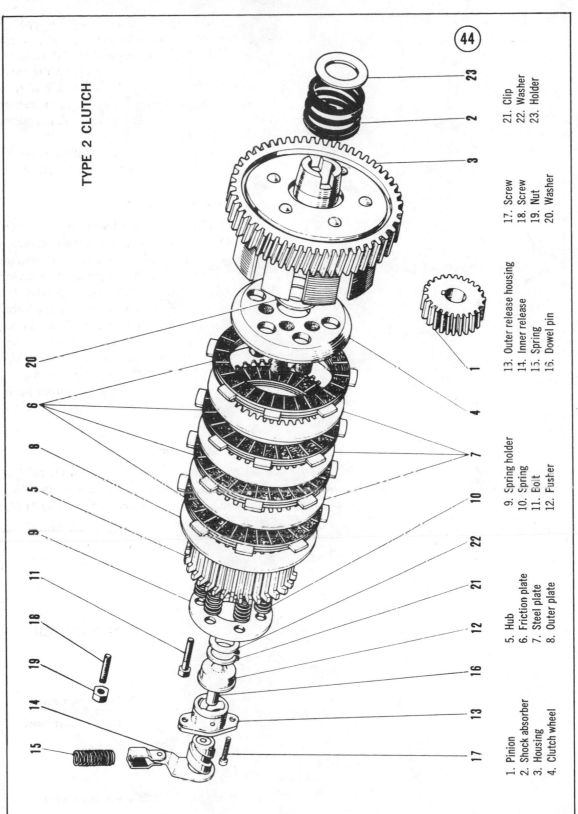

TYPE 2 CLUTCH

1. Pinion
2. Shock absorber
3. Housing
4. Clutch wheel

5. Hub
6. Friction plate
7. Steel plate
8. Outer plate

9. Spring holder
10. Spring
11. Bolt
12. Pusher

13. Outer release housing
14. Inner release
15. Spring
16. Dowel pin

17. Screw
18. Screw
19. Nut
20. Washer

21. Clip
22. Washer
23. Holder

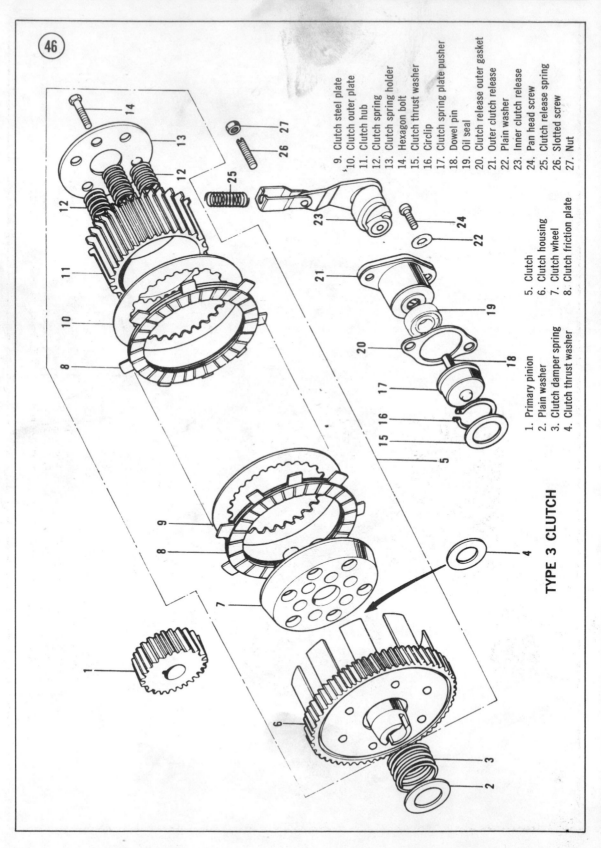

46

9. Clutch steel plate
10. Clutch outer plate
11. Clutch hub
12. Clutch spring
13. Clutch spring holder
14. Hexagon bolt
15. Clutch thrust washer
16. Circlip
17. Clutch spring plate pusher
18. Dowel pin
19. Oil seal
20. Clutch release outer gasket
21. Outer clutch release
22. Plain washer
23. Inner clutch release
24. Pan head screw
25. Clutch release spring
26. Slotted screw
27. Nut

1. Primary pinion
2. Plain washer
3. Clutch damper spring
4. Clutch thrust washer
5. Clutch
6. Clutch housing
7. Clutch wheel
8. Clutch friction plate

TYPE 3 CLUTCH

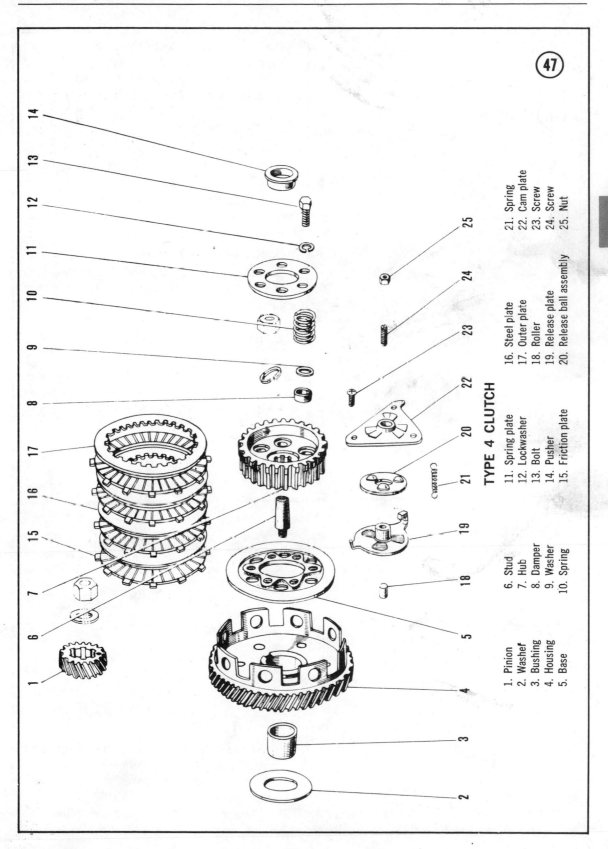

47

TYPE 4 CLUTCH

1. Pinion
2. Washer
3. Bushing
4. Housing
5. Base
6. Stud
7. Hub
8. Damper
9. Washer
10. Spring
11. Spring plate
12. Lockwasher
13. Bolt
14. Pusher
15. Friction plate
16. Steel plate
17. Outer plate
18. Roller
19. Release plate
20. Release ball assembly
21. Spring
22. Cam plate
23. Screw
24. Screw
25. Nut

3

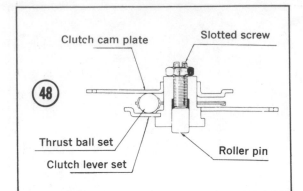

48

Clutch cam plate
Slotted screw
Thrust ball set
Clutch lever set
Roller pin

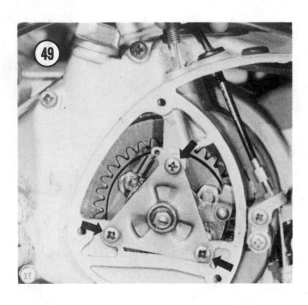

49

necessary to disassemble the clutch if service on it is not required, as in the case of removal in preparation for crankcase disassembly. In such cases, it is only necessary to remove the clutch retaining hardware, then pull the entire assembly free.

1. Remove nuts, clutch spring plate, and springs (**Figure 52**).

2. Feed a rolled-up rag between both primary reduction gears to prevent the clutch from turning, then remove the clutch hub nut.

3. Remove clutch hub, pressure plate, steel plates, and friction plates (**Figure 53**).

4. Remove clutch housing (**Figure 54**).

5. Slide clutch bushing and thrust washer from shaft. Take care to note how thrust washer is installed.

Clutch Inspection

Measure free length of each clutch spring, as shown in **Figure 55**. If free length is shorter than the standard length by the amount of the wear limit specified in **Table 5**, replace all springs.

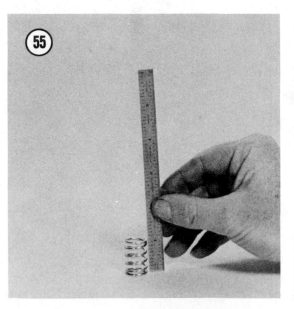

55

and replace any that are worn or damaged.

Reverse the removal procedure to install the clutch release mechanism.

Type 5 Clutch

Figure 50 is an exploded view of this clutch. Operation and service is similar to that of type 4 clutches.

Type 6 Clutch

Figure 51 is an exploded view of this clutch. Service is similar to that of other models. It is released by a rack and pinion (items 6 and 7) pushrod.

Clutch Disassembly

Clutch removal and disassembly is generally similar for all models. Note that it is usually not

Measure thickness of each friction disc at several places, as shown in **Figure 56**. Replace any disc that is worn unevenly, or more than the wear tolerance listed in **Table 6**.

Measure gap (A) between the splines on the clutch friction discs and the clutch housing

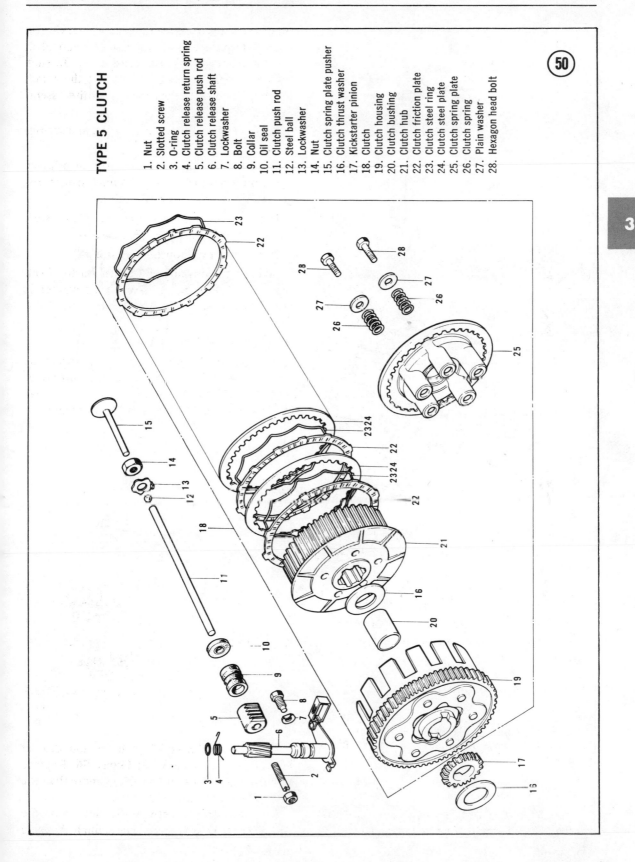

TYPE 5 CLUTCH

1. Nut
2. Slotted screw
3. O-ring
4. Clutch release return spring
5. Clutch release push rod
6. Clutch release shaft
7. Lockwasher
8. Bolt
9. Collar
10. Oil seal
11. Clutch push rod
12. Steel ball
13. Lockwasher
14. Nut
15. Clutch spring plate pusher
16. Clutch thrust washer
17. Kickstarter pinion
18. Clutch
19. Clutch housing
20. Clutch bushing
21. Clutch hub
22. Clutch friction plate
23. Clutch steel ring
24. Clutch steel plate
25. Clutch spring plate
26. Clutch spring
27. Plain washer
28. Hexagon head bolt

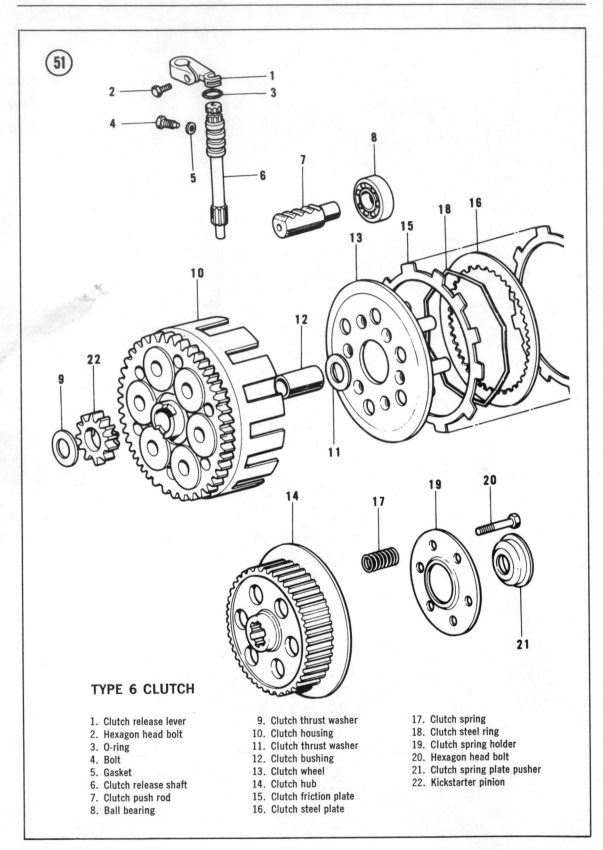

51

TYPE 6 CLUTCH

1. Clutch release lever
2. Hexagon head bolt
3. O-ring
4. Bolt
5. Gasket
6. Clutch release shaft
7. Clutch push rod
8. Ball bearing

9. Clutch thrust washer
10. Clutch housing
11. Clutch thrust washer
12. Clutch bushing
13. Clutch wheel
14. Clutch hub
15. Clutch friction plate
16. Clutch steel plate

17. Clutch spring
18. Clutch steel ring
19. Clutch spring holder
20. Hexagon head bolt
21. Clutch spring plate pusher
22. Kickstarter pinion

Table 5   CLUTCH SPRING SPECIFICATIONS

Model	Standard Length Inch (mm)		Wear Limit Inch (mm)	
J1	0.98	(24.8)	0.03	(0.8)
G1, G1M	0.98	(24.8)	0.03	(0.8)
G Series	0.85	(21.6)	0.08	(2.0)
M Series	0.85	(21.6)	0.08	(2.0)
C1D, C2SS	0.85	(21.6)	0.08	(2.0)
KE, KH, KV100	0.85	(21.6)	0.06	(1.6)
B1L	0.96	(24.5)	0.09	(2.2)
B1L-A	1.08	(27.5)	0.10	(2.5)
KD, KE, KS, KX125	1.30	(33.1)	0.06	(1.5)
KE175	1.36	(34.5)	0.06	(1.5)
F6, F7	1.36	(34.5)	0.14	(3.5)
F2, F3, F4, F21M	0.96	(24.5)	0.09	(2.2)
F8, F9	1.32	(33.6)	0.14	(3.5)
KT250	1.30	(33.1)	0.06	(1.5)
KX250	1.32	(33.6)	0.14	(3.5)
KX400	1.42	(36.0)	0.06	(1.5)
KX450	1.42	(36.0)	0.06	(1.5)

(**Figure 57**) using a feeler gauge. Gap must be 0.0016-0.012 in. (0.04-0.3mm) to prevent noisy operation. Replace the friction plates if the gap is too large.

Check the gear teeth on the clutch housing for burrs, nicks, or damage. Smooth any such defects with an oilstone. If the oilstone doesn't smooth out the damage, replace clutch housing.

Table 6   CLUTCH PLATE SPECIFICATIONS

Model	Standard Thickness Inch (mm)	Wear Limit Inch (mm)
J1, G1	0.17 (4.3)	0.016 (0.4)
G, M Series	0.13 (3.2)	0.010 (0.3)
C1D, C2SS	0.15 (3.7)	0.016 (0.4)
KE, KH, KV100	0.12 (3.1)	0.010 (0.3)
B1L, B1L-A	0.16 (4.0)	0.016 (0.4)
KD, KE, KS, KX125	0.12 (3.1)	0.024 (0.6)
F2, F3, F4, F6	0.16 (4.0)	0.016 (0.4)
KE175	0.12 (3.1)	0.024 (0.6)
F21M	0.16 (4.0)	0.016 (0.4)
F7	0.12 (3.1)	0.010 (0.3)
KT250, KX250	0.12 (3.1)	0.024 (0.6)
F5, F8, F9, K81M	0.11 (2.8)	0.010 (0.3)
KX400, KX450	0.12 (3.1)	0.024 (0.6)

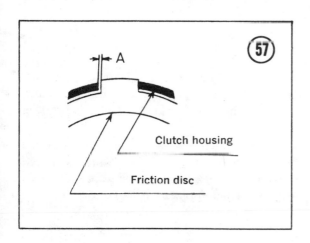

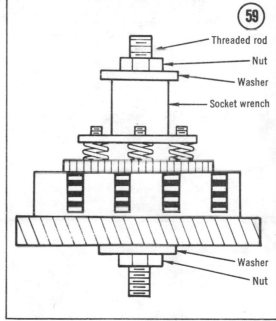

Insert the bushing into the needle bearing in the clutch housing (**Figure 58**). Replace the bushing if there is noticeable play. Excessive play results in gear noise.

Clutch Installation

Reverse the applicable disassembly procedure to reassemble the clutch. Be sure that all thrust washers are in position. An easy way to compress the clutch assembly during reassembly is to make a simple tool from a socket wrench of appropriate diameter, large washers, and a length of threaded rod or bolt of suitable length (**Figure 59**).

Clutch Adjustment (Types 1 and 2)

Figure 60 is a sectional view of a typical clutch adjustment mechanism on these machines. Refer to this illustration, then proceed as follows.

1. Refer to **Figure 61**. Loosen locknut (a), then back off adjustment screw (A) several turns.

2. Refer to **Figure 62**. Loosen locknut (b), then turn clutch cable adjuster (B) to set the angle of

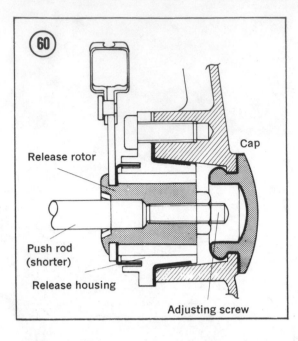

Cap

Release rotor

Push rod
(shorter)

Release housing

Adjusting screw

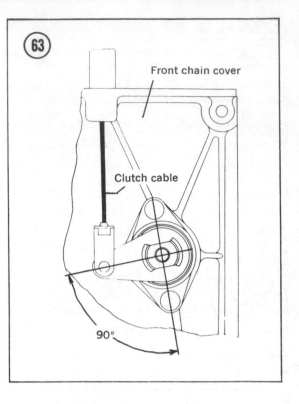

Front chain cover

Clutch cable

90°

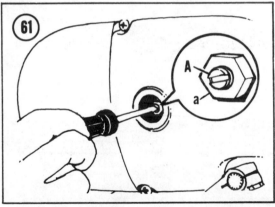

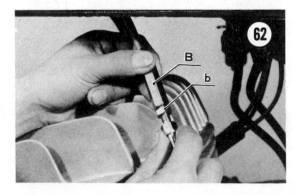

the clutch release lever to 90 degrees, as shown in **Figure 63**.

3. Refer back to Figure 61. Turn adjustment screw (A) clockwise until it seats lightly, then

hold it in that position, and tighten locknut (a). Be sure that screw (A) does not turn any further as you tighten the locknut, or clutch slippage may result.

4. Refer to **Figure 64**. Adjust play at the clutch lever to 0.5-0.7 in. (13-18mm). To do so, loosen locknut (c), then rotate cable adjuster (C) as required. Don't forget to tighten the locknut.

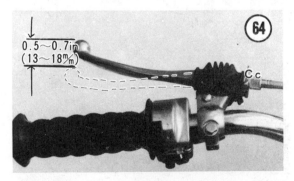

0.5~0.7in
(13~18m/m)

The illustrations for the foregoing procedure apply to F5, F8, F9, and F81M models. Remove the breaker contact cover to gain access to the adjustment screw on F6 and F7 models. On G series models, remove the carburetor cover. The adjustment procedure is similar for all models.

Clutch Adjustment (Type 4)

To adjust the clutch on these models, proceed as follows.

1. Refer to **Figure 65**. Loosen locknut (D) and cable adjustment screw (C).

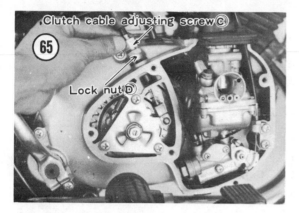

2. Refer to **Figure 66**. Loosen locknut (B), then turn adjusting screw (A) until the clutch release cable is completely slack.

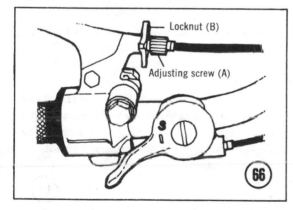

3. Refer to **Figure 67**. Loosen locknut (F). Turn adjustment screw (E) in until it seats, then back it out ¼-½ turn. Tighten locknut (F) securely.

4. Adjust play in the clutch lever to 0.5-0.7 in. (13-18mm). Loosen locknut (c), then rotate cable adjuster (C) as required. Tighten locknut.

Clutch Adjustment (Type 3)

To adjust the clutch on these models, proceed as follows.

1. Remove the carburetor cover.

2. Refer to **Figure 68**. Loosen the locknut, turn the adjuster in fully to give play to the cable, then tighten the locknut.

3. Refer to **Figure 69**. Loosen the locknut, then back out the adjusting screw several turns.

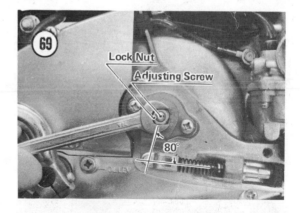

4. Refer to **Figure 70**. Loosen the locknut, then turn the adjusting nut as required until the angle between the clutch release lever and clutch cable is 80 degrees. Tighten the locknut.

5. Refer back to Figure 69. Turn in the adjusting screw until there is approximately 1/16-1/8 in. (2-3mm) play at the clutch lever (**Figure 71**). Be sure to tighten the locknut.

6. Minor adjustments may be made at the clutch hand lever.

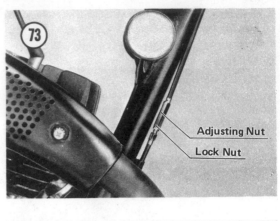

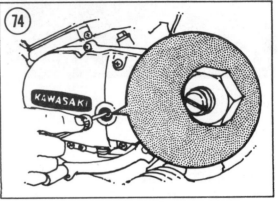

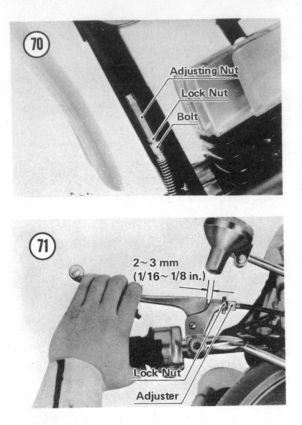

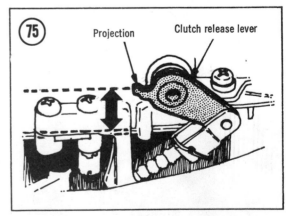

Clutch Adjustment (Type 5)

1. Slide clutch lever dust cover out of the way.

2. Refer to **Figure 72**. Loosen locknut slightly, then turn the adjuster to provide 0.20-0.24 in. (5-6mm) gap between the adjuster and locknut.

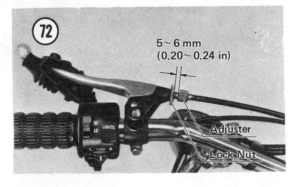

3. Refer to **Figure 73**. Loosen the locknut, then turn the adjusting nut to provide plenty of free play in the cable.

4. Remove the clutch adjustment hole cover.

5. Refer to **Figure 74**. Loosen the locknut. Back out the adjustment screw until it turns freely if it does not already do so.

6. Refer back to Figure 73. Turn the adjusting nut in the cable until the projection on the clutch release lever (**Figure 75**) is parallel with the seam between the left engine cover and left crankcase half.

7. Turn the adjustment screw (**Figure 76**) in until it seats lightly, then tighten the locknut. Do not allow the screw to turn when tightening the locknut.

Clutch Release Adjuster
57001-159

8. Refer back to Figure 73. Remove any play at the clutch hand lever by turning the cable adjustment nut. Then tighten the locknut.

9. Refer back to Figure 71. Adjust hand lever play to 1/16-1/8 in. (2-3mm) using the adjuster, then tighten the locknut.

10. Replace both covers.

Clutch Adjustment (Type 6)

1. Loosen the locknuts at each end of the clutch cable, then turn each adjuster to provide plenty of cable play.

2. Refer to **Figure 77**. Remove the release lever mounting bolt, then remove the release lever from its shaft.

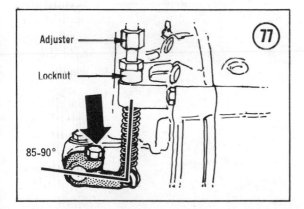

Adjuster

Locknut

85-90°

3. Replace the lever on its shaft so that it forms an angle of 85 to 90 degrees with the cable. Tighten the mounting bolt.

4. Turn the adjuster at the lower end of the cable to provide 1/16-1/8 in. (2-3mm) play at the clutch hand lever, then tighten the lower cable locknut.

5. Tighten the upper cable locknut.

6. Minor adjustments may be made with the upper cable adjuster.

ROTARY VALVE

The rotary valve system consists of the crankshaft, disc valve, crankcase, and disc cover. **Figure 78** is a sectional view of the valve mechanism.

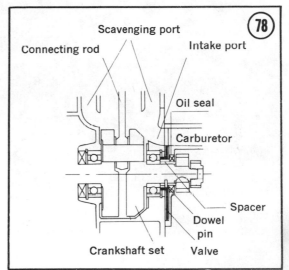

Scavenging port
Connecting rod
Intake port
Oil seal
Carburetor
Spacer
Dowel pin
Crankshaft set
Valve

On all rotary valve models but F5, F8, and F9, the disc is made from phenolic resin. The boss in the center of the disc is of steel, and is attached to the crankshaft with a dowel pin. Valve discs on models F5, F8, and F9 are of steel.

The valve floats back and forth a distance of 0.012 in. (0.3mm). This floating action permits the valve to seat against the O-ring on the valve cover, and thereby seal the crankcase during the down stroke of the piston.

Removal

To remove the rotary valve, proceed as follows.

1. Remove the valve cover retaining screws, then pull off the valve cover (**Figure 79**).

2. Slide the valve disc (**Figure 80**) from its shaft.

3. Remove the spacer, O-ring, and dowel from the crankshaft (**Figure 81**).

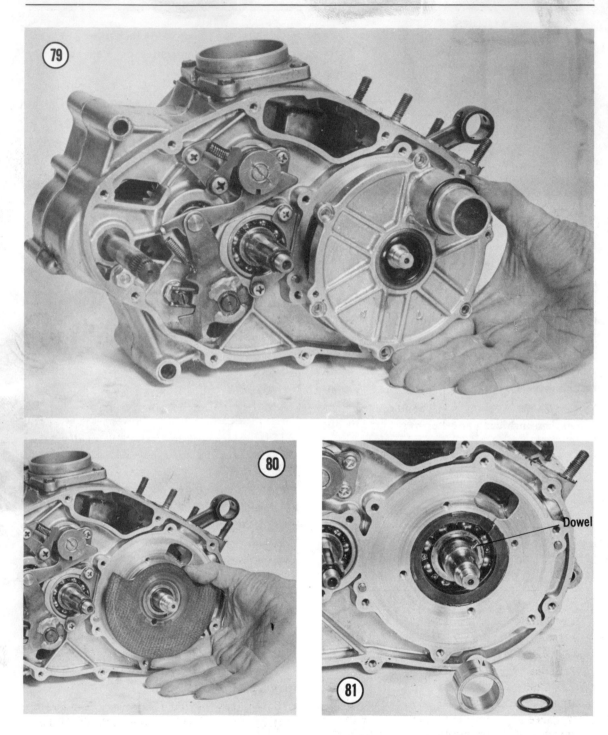

Inspection

Figure 82 illustrates the valve cover. Examine the oil seal for scratches, lip deformation, or other damage. Check for any damage to the O-ring. Replace the valve cover in the event of deep scratches, or if it is worn more than the wear limit specified in the following table. **Figure 83** illustrates the measurement. **Table 7** specifies wear limits.

Measure thickness of the valve disc, as shown in **Figure 84**. Replace the disc if it is worn beyond the wear limit, or if there are any scratches

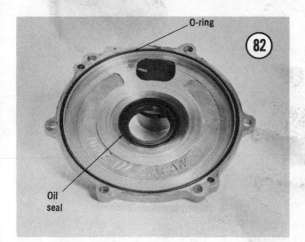

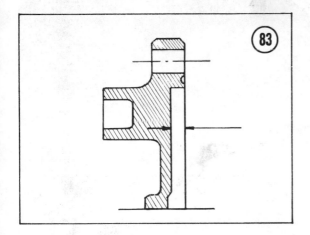

Table 7   VALVE COVER SPECIFICATIONS

Model	Standard Depth		Wear Limit	
	Inch	(mm)	Inch	(mm)
J1	0.13	(3.4)	0.16	(4.0)
G, M Series	0.13	(3.4)	0.16	(4.0)
G31M-A	0.14	(3.5)	0.16	(4.0)
KE, KH, KV100	0.14	(3.5)	0.16	(4.0)
B1 Series	0.14	(3.5)	0.16	(4.0)
C1D, C2SS	0.14	(3.5)	0.16	(4.0)
KD, KE, KS, KX125	0.03	(0.8)	0.05	(1.2)
F2, F3, F6	0.14	(3.5)	0.16	(4.0)
KE175	0.05	(1.2)	0.06	(1.5)
F4, F7	0.14	(3.5)	0.16	(4.0)
F5, F8, F81M, F9	0.03	(0.8)	0.01	(0.2)

or damage on its surface. Thickness should be as specified in **Table 8**.

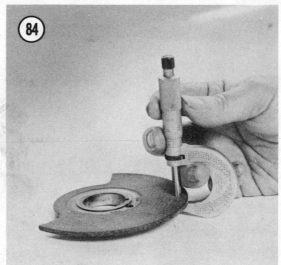

Table 8   VALVE DISC SPECIFICATIONS

Model	Standard Thickness		Wear Limit	
	Inch	(mm)	Inch	(mm)
KD, KE, KS125	0.16	(4.0)	0.15	(3.7)
B1L-A	0.16	(4.0)	0.15	(3.7)
F5, F8, F9, F81M	0.02	(0.5)	0.01	(0.4)
All others	0.12	(3.1)	0.11	(2.9)

Installation

Reverse the removal procedure to install the rotary valve. Observe the following notes.

1. Apply engine oil to both sides of the valve disc before installation.

2. Insert the smaller O-ring into the spacer on the crankshaft. Install the larger O-ring in the groove on the valve cover.

3. Tighten the valve cover screws in the order shown in **Figure 85**.

4. On models F6 and F7, be sure to align the mark on the valve with the pin on the crankshaft.

GEARSHIFT MECHANISM

Figure 86 illustrates external parts of a typical gearshift mechanism. As the rider presses the gearshift pedal, the shaft turns, and moves the change lever. The change lever meshes with pins

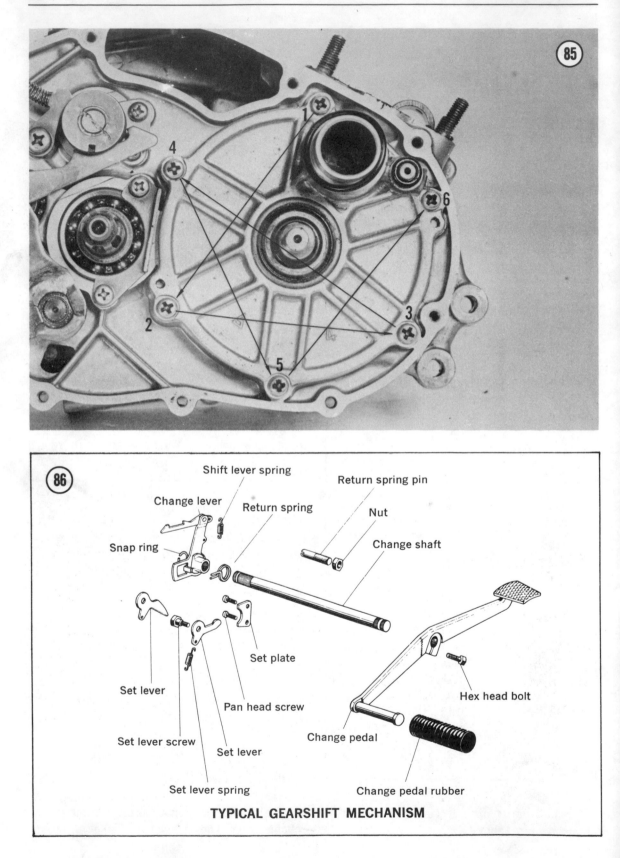

TYPICAL GEARSHIFT MECHANISM

on the shift drum (part of the transmission assembly). Therefore, as the pedal is moved, the shift drum rotates. Grooves on the shift drum cause shift forks in the transmission to slide from side to side, thereby selecting the various gear ratios (**Figure 87**).

The set levers are also meshed with the pins on the change drums. They keep the drum in position after each step of rotation of the drum.

Removal

To remove the gearshift mechanism, proceed as follows.

1. Carefully note how both set levers are installed (**Figure 88**).

2. Remove the shifter shaft retaining clip (**Figure 89**) and thrust washer.

3. Disengage set levers from gear change drum.

4. Pull out shifter shaft and levers as an assembly (**Figure 90**).

5. Note how return spring is installed, then remove it (**Figure 91**).

Inspection

Check return spring tension. Replace the spring if it is weak or cracked. Inspect the set lever spring for cracks or weakness. Be sure that the return spring set pin is not loose. If it is, missed shifts will result. Be sure that the locknut is tight.

Retaining clip

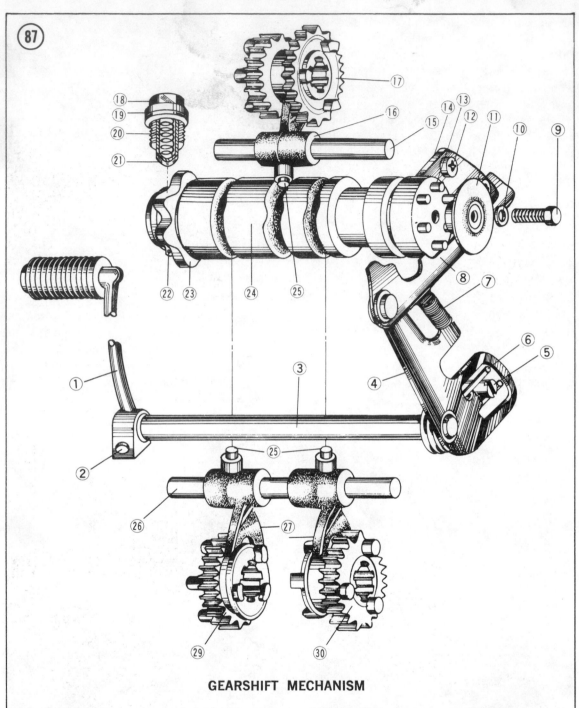

GEARSHIFT MECHANISM

1. Shift pedal	9. Screw	17. 3rd & 4th gear	24. Shift drum
2. Bolt	10. Washer	18. Drum positioning bolt	25. Guide pin
3. Gear change shaft	11. Drum pin holder	19. Gasket	26. Long shift rod
4. Arm	12. Screw	20. Spring	27. Shift fork
5. Return spring pin	13. Drum pin	21. Drum positioning pin	28. Shift fork
6. Return spring	14. Shift drum stopper	22. Circlip	29. 6th gear
7. Spring	15. Short shift rod	23. Drum operating disc	30. 5th gear
8. Shift pawl	16. Shift fork		

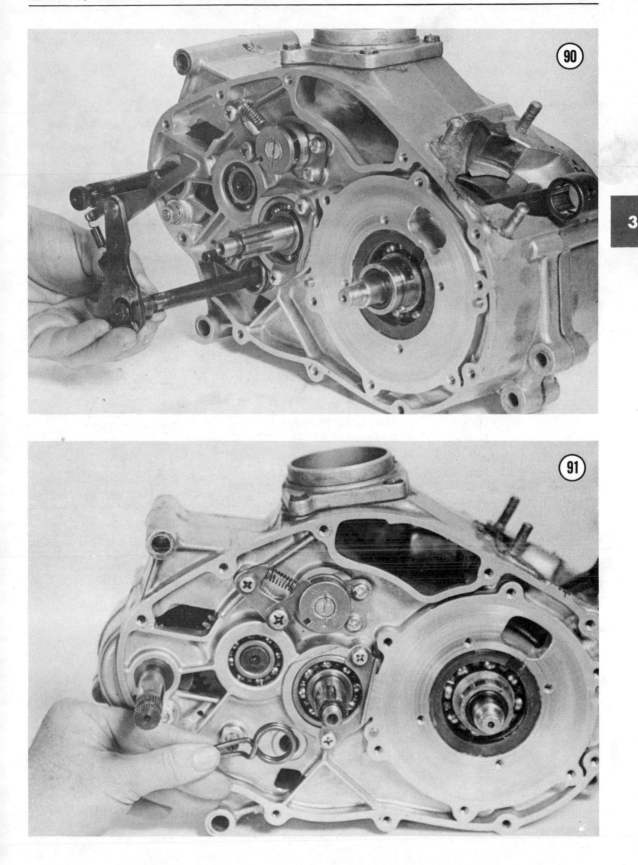

Installation

Reverse the removal procedure to install the shift mechanism. Observe the following notes.

1. Be sure to install each spring correctly.

2. On F series models, adjust shift lever position by turning the return spring setting pin as required.

CRANKCASE

The crankcase is made in 2 halves of diecast aluminum alloy. They are assembled without a gasket; only gasket cement, such as Kawasaki bond is used. Two dowel pins hold the crankcase halves in alignment when they are bolted together. **Figure 92** is an exploded view of a typical crankcase assembly.

Crankcase Disassembly

Crankcase disassembly is generally similar for all models. Note that M, KE, KS, KT, and KX series require a crankcase splitting tool.

1. Remove neutral indicator switch. Also remove snap rings from gearshift rods on models so equipped.

2. Remove air cleaner adapter (**Figure 93**).

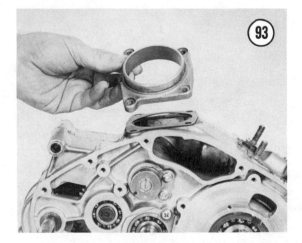

3. Remove the shift drum retaining plate (**Figure 94**).

4. Remove all crankcase screws. An impact tool will make this job much easier.

5. Using a rawhide mallet, alternately tap the left end of the crankshaft and transmission output shaft to split both crankcase halves, or use a crankcase splitting tool for those models mentioned.

6. Lift left crankcase away (**Figure 95**). Leave all internal components in the right crankcase half (**Figure 96**).

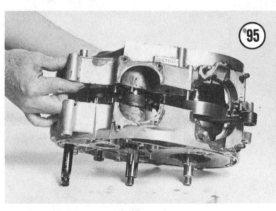

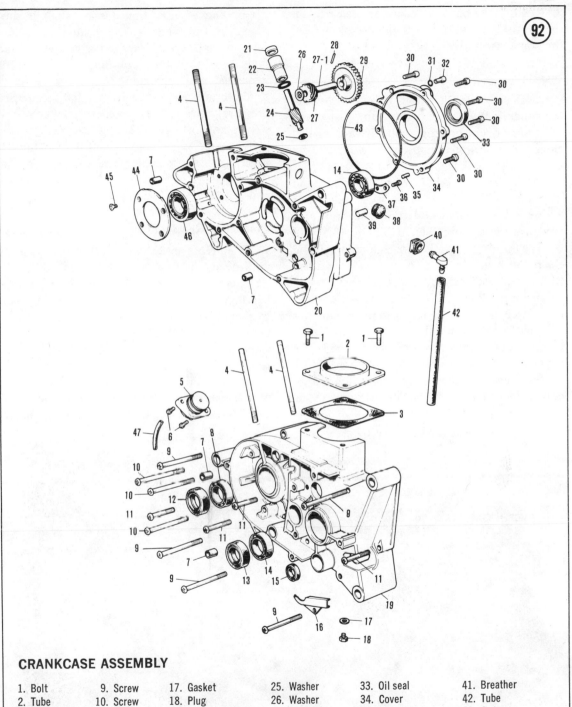

CRANKCASE ASSEMBLY

1. Bolt	9. Screw	17. Gasket	25. Washer	33. Oil seal	41. Breather
2. Tube	10. Screw	18. Plug	26. Washer	34. Cover	42. Tube
3. Gasket	11. Screw	19. Left crankcase	27. Gear	35. Dowel pin	43. O-ring
4. Stud	12. Oil seal	20. Right crankcase	28. Dowel pin	36. Screw	44. Bearing retainer
5. Pump	13. Oil seal	21. Oil seal	29. Gear	37. Bearing retainer	45. Screw
6. Screw	14. Bearing	22. Bushing	30. Screw	38. Grommet	46. Bearing
7. Dowel pin	15. Oil seal	23. O-ring	31. O-ring	39. Dowel pin	47. Tube
8. Bearing	16. Cover	24. Gear	32. Check valve	40. Grommet	

7. Remove the bearing retainers, then pry out the oil seals. Finally, press the bearings from the crankcase halves.

Inspection

Check each oil supply hole. If any are clogged, blow them out with compressed air. Also check the transmission breather hole. If dust or dirt clogs this hole, internal pressure will build up and cause oil leakage.

Check the crankshaft main bearings and transmission bearings for rust, wear, pitting, or excess radial clearance. If radial clearance of any bearing is more than 0.002 in. (0.5mm), replace the bearings. Before examining them, clean the bearings with solvent and dry them with compressed air. Do not spin bearings with an air blast. Transmission bearings are particularly susceptible to damage from metal particles or other foreign material in the transmission oil. Crankshaft bearings may become damaged if the air filter is damaged or missing. **Figure 97** illustrates a crankshaft bearing which failed after only a few miles of operation without an air filter.

One end of each transmission shaft is supported in a bushing. These bushings are lubricated by oil carried through a groove on the shaft. Examine these bushings carefully for wear, and replace them if necessary.

The crankcase oil seals maintain crankcase pressure. If these seals leak, primary compression leakage will occur and lead to poor engine performance and possible crankshaft failure. It is good practice to replace these seals each time the engine is overhauled. Also, check the oil seals on the transmission and shifter shafts.

Crankcase Reassembly

1. Begin reassembly by pressing in each bearing until its side is flush with the inner side of the crankcase, as shown in **Figure 98**. Lubricate the bearings with engine oil during installation. This work will be easier if the crankcase is heated to approximately 200°F in an oven. Do not use a torch for heating, as warping or cracking may result.

2. Press the oil seals in from the magneto side until they are flush with the outside of the crankcase, as shown in **Figure 99**. Markings on the oil

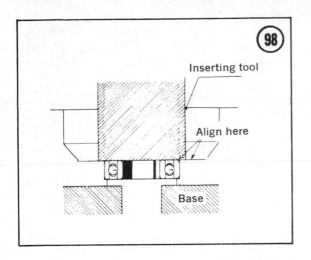

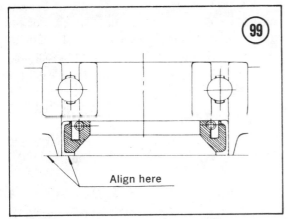

seals should be toward the magneto, or visible after they are installed. Always install new oil seals when replacing bearings. Lubricate seal lips with engine oil upon installation.

3. On machines so equipped, lubricate the needle bearing, then press it in until it stops.

4. Lubricate the transmission drive shaft bushing then press it in from the gearshift pedal side.

5. Install the crankshaft into the right crankcase half, except on M Series. If the crankshaft must be pressed in, use a wedge between crank wheels to maintain crankshaft alignment.

6. Insert the kick shaft.

7. Install the transmission and shifter drum as a unit. On models with a ball on the end of the transmission drive shaft, a little grease will hold the ball in position during assembly.

8. Apply gasket cement to the mating surfaces of the crankcase halves.

9. On G series models, install the ball and shim at the end of the transmission drive shaft.

10. Assemble both crankcase halves. Tap the left half with a plastic mallet to seat it against the right half. Take care not to damage oil seals.

11. Install and tighten the crankcase screws.

After assembly, be sure that the crankshaft and transmission gears rotate smoothly. Check the gearshift mechanism for smoothness and positive operation. Be sure that the kick gear and kick ratchet operate properly.

KICKSTARTER

Several different types of kickstarter mechanisms are used on Kawasaki machines. Refer to the applicable section for the procedure to follow for your machine.

To remove the kickstarter, first take careful note of how it is installed, then lift it from the crankcase (**Figure 100**).

Type 1 Kickstarter

Figure 101 is an exploded view of this kickstarter mechanism. As the rider presses the kickstarter pedal, the kick shaft rotates clockwise (**Figure 102**). As the kick shaft rotates, the kick pawl spring and kick pawl pin push the kick pawl away from the kick pawl stopper, and into engagement with the internal teeth of the kick gear. After the engine starts, and the kick pedal

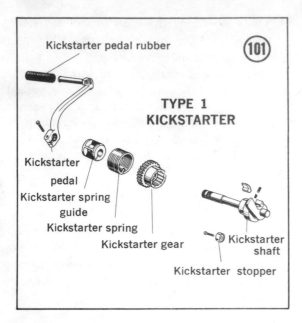

Kickstarter pedal rubber

TYPE 1 KICKSTARTER

Kickstarter pedal

Kickstarter spring guide

Kickstarter spring

Kickstarter gear

Kickstarter shaft

Kickstarter stopper

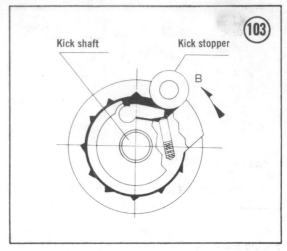

Kick shaft   Kick stopper

B

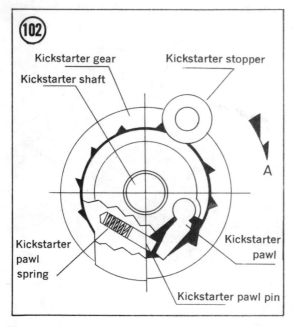

Kickstarter gear   Kickstarter stopper

Kickstarter shaft

A

Kickstarter pawl spring

Kickstarter pawl

Kickstarter pawl pin

3. Remove the kick stopper from the left crankcase half.

After disassembly, inspect the following items.
1. Check the inner teeth of the kick gear for wear. If these teeth are worn or rounded, the pawl will slip. Replace the gear if the teeth are worn or damaged.
2. Check for wear on the tip of the kick pawl. Wear results in slippage. Replace the pawl if the tip is worn.
3. Be sure that there is no foreign material in the pawl pin hole. Check for freedom of movement of the pawl pin and pawl spring.

Installation is generally the reverse of removal. Observe the following notes.
1. Install the kick stopper into the left crankcase half.
2. Insert the pawl spring, then the pawl pin, into the hole in the kick shaft.
3. Install the kick pawl. Hold the kick pawl down, then install the kick gear.
4. Insert one end of the kick spring into the hole in the right crankcase half. Twist the outer end of the spring clockwise approximately 120 degrees and insert it into the hole on the kick shaft (**Figure 104**).

Type 2 Kickstarter

Figures 105 and 106 are exploded and sectional views of this kickstarter. When the pedal is pressed, the kick gear slides along the kick shaft and meshes with the low gear on the output shaft, thereby turning the engine. When the

is released, the kick shaft returns to its original position. At this time, the kick pawl stopper (**Figure 103**) contacts the kick pawl and holds it away from the kick gear, thereby releasing the mechanism during normal running.

To disassemble this mechanism, proceed as follows.
1. Slide the kick gear from the kickstarter shaft.
2. Disassemble the pawl, pawl pin, and pawl spring.

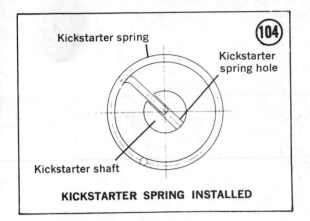

Kickstarter spring

(104)

Kickstarter spring hole

Kickstarter shaft

KICKSTARTER SPRING INSTALLED

engine starts, the kick gear is driven by the gear on the output idle gear, and forced to disengage. When the kick pedal is released, the kick shaft turns clockwise and is stopped by the kick stopper.

To disassemble this kickstarter, proceed as follows.

1. Remove the spring guide, the spring, and both snap rings.

2. Remove the snap rings and the kick gear from the kick shaft.

After disassembly check the following items.

1. Check the kick gear guide and kick gear splines for wear and free movement.

2. Check the kick shaft for bends or cracks.

3. Check the teeth of the kick gear for wear or damage.

Installation is generally the reverse of removal. Observe the following notes.

1. Insert the kick shaft into the right crankcase half. Be sure the shim is in place, then install the snap rings.

2. Insert one end of the spring into the hole in the right crankcase half. Twist the spring clockwise approximately 120 degrees, then insert the other end into the hole in the kick shaft.

3. Slide the spring guide onto the kick shaft.

4. Install the kick gear and gear holder from outside the right crankcase half, then install the snap ring into its groove on the kick shaft.

Type 3 Kickstarter

Figure 107 is an exploded view of this kickstarter. **Figure 108** illustrates its operation. The ratchet slides along the splined portion of the

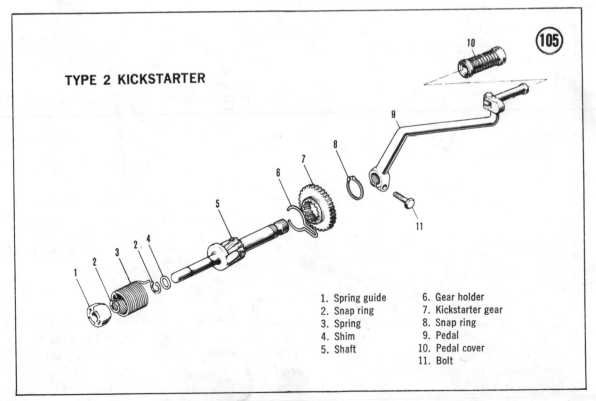

TYPE 2 KICKSTARTER

(105)

1. Spring guide
2. Snap ring
3. Spring
4. Shim
5. Shaft
6. Gear holder
7. Kickstarter gear
8. Snap ring
9. Pedal
10. Pedal cover
11. Bolt

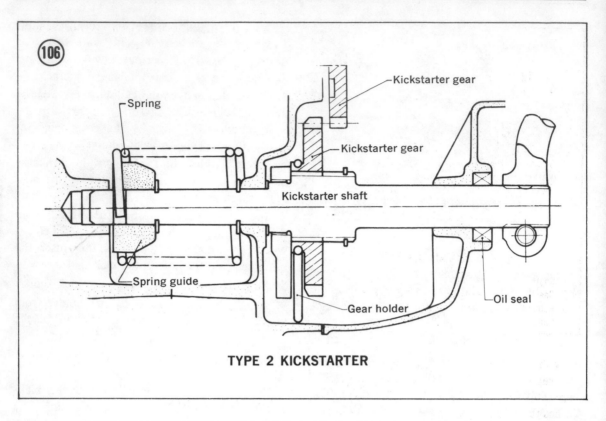

TYPE 2 KICKSTARTER

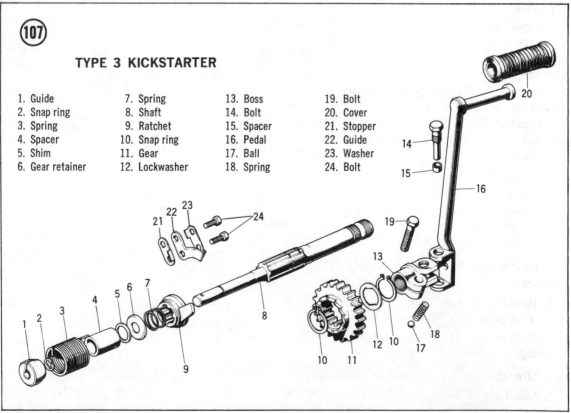

TYPE 3 KICKSTARTER

1. Guide	7. Spring	13. Boss	19. Bolt
2. Snap ring	8. Shaft	14. Bolt	20. Cover
3. Spring	9. Ratchet	15. Spacer	21. Stopper
4. Spacer	10. Snap ring	16. Pedal	22. Guide
5. Shim	11. Gear	17. Ball	23. Washer
6. Gear retainer	12. Lockwasher	18. Spring	24. Bolt

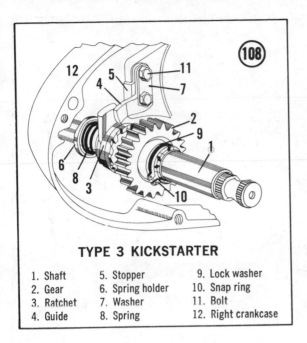

TYPE 3 KICKSTARTER

1. Shaft	5. Stopper	9. Lock washer
2. Gear	6. Spring holder	10. Snap ring
3. Ratchet	7. Washer	11. Bolt
4. Guide	8. Spring	12. Right crankcase

kick shaft. When the rider presses the kick pedal, the ratchet slides past the kick guide until it separates from the guide plate. The spring then forces the ratchet against the teeth on the side of the kick gear, causing the kick gear to turn. The kick gear is always meshed with the kickstarter idler gear in the transmission.

When the engine starts, the kick gear is driven by the kick idler gear in the transmission. The teeth on the side of the kick gear slide over the teeth on the ratchet until the kick starter pedal is released. When the kickstarter pedal is released, the ratchet is forced to move away from the kick gear by the guide plate.

> NOTE: *F8 and early F5 models before engine No. 07269 do not use the kick guide plate. Helical splines on the kick shaft force the ratchet against the side of the kick gear.*

To disassemble this mechanism, proceed as follows.

1. Remove the kick gear snap ring, then pull the kick gear from the kick shaft.

2. Remove the ratchet, spring holder plate, and spring.

After disassembly, check the following items.

1. Check that the ratchet slides against the kick guide properly.

2. Be sure that the kick shaft is not bent or scratched.

3. Check for worn or damaged teeth on the kick gear.

Installation is generally the reverse of removal. Observe the following notes.

1. Install the kick guide and kick stopper into the crankcase. Be sure both screws are tight.

2. Insert the kick shaft into its hole.

3. Install the spring holder, shim, spacer, and snap ring.

4. Insert one end of the return spring into the hole in the crankcase. Twist the spring approximately 120 degrees and insert the other end into the hole in the kick shaft.

5. Slide the spring guide onto the kick shaft.

6. Slide the ratchet onto the kick shaft. Be sure that the marks on the kick shaft and the ratchet are aligned.

7. Install the kick gear and kick gear snap ring.

Type 4 Kickstarter

Figure 109 is an exploded view of this kickstarter. Operation, disassembly, service, and installation are similar to Type 3 kickstarter.

Type 5 Kickstarter

Figure 110 is an exploded view of this kickstarter. Its operation, disassembly, service, and installation are similar to that of Type 3.

CRANKSHAFT

The crankshaft operates under conditions of high stress. Dimensional tolerances are critical. It is necessary to locate and correct defects in the crankshaft to prevent more serious trouble later. **Figure 111** illustrates parts of a typical crankshaft assembly.

To remove the crankshaft, first be sure that the dowel (**Figure 112**) has been removed. Start it by tapping its end with a rawhide mallet, then lift it out (**Figure 113**).

Inspection

There are several measurement locations on the crankshaft assembly. Measurements to be

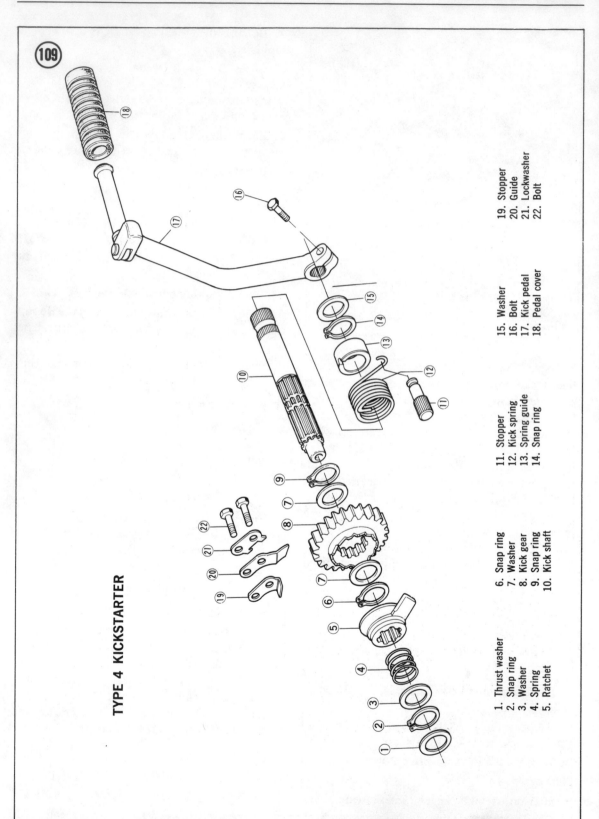

109

TYPE 4 KICKSTARTER

1. Thrust washer
2. Snap ring
3. Washer
4. Spring
5. Ratchet

6. Snap ring
7. Washer
8. Kick gear
9. Snap ring
10. Kick shaft

11. Stopper
12. Kick spring
13. Spring guide
14. Snap ring

15. Washer
16. Bolt
17. Kick pedal
18. Pedal cover

19. Stopper
20. Guide
21. Lockwasher
22. Bolt

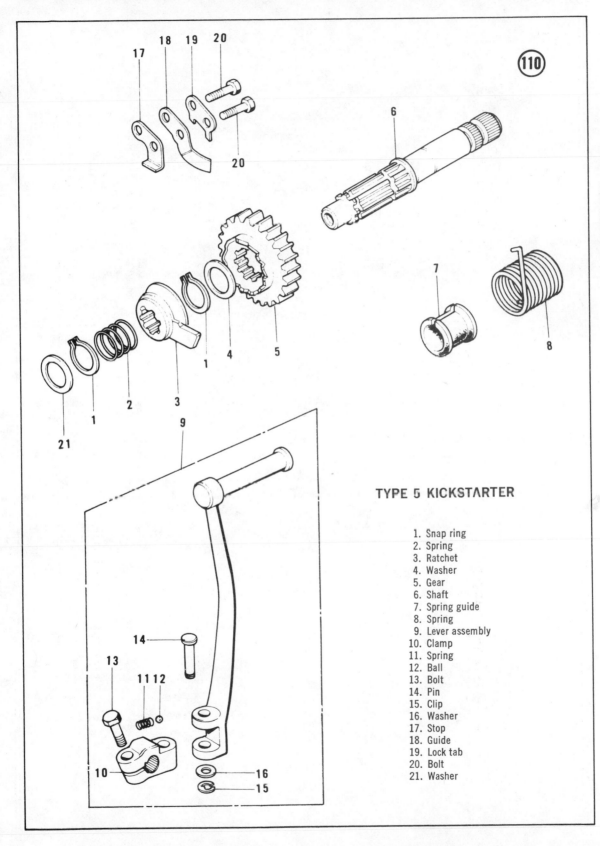

TYPE 5 KICKSTARTER

1. Snap ring
2. Spring
3. Ratchet
4. Washer
5. Gear
6. Shaft
7. Spring guide
8. Spring
9. Lever assembly
10. Clamp
11. Spring
12. Ball
13. Bolt
14. Pin
15. Clip
16. Washer
17. Stop
18. Guide
19. Lock tab
20. Bolt
21. Washer

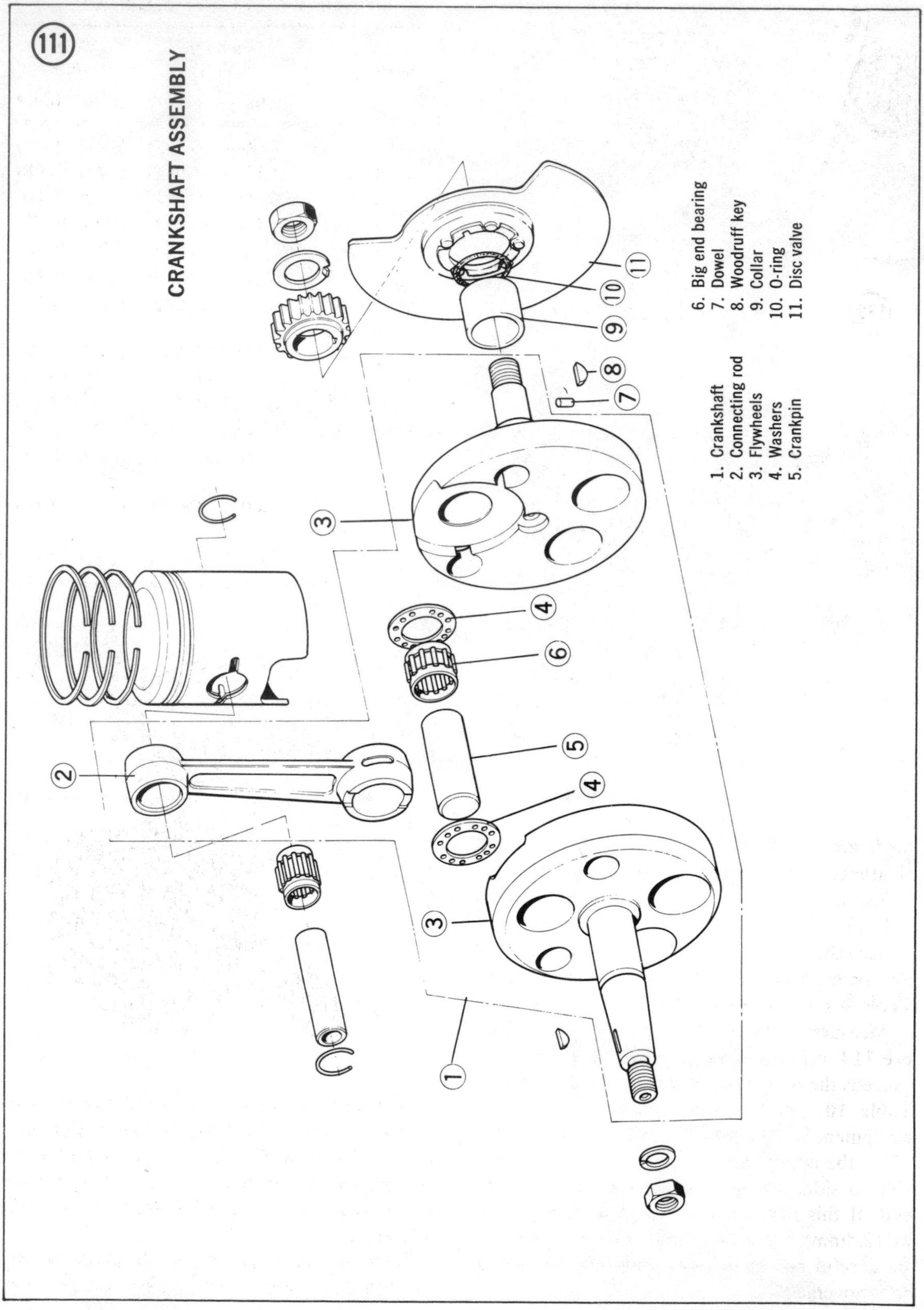

CRANKSHAFT ASSEMBLY

1. Crankshaft
2. Connecting rod
3. Flywheels
4. Washers
5. Crankpin
6. Big end bearing
7. Dowel
8. Woodruff key
9. Collar
10. O-ring
11. Disc valve

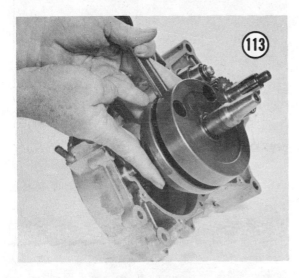

Table 9	BIG END CLEARANCE			
Model	Standard Play		Wear Limit	
	Inch	(mm)	Inch	(mm)
J1	0.0008	(0.021)	0.008	(0.20)
M Series	0.0011	(0.029)	0.003	(0.08)
G Series	0.0009	(0.022)	0.008	(0.20)
G4TR	0.0006	(0.014)	0.002	(0.05)
KE, KH, KV100	0.0011	(0.029)	0.003	(0.08)
C1D, C2SS	0.0009	(0.022)	0.002	(0.05)
B1 Series	0.0007	(0.020)	0.002	(0.05)
KD, KE, KS, KX125	0.0008	(0.021)	0.008	(0.02)
KE175	0.0006	(0.014)	0.003	(0.08)
KT250	0.0020	(0.052)	0.004	(0.10)
F2, F3, F6, F7	0.0006	(0.014)	0.008	(0.20)
F4, F21M	0.0019	(0.050)	0.004	(0.10)
F5, F8, F81M, F9	0.0019	(0.050)	0.004	(0.10)
KX250, 400, 450	0.0015	(0.037)	0.004	(0.10)

made are big end radial clearance, big end side clearance, and small end radial clearance.

Measure big end radial clearance with a dial indicator. If clearance exceeds the wear limit, replace the crankpin and needle bearing. It may also be necessary to replace the connecting rod. **Table 9** specifies wear limits.

Measure side clearance as shown in **Figure 114**, using a feeler gauge. If side clearance exceeds the wear limit, replace the side washers. **Table 10** specifies wear limits. If measuring equipment is not available, refer to **Figure 115**. Move the upper end of the connecting rod from side to side. Measure movement of the upper end. If this movement is no greater than 0.10 in. (2.5mm), the lower end bearing is not worn. Be careful not to mistake side play for upper end movement.

Measure piston pin radial clearance at measurement location (A) in **Figure 116**. If clearance exceeds 0.002 in. (0.05mm), replace the needle bearing and piston pin. Standard clearance for all models is 0.00012-0.00086 in. (0.003-0.022mm).

If this measurement is difficult, clean and dry the piston pin, upper end bearing, and connect-

Table 10 CONNECTING ROD SIDE CLEARANCE

Model	Standard Clearance		Wear Limit	
	Inch	(mm)	Inch	(mm)
J1	0.016	(0.40)	0.024	(0.60)
M Series	0.016	(0.40)	0.024	(0.60)
G4TR	0.011	(0.28)	0.018	(0.45)
C1D, C2SS	0.011	(0.28)	0.018	(0.45)
KE, KH, KV100	0.021	(0.53)	0.024	(0.60)
B1 Series	0.011	(0.28)	0.018	(0.45)
KD, KE, KS, KX125	0.015	(0.38)	0.024	(0.60)
KE175	0.016	(0.40)	0.024	(0.60)
KT250	0.020	(0.50)	0.027	(0.70)
F2, F3, F6, F7	0.015	(0.38)	0.024	(0.60)
F4, F21M	0.017	(0.43)	0.024	(0.60)
F5, F8, F9, F81M	0.017	(0.43)	0.024	(0.60)
KX250	0.016	(0.40)	0.031	(0.80)
KX400, 450	0.020	(0.50)	0.039	(1.00)

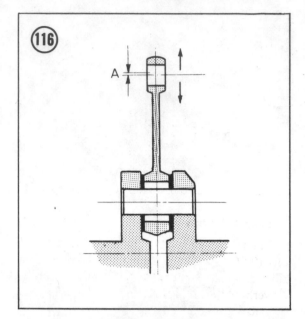

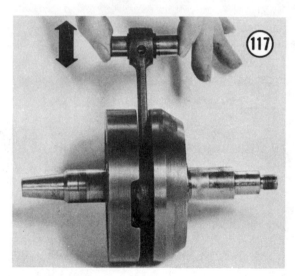

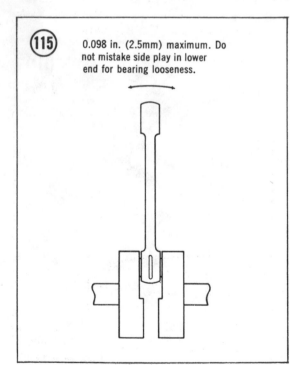

0.098 in. (2.5mm) maximum. Do not mistake side play in lower end for bearing looseness.

ing rod. Assemble them without lubrication. Then check for any perceptible play in the upper end (**Figure 117**). If any exists, replace the piston pin and bearing. In extreme cases it may be necessary to replace the connecting rod also.

Crankshaft Runout

Mount the crankshaft in a lathe, V-blocks, or other suitable centering device. Rotate the crankshaft through a complete revolution and measure runout at the main bearing journals, as shown in **Figure 118**. If the dial indicator reading is greater than the repair limit, disassemble the crankshaft and replace the crankpin. If runout exceeds the standard limit, but does not exceed the repair limit, it may be corrected. Standard runout limit for all models is 0.0012 in. (0.03mm). The repair limit is 0.004 in. (0.10mm) for all models.

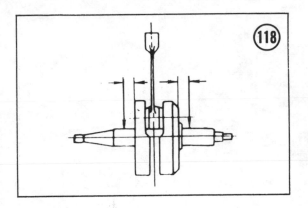

Crankshaft Overhaul

Crankshaft overhaul requires a press of 10-12 tons (9,000-11,000 kg) capacity, holding jigs, and a crankshaft alignment jig. Do not attempt to overhaul the crankshaft unless this equipment is available.

1. Place the crankshaft assembly in a suitable jig, then press out the crankpin from the drive side first (**Figure 119**).

2. Remove the spacers, connecting rod, and lower end bearing (**Figure 120**).

3. Press the crankpin out from the magneto side (**Figure 121**).

4. Carefully remove all residue from the crank wheels.

5. Using a suitable alignment fixture, press the replacement crankpin into the magneto side crank wheel (**Figure 122**) until the end of the crankpin is flush with the outside of the crank wheel.

6. Install a side washer, then the bearing.

7. Install the connecting rod then the remaining side washer. There is no front or back to the connecting rod; it fits either way.

8. Using a small square for initial alignment (**Figure 123**), start pressing the drive side crank wheel onto the crankpin.

9. Select a feeler gauge of appropriate thickness (Table 10), then insert it between the upper spacer and drive side crank wheel. Continue pressing the drive side crank wheel onto the crankpin until the feeler gauge fits tightly.

10. Release all pressure from the press. The feeler gauge will then slip out easily.

3

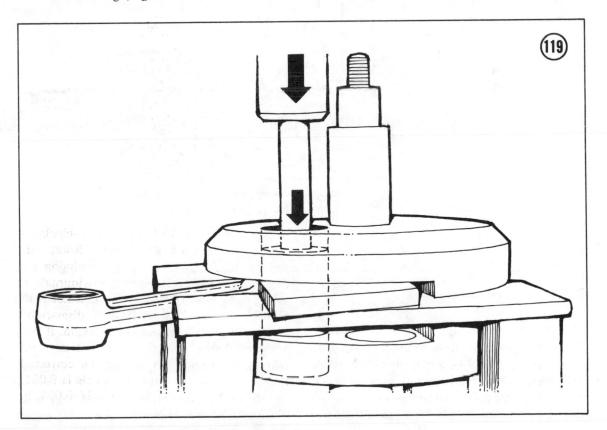

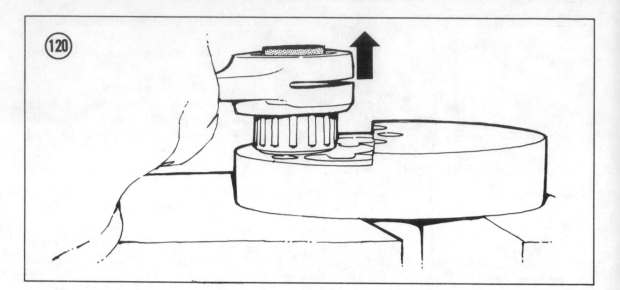

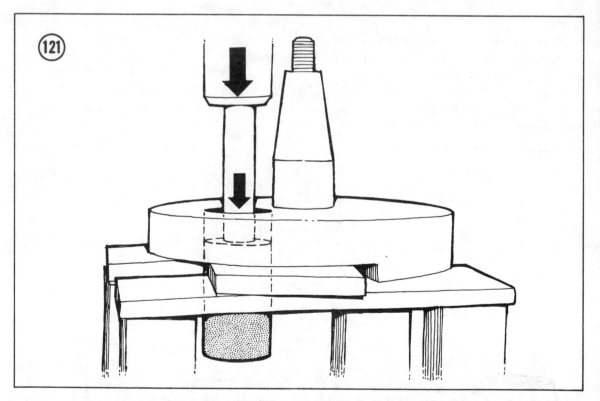

11. Align the crankshaft assembly.

If after a crankshaft seizure, either crankshaft half is damaged, replace the entire crankshaft assembly. Otherwise, disassemble the crankshaft and replace the connecting rod, needle bearing, side washers, and crankpin.

Defective crankshaft seals are the most common cause of catastrophic crankshaft failures.

Always replace crankcase oil seals when the crankshaft is removed for service.

Crankshaft Alignment

After any crankshaft service, it is necessary to align the assembly so that both crank wheels and the shafts extending from them all rotate on a common center. Mount the assembled crank-

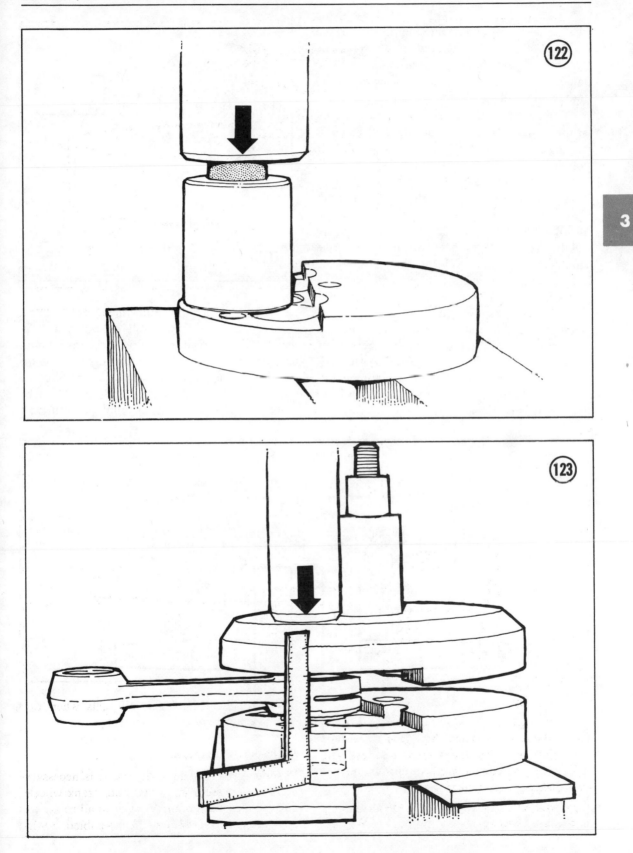

shaft in a suitable alignment fixture, as described under *Crankshaft Runout*, then slowly rotate the crankshaft through one or more complete turns, and observe both dial indicators. One of several indications will be observed.

1. Neither dial indicator needle begins its swing at the same time, and the needles will move in opposite directions during part of the crankshaft rotation cycle. Each needle will probably indicate a different amount of total travel. This condition is caused by eccentricity (both crank wheels not being on the same center), as shown in **Figure 124**. To correct this situation, slowly rotate the crankshaft assembly until the drive side dial gauge indicates its maximum. Mark the rim of the drive side crank wheel at the point in line with the plungers on both dial gauges. Remove the crankshaft assembly from the jig, then while holding the magneto side crank wheel in one hand, strike the chalk mark a sharp blow with a brass or lead mallet (**Figure 125**). Recheck alignment after each blow, and continue this procedure until both dial gauges begin and end their swings at the same time.

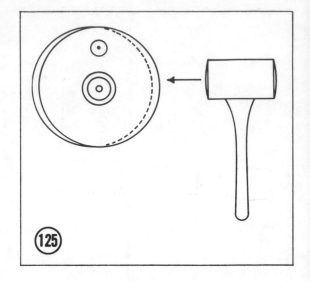

2. After the foregoing adjustment is completed, the crank wheels may still be pinched (**Figure 126**), or spread (**Figure 127**). Both dial indicators will indicate maximum travel when the crankpin is toward the dial gauges if the crank wheels are pinched. Correct this condition by removing the crankshaft assembly, then drive a

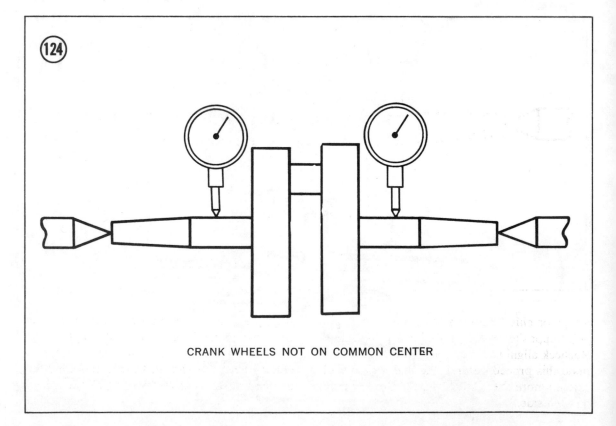

CRANK WHEELS NOT ON COMMON CENTER

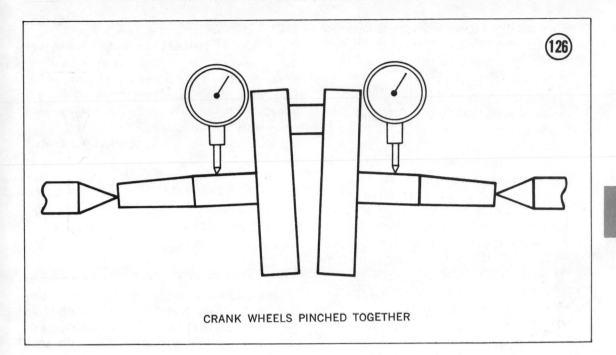

CRANK WHEELS PINCHED TOGETHER

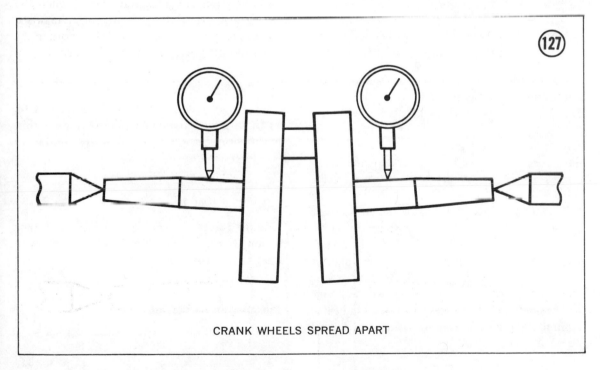

CRANK WHEELS SPREAD APART

wedge or chisel between the crank wheels at a point opposite maximum dial gauge indication. Recheck alignment after each adjustment. Continue this procedure until the dial gauges indicate no more than 0.0012 in. (0.03mm) runout on each side.

If the dial gauges indicate their maximum when the crankpin is on the side of the alignment test jig away from the dial gauges, the crank wheels are spread. Correct this condition by tapping the outside of one of the wheels toward the other with a brass or lead mallet.

Recheck alignment after each blow. Continue adjustment until runout is within the tolerance specified in the foregoing paragraph.

> NOTE: *It may be necessary to repeat the correction for eccentricity during the correction procedure for pinch or spread.*

TRANSMISSION

Kawasaki bikes are variously equipped with 4-, 5-, and 6-speed transmissions. Although service procedures for the various transmissions are similar, individual gear ratios differ, depending on transmission usage. Service procedures are similar for all models; differences will be pointed out where they exist.

Type 1 Transmission

Figures 128 and 129 are exploded and sectional views of this transmission, which is used on G series models, except for G4.

As the gearshift mechanism rotates the shift drum, the shift forks move in slots in the drum to position the shift forks, and thereby select the different gear positions within the transmission. The change drum is provided with 6 pins. Each time the gearshift pedal is operated, the drum rotates ⅙ of a revolution. Each step selects one gear ratio.

The steel ball at the end of the drive shaft eliminates the influence of thrust produced by clutch action, and makes gear changes easier. The idler gears transmit the kick gear rotation to the primary gear, through the gear in the clutch housing. The transmission switch mounts on the crankcase. It causes the neutral indicator lamp to light when the transmission is in neutral position.

Type 2 Transmission

Figure 130 is an exploded view of this transmission. It features dual-range operation, which provides greater reduction for off-road operations.

Type 3 Transmission

Figures 131 and 132 are exploded and sectional views of this transmission used on the F series models. The selector forks slide along guide bars, instead of sliding on the shift cam. The pins on the shift forks are inserted into grooves on the shift drum. Rotation of the shift drum moves the shift forks to select the desired gear ratio.

Three balls are spaced every 120 degrees around the output shaft. They are used to set the neutral position, which is between first and second gear position.

Type 4 Transmission

Figure 133 is an exploded view of this transmission. The shift drum is provided with 5 pins. Each movement of the gearshift pedal rotates the drum ⅕ revolution. Each step selects one gear position or neutral. The shift forks move in grooves in the shift drum to select the gear ratios.

Type 5 Transmission

This transmission has 6 speeds. **Figures 134 and 135** are sectional and exploded views of this transmission. Service procedures are similar to those of other transmissions.

Type 6 Transmission

Figure 136 is an exploded view of this transmission. Note that all shift forks slide on rails rather than on the shift cam itself.

Transmission Disassembly

1. Lift transmission from crankcase as a unit (**Figure 137**).

2. Remove shift forks from shift drum by removing cotter pins and shift fork pins.

3. On some models the shift forks slide on guide rods. They are removed when the shift fork pins are removed from the shift drum.

4. Remove each gear (**Figure 138**) by removing its associated snap ring and thrust washer.

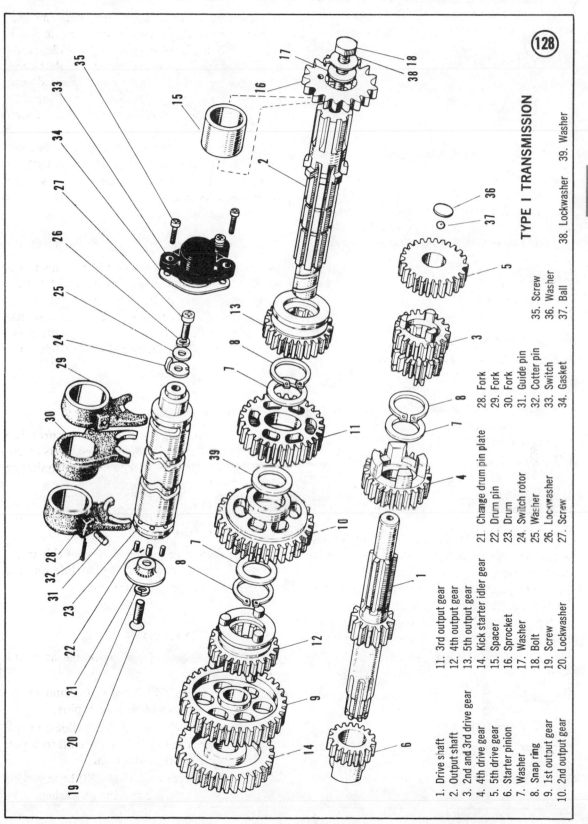

(128)

TYPE I TRANSMISSION

1. Drive shaft
2. Output shaft
3. 2nd and 3rd gear
4. 4th drive gear
5. 5th drive gear
6. Starter pinion
7. Washer
8. Snap ring
9. 1st output gear
10. 2nd output gear
11. 3rd output gear
12. 4th output gear
13. 5th output gear
14. Kick starter idler gear
15. Spacer
16. Sprocket
17. Washer
18. Bolt
19. Screw
20. Lockwasher
21. Change drum pin plate
22. Drum pin
23. Drum
24. Switch rotor
25. Washer
26. Lockwasher
27. Screw
28. Fork
29. Fork
30. Fork
31. Guide pin
32. Cotter pin
33. Switch
34. Gasket
35. Screw
36. Washer
37. Ball
38. Lockwasher
39. Washer

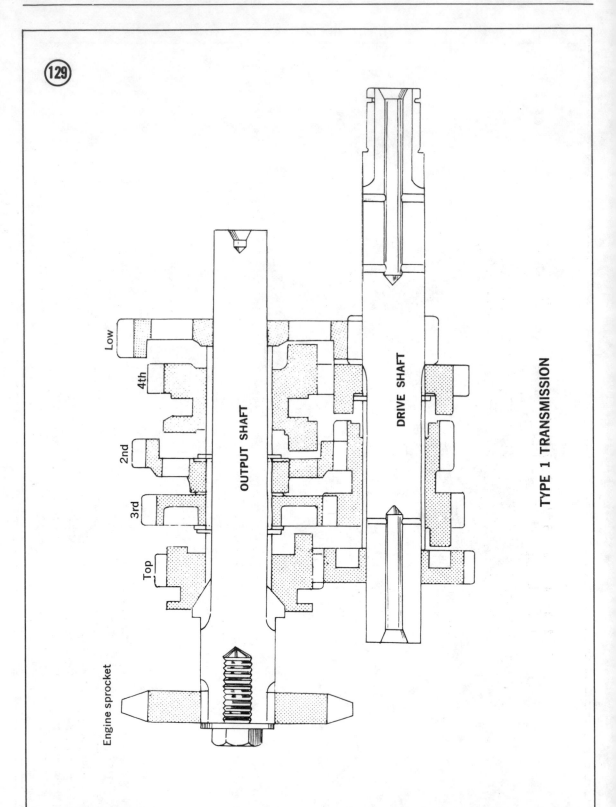

Engine sprocket

OUTPUT SHAFT

Low

4th

2nd

3rd

Top

DRIVE SHAFT

TYPE 1 TRANSMISSION

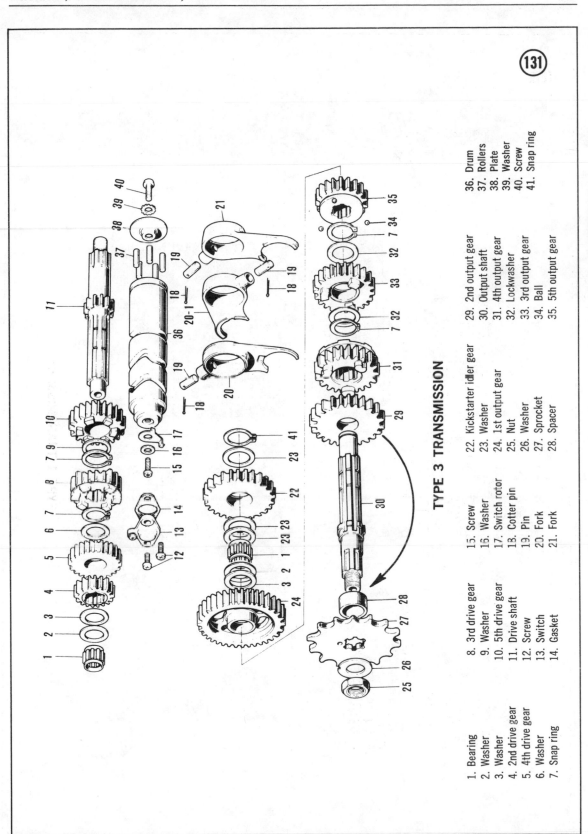

(131)

TYPE 3 TRANSMISSION

1. Bearing
2. Washer
3. Washer
4. 2nd drive gear
5. 4th drive gear
6. Washer
7. Snap ring

8. 3rd drive gear
9. Washer
10. 5th drive gear
11. Drive shaft
12. Screw
13. Switch
14. Gasket

15. Screw
16. Washer
17. Switch rotor
18. Cotter pin
19. Pin
20. Fork
21. Fork

22. Kickstarter idler gear
23. Washer
24. 1st output gear
25. Nut
26. Washer
27. Sprocket
28. Spacer

29. 2nd output gear
30. Output shaft
31. 4th output gear
32. Lockwasher
33. 3rd output gear
34. Ball
35. 5th output gear

36. Drum
37. Rollers
38. Plate
39. Washer
40. Screw
41. Snap ring

3

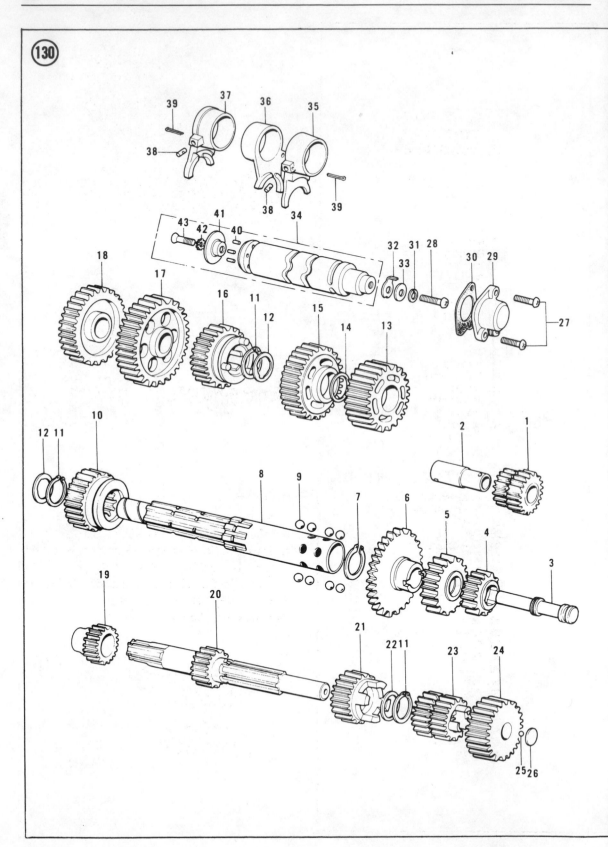

TYPE 2
TRANSMISSION

1. Gear
2. Countershaft
3. Rod
4. Gear
5. Gear
6. Engine sprocket
7. Snap ring
8. Shaft
9. Ball
10. Gear
11. Snap ring
12. Thrust washer
13. 3rd gear
14. Thrust washer
15. 2nd gear
16. 4th gear
17. Low gear
18. Idle gear
19. Pinion
20. Drive shaft
21. 4th gear
22. Thrust washer
23. 2nd and 3rd gear
24. Gear
25. Ball
26. Thrust washer
27. Screw
28. Screw
29. Switch
30. Gasket
31. Washer
32. Rotor
33. Washer
34. Drum
35. Fork
36. Fork
37. Fork
38. Pin
39. Pin
40. Pin
41. Plate
42. Lockwasher
43. Screw

Inspection

1. Measure clearance between each shift fork and the groove on its associated gear as shown in **Figure 139**. Standard clearance is 0.004–0.01 in. (0.1-0.25mm). Replace the gear and/or the fork if the clearance exceeds 0.024 in. (0.6mm). Replace the shift fork if there are any burrs or other damage.

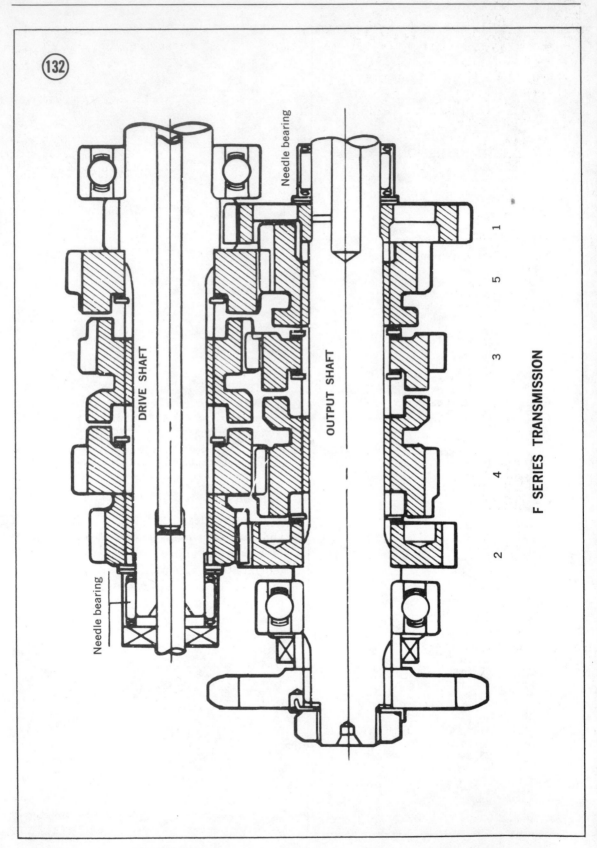

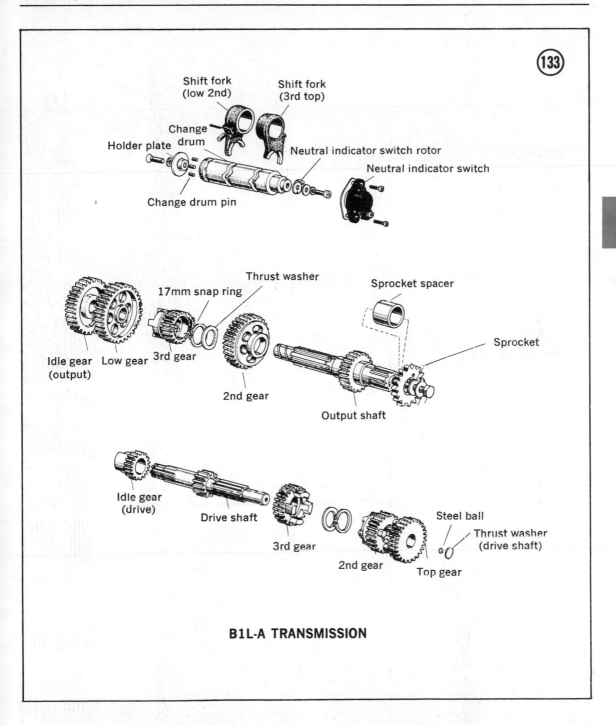

B1L-A TRANSMISSION

2. Any burrs, pits, or roughness on the gear teeth will cause wear on the mating gear. Replace any gear with such defects. Examine its mating gear carefully and replace it if there is any doubt about its condition.

3. Check dog clutch teeth (**Figure 140**) for wear or damage.

4. Be sure that all sliding gears operate smoothly on their splines.

Transmission Assembly

To assemble the transmission, reverse the disassembly procedure. Observe the following notes.

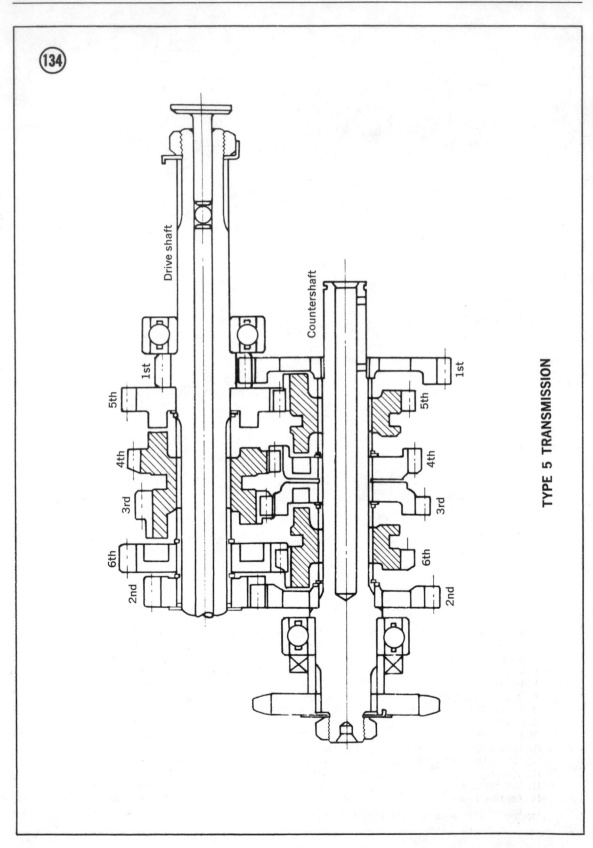

TYPE 5 TRANSMISSION

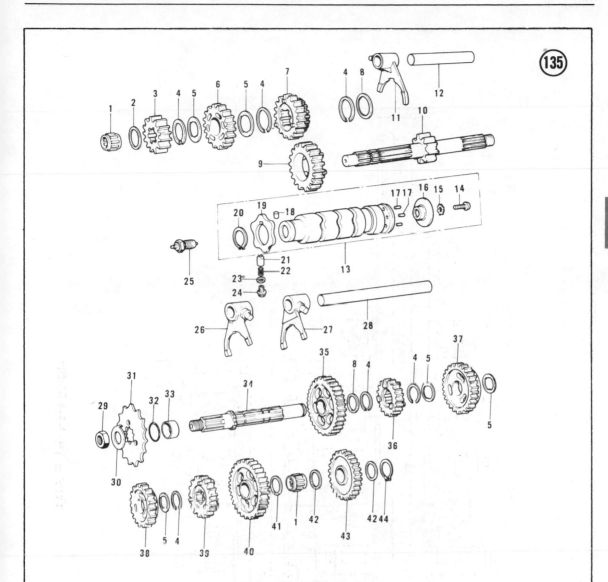

TYPE 5 TRANSMISSION

1. Needle bearing
2. Thrust washer
3. Drive shaft 2nd gear
4. Snap ring
5. Lockwasher
6. Drive shaft top gear
7. Drive shaft 3rd and 4th gear
8. Thrust washer
9. Drive shaft 5th gear
10. Drive shaft
11. 5th and top selector fork
12. Shift rod
13. Gear change drum
14. Pan head screw
15. Lockwasher

16. Gear change drum pin plate
17. Gear change drum pin
18. Dowel
19. Gear change drum operating disc
20. Snap ring
21. Neutral positioning pin
22. Neutral positioning pin spring
23. Gasket
24. Bolt
25. Neutral switch
26. 2nd and 3rd selector fork
27. Low and 4th selector fork
28. Shift rod
29. Nut
30. Lockwasher

31. Engine sprocket
32. O-ring
33. Engine sprocket collar
34. Output shaft
35. 2nd gear, output shaft
36. Top gear, output shaft
37. 3rd gear, output shaft
38. 4th gear, output shaft
39. 5th gear, output shaft
40. Low gear, output shaft
41. Thrust washer
42. Plain washer
43. Kickstarter idle gear
44. Snap ring

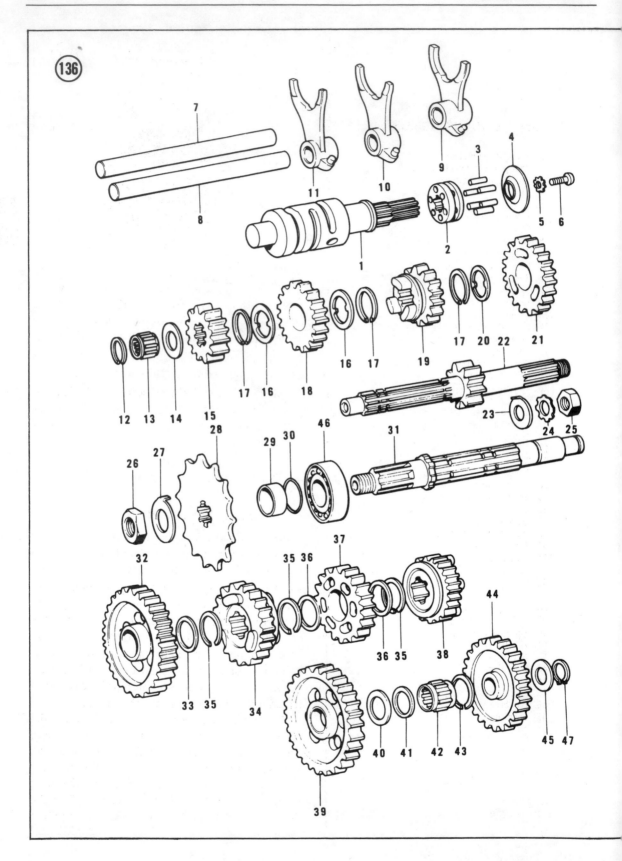

TYPE 6 TRANSMISSION

1. Gear change drum
2. Change drum operating disc
3. Gear change drum pin
4. Gear change drum pin holder
5. Lockwasher
6. Pan head screw
7. Shift rod
8. Shift rod
9. Selector fork, low
10. Selector fork, 2nd and 3rd
11. Selector fork, 4th and top
12. Snap ring
13. Needle bearing
14. Thrust washer
15. Drive shaft 2nd gear
16. Lockwasher
17. Snap ring
18. Drive shaft 4th gear
19. Drive shaft 3rd gear
20. Thrust washer
21. Drive shaft top gear
22. Drive shaft
23. Lockwasher
24. Lockwasher
25. Locknut
26. Nut
27. Lockwasher
28. Engine sprocket
29. Engine sprocket collar
30. O-ring
31. Output shaft
32. Output shaft 2nd gear
33. Thrust washer
34. Output shaft 4th gear
35. Snap ring
36. Lockwasher
37. Output shaft 3rd gear
38. Output shaft top gear
39. Output shaft low gear
40. Thrust washer
41. Thrust washer
42. Needle bearing
43. Snap ring
44. Kickstarter idle gear
45. Thrust washer
46. Ball bearing
47. Snap ring

Check dog clutch teeth for wear

1. Position the shift forks in the grooves in the gears, then insert the transmission and shift drum into right crankcase half as an assembly.

2. On G series models, be sure that the kick gear and both idler gears are completely engaged.

3. Clean the steel balls (F series) with cleaning solvent, then grease them to hold them in position during installation. Be sure that the balls move properly.

4. Secure the gearshift drum to the right crankcase half with the setting plate.

DRAIN PUMP

Some models are equipped with a drain pump which removes any gasoline and oil which may accumulate inside the carburetor chamber. **Figure 141** is a sectional view of the pump. Upward movement of the piston causes a lowered pressure in the crankcase, consequently, the diaphragm is pulled inward toward the crankcase. As the diaphragm moves inward, inlet valve (A) opens and exhaust valve (B) closes. As the inlet valve opens, contents of the carburetor chamber are drawn into the pump.

As the piston moves down in the cylinder, the crankcase is pressurized. Crankcase pressure forces the diaphragm away from the crankcase. Pressure built up in the pump by the outward movement of the diaphragm closes the inlet valve and opens the discharge valve. When the discharge valve opens, contents of the pump are expelled.

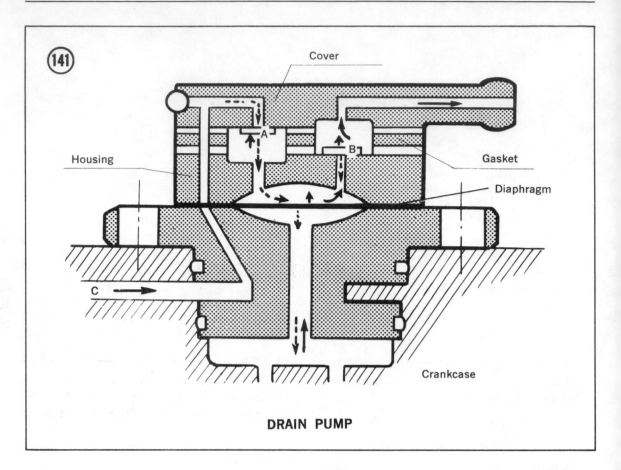

(141)

Cover

Housing

A

B

Gasket

Diaphragm

C

Crankcase

DRAIN PUMP

CHAPTER FOUR

ELECTRICAL SYSTEM

This chapter discusses operating principles and maintenance of the ignition, lighting, and charging systems.

FLYWHEEL MAGNETO

A flywheel magneto provides electrical power for the ignition and electrical systems of most of the machines covered by this manual. Separate coils within the magneto supply current for ignition, daytime and nighttime operation, and battery charging. Alternating current produced by the magneto is used for ignition and lights, except for stoplights and turn signals. A rectifier converts this alternating current into direct current for charging the battery and operating the horn and turn signals. **Figure 1** illustrates a typical magneto.

Figure 2 is a circuit diagram of a typical magneto which operates the ignition, charging, and lighting systems. As the flywheel rotates, permanent magnets attached to the flywheel revolve past the various windings in the magneto, thereby inducing current in the windings.

When the contact breaker points are closed, the current (approximately 4 amperes) developed in the ignition coil is grounded, and no current is delivered to the ignition coil. When the points open, this current is delivered to the pri-

mary winding of the ignition coil. The 200 or 300 volts across the coil primary winding is stepped up to the very high voltage of 10,000 to 15,000 volts required to jump the spark plug gap. A capacitor (condenser) is connected across the ignition points to prevent them from arcing as they open.

Nighttime riding imposes an additional load on the magneto because of the use of lights. To accommodate different current requirements, the lighting coil is tapped for both day and night loads.

The rectifier serves 2 purposes. It converts alternating current generated by the magneto into direct current for charging the battery, and it also prevents the battery from discharging through the magneto when the magneto output voltage is too low to charge the battery.

Magnetos on some models have 3 charging taps. The pink wire is used during night operation. The blue or yellow/green wires are used for day operation. In cases where the battery is chronically undercharged, connect the blue wire from the magneto to the blue wire at the main switch. Connect the yellow/green wire to the blue wire at the main switch when the battery is overcharged.

Figure 3 is a simplified diagram of the system on F5 and F9 models. The silicon voltage regu-

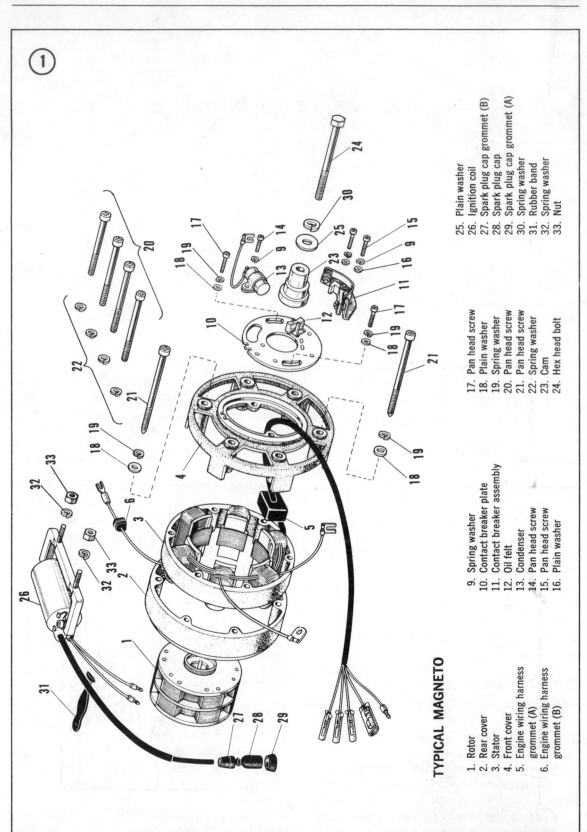

TYPICAL MAGNETO

1. Rotor
2. Rear cover
3. Stator
4. Front cover
5. Engine wiring harness grommet (A)
6. Engine wiring harness grommet (B)
9. Spring washer
10. Contact breaker plate
11. Contact breaker assembly
12. Oil felt
13. Condenser
14. Pan head screw
15. Pan head screw
16. Plain washer
17. Pan head screw
18. Plain washer
19. Spring washer
20. Pan head screw
21. Pan head screw
22. Spring washer
23. Cam
24. Hex head bolt
25. Plain washer
26. Ignition coil
27. Spark plug cap grommet (B)
28. Spark plug cap
29. Spark plug cap grommet (A)
30. Spring washer
31. Rubber band
32. Spring washer
33. Nut

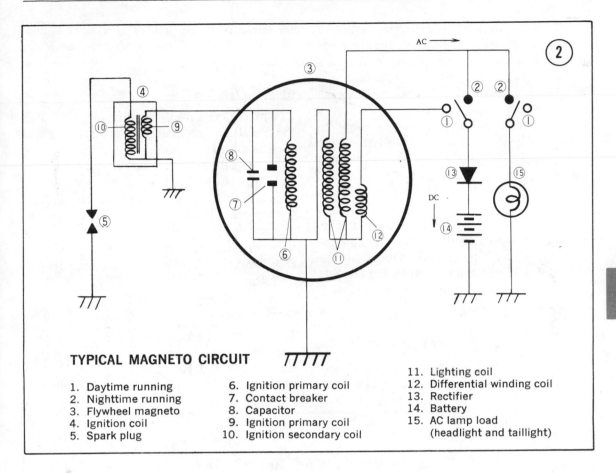

TYPICAL MAGNETO CIRCUIT

1. Daytime running
2. Nighttime running
3. Flywheel magneto
4. Ignition coil
5. Spark plug
6. Ignition primary coil
7. Contact breaker
8. Capacitor
9. Ignition primary coil
10. Ignition secondary coil
11. Lighting coil
12. Differential winding coil
13. Rectifier
14. Battery
15. AC lamp load
    (headlight and taillight)

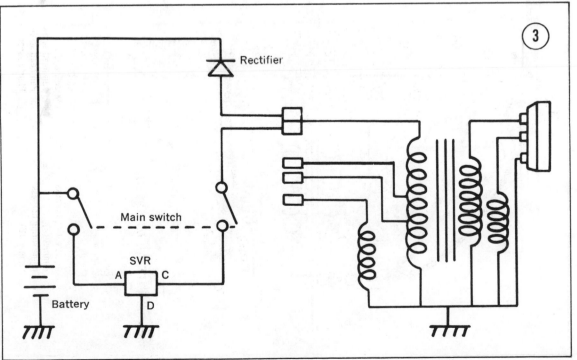

lator (SVR) serves to control charging voltage in the day riding condition. Note that the SVR is not in the circuit during night riding conditions.

If the DC load is reduced, as is the case of a burned-out brake light, the battery may be overcharged.

Note that the lighting coil serves mainly to operate the headlight, but it also furnishes power to the speedometer, tachometer, and high beam indicator bulbs. If the headlight burns out, the other bulbs will burn out also because of excess voltage.

Magnetos on models F5, F7, and F9 (Figure 4) are basically similar to those on conventional magneto-ignition models, except that the ignition coil is replaced with an exciter coil and a signal coil to meet requirements of the capacitor discharge ignition system.

MAGNETO TROUBLESHOOTING

In the event that an ignition malfunction is believed to be caused by a defective magneto on models with breaker points, check the coils, condenser, and breaker points as described in the following paragraphs.

Magneto Ignition Coil

With the magneto wiring disconnected, block the breaker points open with a piece of paper such as a business card.

Measure the resistance between the black wire and ground with a low-range ohmmeter. If resistance is approximately 0.5 ohm, the coil is good.

Disconnect the ground wire between the ignition coil and the magneto base. Measure insulation resistance between the iron core and the coil. Insulation resistance should be at least 5 megohms.

Condenser

Measure capacity of the condenser, using a condenser tester. The value should be 0.18-0.25 microfarad. With the condenser ground wire disconnected, measure insulation resistance be-

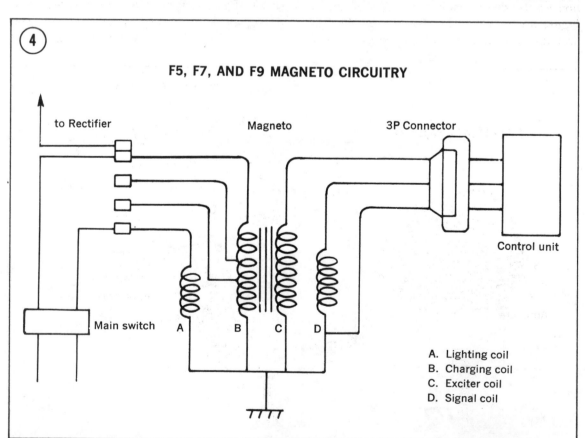

F5, F7, AND F9 MAGNETO CIRCUITRY

to Rectifier   Magneto   3P Connector

Control unit

Main switch   A   B   C   D

A. Lighting coil
B. Charging coil
C. Exciter coil
D. Signal coil

tween the outer case and the positive terminal. Insulation resistance should be over 5 megohms.

In the event that no test equipment is available, a quick test of the condenser may be made by connecting the negative lead or case to the negative terminal of a 6-volt battery, and the positive lead to the positive terminal. Allow the condenser to charge for a few seconds, then quickly disconnect the battery and touch the condenser leads together. If you observe a spark as the leads touch, you can assume that the condenser is good.

Arcing between the breaker points is a common symptom of a defective condenser.

Breaker Points

Refer to Chapter Two for details of breaker point service and ignition timing.

STARTER-GENERATOR

Some models are equipped with a combination starter-generator instead of a magneto. **Figure 5** is an exploded view of this unit. The armature rotates with the engine crankshaft.

Attached to the end of the armature shaft is the breaker cam. The unit operates as a generator when the engine is running, and as a starting motor when the engine is stopped. Associated with the starter-generator is a cut-out relay, voltage regulator, and starter relay. **Figure 6** is a schematic diagram of the associated circuitry. Refer to this diagram during the following discussion.

Starter Relay

The starter relay is enclosed within the voltage regulator unit. **Figure 7** illustrates the relay circuit. Pressing the starter switch energizes the relay coil and closes the relay contacts. Current then flows from the battery, through the relay contacts, and finally through the series field winding (M) of the starter-generator.

Cut-Out Relay

When the engine is off, or running at low speed, the battery must be disconnected from the generator to prevent it from discharging. The cut-out relay performs this function. As engine

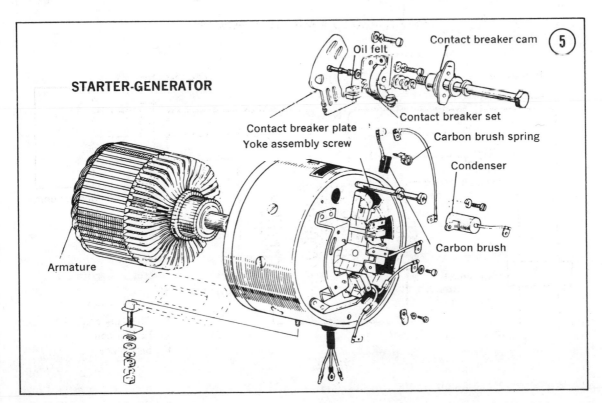

STARTER-GENERATOR

Oil felt
Contact breaker cam ⑤
Contact breaker plate
Yoke assembly screw
Contact breaker set
Carbon brush spring
Condenser
Carbon brush
Armature

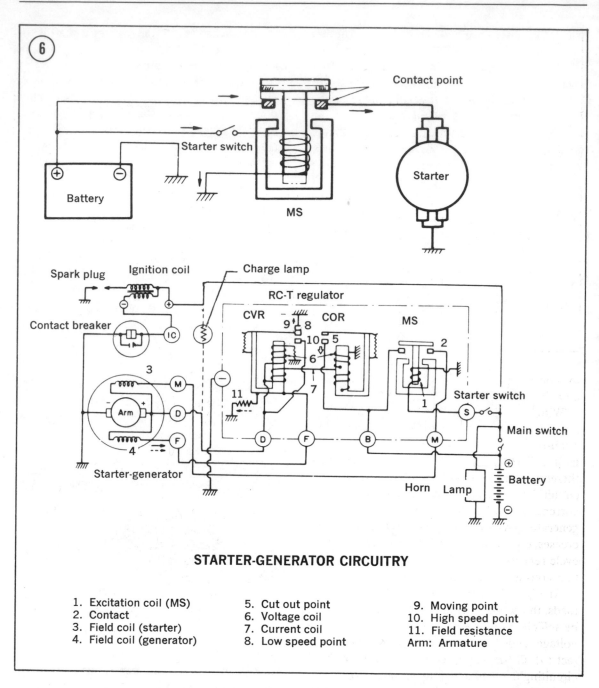

STARTER-GENERATOR CIRCUITRY

1. Excitation coil (MS)	5. Cut out point	9. Moving point
2. Contact	6. Voltage coil	10. High speed point
3. Field coil (starter)	7. Current coil	11. Field resistance
4. Field coil (generator)	8. Low speed point	Arm: Armature

speed increases, output voltage of the generator increases to a value sufficient to charge the battery. When this occurs, a voltage sensing coil in the cut-out relay closes the relay contacts, permitting current to flow from the generator to the battery and external loads. As the engine slows down, generator output decreases, and current tends to flow from the battery to the generator. A second coil in the cut-out relay senses this reverse current and allows the contacts to again open, thereby disconnecting the battery and generator.

Voltage Regulator

Varying engine speeds and electrical loads affect generator output. The voltage regulator maintains the output voltage at a constant level

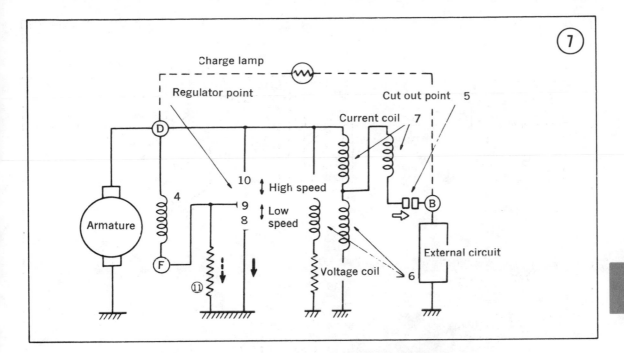

by controlling the field current in the generator. Figure 7 illustrates its operation.

With contacts (8) and (9) closed, the field is grounded and the generator produces its maximum output. As the output rises, voltage regulator coil (6) pulls contacts (8) and (9) apart, thereby inserting resistance (10) into the field circuit. The resistance decreases generator field current, which results in less output from the generator. As output from the generator decreases, contacts (8) and (9) close again and the cycle repeats. The cycling action tends to maintain constant generator output.

At higher engine speeds and light electrical loads, the action of contacts (8) and (9) may not be sufficient to limit generator output. If output voltage tends to go very high, coil (6) pulls contact (9) all the way to contact (10), thus short-circuiting the field and causing generator output to decrease to almost zero. Voltage regulation is then effected by cycling of contact (9) between midposition and contact (10).

Starter-Generator
Removal/Installation

1. Remove shift pedal.
2. Remove left crankcase cover.
3. Remove breaker cam (**Figure 8**).

4. Remove yoke retaining screws, then pull yoke from engine (**Figure 9**).

5. Using a suitable puller, remove armature (**Figure 10**).

6. Remove Woodruff key from crankshaft.

Reverse the removal procedure to install the starter-generator. If brushes were removed, don't install them until after the yoke assembly is in position. If the brushes were not removed, it will be necessary to position them as shown in

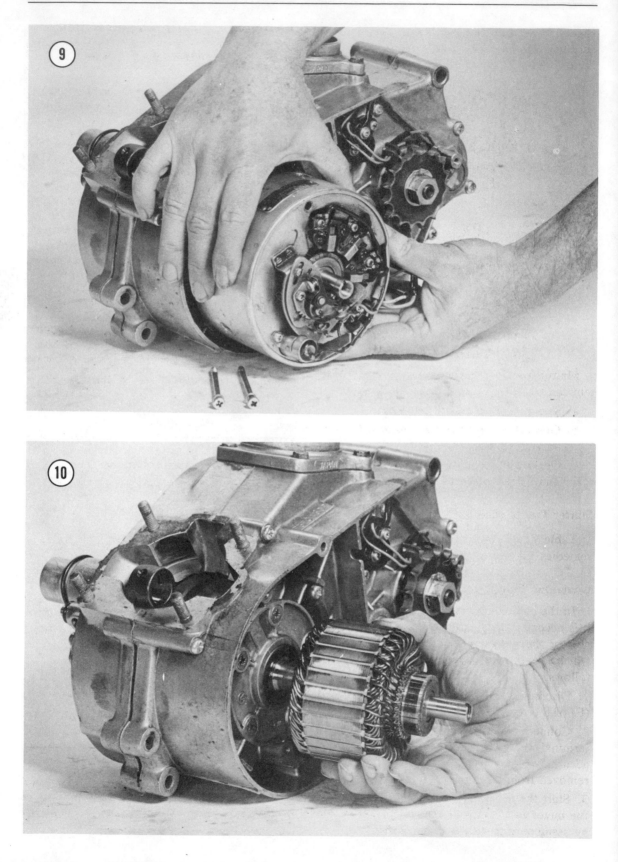

Figure 11 before the yoke can be installed. Be sure to snap them into position before starting the engine.

1. Brush in position for installation
2. Brush in normal position

STARTER-GENERATOR TROUBLESHOOTING

Malfunctions within the starter-generator system can be divided into 3 main categories:

a. Starter does not work properly.

b. Generator output is too low, resulting in an undercharged battery.

c. Generator output is too high, resulting in an overcharged battery.

Starter Troubleshooting

Table 1 lists symptoms, probable causes, and remedies for starter malfunctions.

Generator Troubleshooting

In the case of charging system malfunctions, it is necessary to determine whether the generator or the regulator is at fault. To determine which, refer to **Figure 12**, then proceed as follows.

1. Disconnect the wires from terminal (D) and (F) of the regulator.

2. Connect the wire which was removed from terminal (F) to a good ground. Connect an accurate voltmeter (0-20 VDC) between the wire removed from terminal (D) and ground.

3. Start the engine and run it at 2,200 rpm. If the meter indicates more than 13 volts, it can be assumed that the generator is OK.

Table 1   **STARTER TROUBLESHOOTING**

Symptom	Probable Cause	Remedy
Starter does not work	Low battery	Recharge battery
	Worn brushes	Replace brushes
	Internal short	Repair or replace defective component
	Relay inoperative	Replace voltage regulator
	Defective wiring or connections	Repair wire or clean and tighten
	Defective switch	Replace switch
Starter action is weak	Low battery	Recharge battery
	Pitted relay contacts	Clean contacts or replace voltage regulator
	Brushes worn	Replace brushes
	Defective wiring or connections	Repair wire or clean and tighten connections
	Short in commutator	Replace armature
Starter runs continuously	Stuck relay	Dress contacts or replace voltage regulator

If the meter indications are not as specified, the starter-generator is faulty.

Checking the Yoke

Clean the yoke assembly of all foreign material, and remove it from the machine.

1. Use an ohmmeter to measure insulation resistance between positive brush and ground. If the meter indicates continuity, check for a short circuit at the brush holder or terminal (D). Note that the negative brush holder is not insulated.

2. Measure field coil resistance between terminals (F) and (D). Field coil resistance should be between 5-8 ohms.

3. Set the ohmmeter to its highest range. Measure insulation resistance between terminal (F) and a good ground. Insulation resistance should be essentially infinite.

If the measurements obtained in Steps 2 or 3 are not as specified, replace the yoke. If the yoke assembly is good, check the brushes and the armature.

4

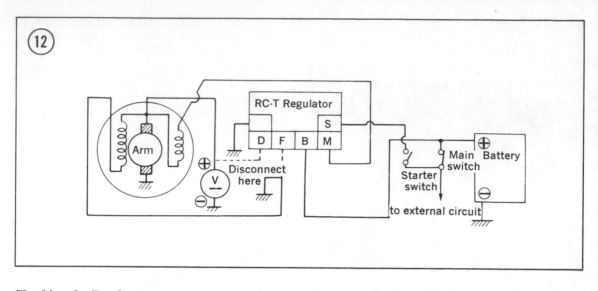

Checking the Brushes

Poor brush condition is one of the most frequent causes of low generator output. Remove the brushes and examine them carefully. Each brush must contact the commutator with at least 3 quarters of its contact surface. If either brush is worn excessively, replace both brushes.

If the brushes and the commutator are rough, misalignment of the armature and crankshaft may be the cause. Check the tapered bore of the armature and smooth it if there are any burrs.

When replacing brushes, be sure that the positive brush lead doesn't touch the brush holder or the edge of the breaker plate. Also be sure that the negative brush lead doesn't touch the positive brush spring.

Checking the Armature

1. Clean the commutator of oil, dust, and foreign material.

2. If the commutator is rough or covered with carbon dust, polish it with fine emery paper. If a light polishing does not clean up the surface, remove the armature and turn the commutator in a lathe. Do not reduce commutator diameter by more than 0.08 in. (2.0mm).

3. Undercut the mica segments between the commutator segments with a hacksaw blade to a depth of 0.02-0.04 in. (0.05-1.0mm). Remove the dust between the segments.

4. Use an ohmmeter or armature growler to determine that no commutator segment is shorted to the shaft. If any short exists, replace the armature.

Checking the Regulator

Varying engine speeds and electrical loads affect output of the generator. The regulator controls generator output, and also disconnects the battery from the generator whenever generator output voltage is less than that of the battery, thereby preventing battery discharge through the generator.

Disconnect the wire from terminal (B) at the regulator. Be careful that this wire doesn't become grounded. Connect the voltmeter between terminal (B) of the regulator and ground, as shown in **Figure 13**. Start the engine and run it at 2,500 rpm. The voltmeter should indicate 14.7-15.7 volts.

Observe the contacts on the cut-out relay as you slowly increase engine speed. The contacts should close when the voltmeter indicates 12.5-13.5 volts.

Adjusting the Voltage Regulator

CAUTION
Disconnect the battery before removing the regulator cover. Do not make any adjustments with the battery in place.

Remove the regulator cover and adjust the regulator by bending the adjustment spring. Bending the spring downward raises the voltage

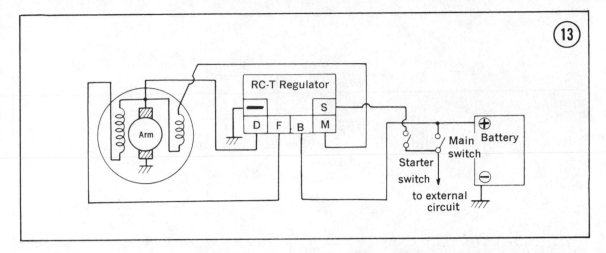

setting. The voltage regulator can be identified by its 2 contact points.

The cut-out relay can be identified by a single set of contacts which are normally open. The relay rarely, if ever, needs adjustment. Usually all that is required is to dress the contacts lightly to remove any corrosion or light pitting.

Should adjustment be required, bend the spring retainer up or down as required. Lowering the spring retainer raises the voltage setting.

Ignition Coil

The ignition coil is a form of transformer which develops the high voltage required to jump the spark plug gap. The only maintenance required is keeping the electrical connections clean and tight, and making sure the coil is mounted securely.

If coil condition is doubtful, there are several checks which should be made.

1. Measure resistance with an ohmmeter between the positive and negative primary terminals. Resistance should indicate approximately 5 ohms for most coils on these machines. Some coils, however, have a primary resistance less than 2 ohms.

2. Measure resistance between either primary terminal and the secondary high voltage terminal. Resistance should be in the range of 5,000-11,000 ohms.

3. Scrape the paint from the coil housing down to bare metal. Measure the resistance between this bare spot and the high voltage terminal.

Insulation resistance must be at least 3 megohms (3 million ohms).

4. If these checks don't reveal any defects, but coil condition is still doubtful, replace the coil with one known to be good.

Be sure that you connect the primary wires correctly.

RECTIFIER

The rectifier serves 2 purposes. First, it converts alternating current generated by the magneto into direct current for battery charging. Second, it prevents the battery from discharging through the charging coil in the magneto when the engine isn't turning fast enough to charge the battery.

To test the rectifier, refer to **Figure 14**. Connect the negative terminal of a 6-volt battery to the blue/white lead on the rectifier. Connect a small 6-volt bulb, such as a taillight bulb, in series with the positive battery lead, then connect the other terminal of the bulb to the brown wire on the rectifier. If the bulb lights, the rectifier is defective and must be replaced. Reverse the rectifier leads so that the negative battery lead is connected to the brown rectifier lead and the positive lead and lamp are connected to the blue/white lead. The lamp should now light. If not, replace the rectifier.

If the bike is operated for extended periods with the battery disconnected, or with the battery circuit fuse blown, rectifier damage may result. Avoid such operation, and check the fuse from time to time.

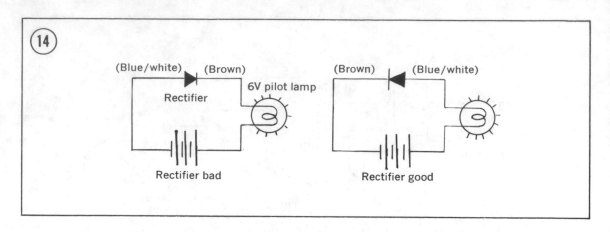

HIGH VOLTAGE CABLE

This cable carries the current from the ignition coil to the spark plug. If it becomes sharply bent or is allowed to chafe against the frame, damage and eventual destruction will occur. Pay particular attention to the routing of this cable.

CAPACITOR DISCHARGE IGNITION SYSTEM OPERATION

Some models are equipped with a capacitor discharge (CD) ignition system. This solid state system, unlike conventional ignition systems, uses no breaker points or other moving parts. **Figure 15** illustrates the capacitor discharge system.

Alternating current from the exciter coil is rectified and used to charge the capacitor. As the piston approaches firing position, a pulse from the signal coil is rectified, shaped, and then used to trigger the silicon controlled rectifier (SCR) which in turn allows the capacitor to discharge quickly into the primary circuit of the ignition coil, where the voltage is stepped up to fire the spark plug.

Refer to Chapter Two for details of ignition timing.

Magneto

To check the magneto, disconnect the wires from the main switch, the rectifier, and the control unit. Measure resistance between each listed lead and the black lead with an ohmmeter. A schematic diagram of the magneto is shown in **Figure 16**. Resistance of each coil should be approximately as specified in **Table 2**.

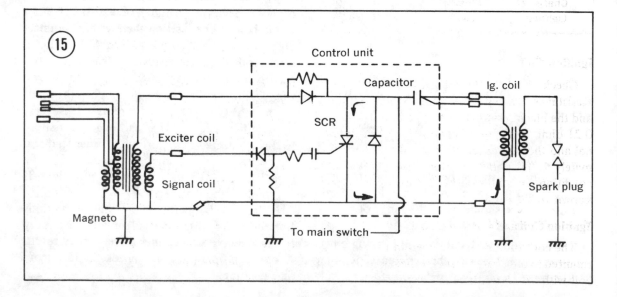

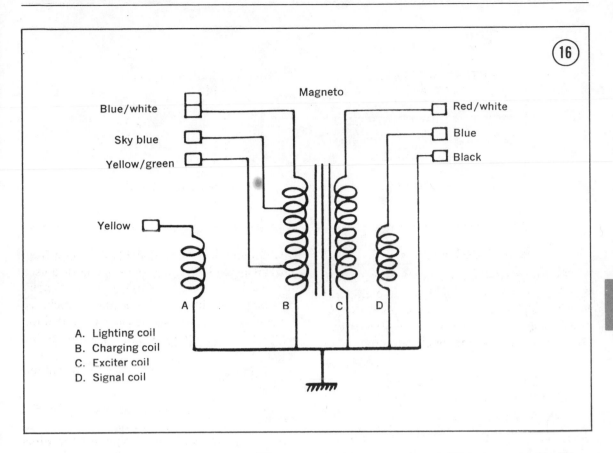

A. Lighting coil
B. Charging coil
C. Exciter coil
D. Signal coil

Table 2   MAGNETO COIL RESISTANCE

Coil	Connection	Resistance (ohms)
Exciter	Red/white	220
Signal	Blue	75
Charging	Blue/white	0.23
Lighting	Yellow	0.23

Ignition Coil

Check the ignition coil with an ohmmeter. Resistance between the green/white terminal and the black terminal should be approximately 0.21 ohm. Resistance between the black terminal and the output terminal should be approximately 1,800 ohms. If after these checks, coil condition is still doubtful, substitute a coil known to be good.

Ignition Coil and Control Unit Tests

The control unit tester shown in **Figure 17** is required to test these units. To check the ignition coil with the tester, proceed as follows.

1. Insert power cord (K) into receptacle (B) on the tester. Connect the power cord into a standard 110-volt outlet. Be sure power switch (D) is OFF.

2. Insert the connector of accessory cord (H) into receptacle (A) on the tester.

3. Insert the high voltage cable of the ignition coil into receptacle (E). Connect the 2-pole connector on cord (H) to the ignition coil.

4. Set switch (L) to COIL.

5. Press rocker switch (D) to ON.

6. Press pushbutton (C). If there is no spark at gap (M), the coil is defective.

After you test the coil, remove it from the tester, then test the control unit.

1. Perform Steps 2 and 3 above.

2. Connect the 3-pole connector on cord (H) to the receptacle on the control unit.

3. Set switch (L) to UNIT.

4. Press switch (D) to ON.

5. Press pushbutton (C). Pilot lamp (G) will light, and there will be a strong spark discharge

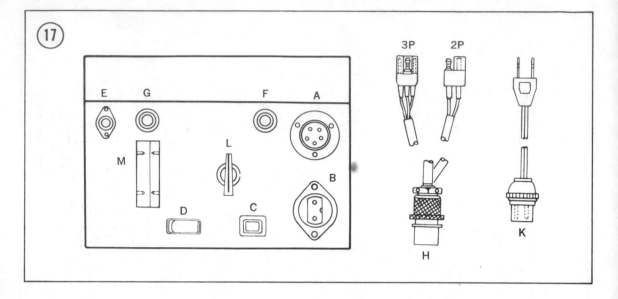

in the 3-needle spark gap if the control is good. If there is no spark, replace the control unit.

It is also possible to test the control unit and ignition coil together.

1. Perform Steps 1 and 2 of the coil test.

2. Connect both the coil and the control unit to the tester using the terminals on cable (H).

3. Connect the high voltage cable from the coil to receptacle (E) on the tester.

4. Set switch (L) to UNIT.

5. Set switch (D) to ON.

6. Press pushbutton (C).

7. If there is a spark discharge at spark gap (M), and pilot lamp (G) lights, both the ignition coil and the control unit are good. If there is no spark, each unit must be tested separately.

SOLID STATE VOLTAGE REGULATOR

Some machines are equipped with a solid state unit which is used as a voltage regulator (SVR in **Figure 18**). This unit consists of a zener diode (ZD), a silicon controlled rectifier (SCR), and 2 resistors, as shown in **Figure 19**. Refer to this illustration during the following discussion.

Assume that the main switch is closed. As engine speed increases, output voltage from the magneto tends to increase. If the battery is fully charged, the voltage at point (A) will tend to rise. If it reaches the zener voltage (7.0 ± 0.5 volts), the zener diode conducts in the reverse direction, thereby triggering the silicon controlled rectifier. When the silicon controlled rectifier conducts, magneto output is grounded, thereby reducing its output voltage to near zero. As the voltage at junction (A) drops, the zener diode ceases to conduct, and removes the trigger signal to the silicon controlled rectifier.

Checking the SVR

Connect a test lamp in series with a 6-volt battery, or use an ohmmeter to determine whether there is continuity between points (C) and (D). The continuity test lamp should not light, or the ohmmeter should show no continuity. Reverse the continuity tester connections to the SVR. If the lamp lights or the ohmmeter indicates continuity, the unit is defective. Also be sure that terminal (C) is not shorted to case.

If the facilities are available, connect the test circuit shown in **Figure 20**. Slowly increase the voltage from the power supply and observe the lamp. The lamp must light when the voltmeter indicates 6.5-7.5 volts. If not, the unit must be replaced.

Reduce the power supply voltage to 1.0 volt below the point where the lamp became lit. Disconnect the battery momentarily, then reconnect it. If the lamp lights, replace the SVR.

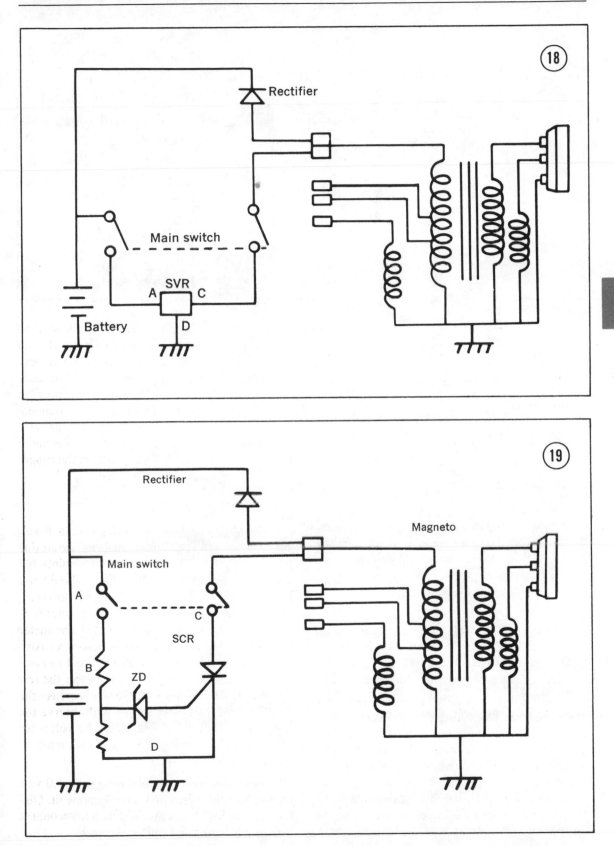

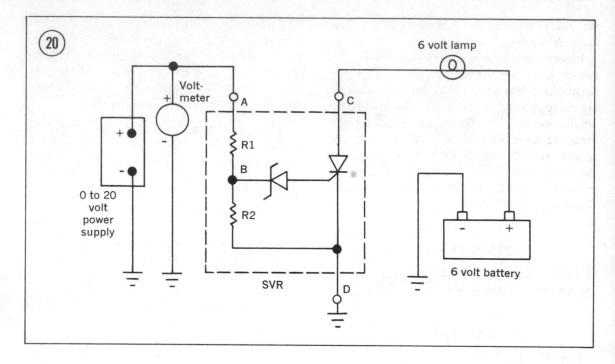

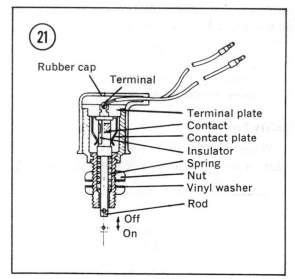

LIGHTS

Machines designed to be ridden on public streets are equipped with lights. Check them periodically to be sure that they are working properly.

Headlight

The headlight unit consists primarily of a lamp body, a dual-filament bulb, a lens and reflector unit, a rim, and a socket. To adjust the headlight, loosen the mounting bolts and move the assembly as required.

Brake Light

Figure 21 illustrates the brake light switch. The switch is actuated by the brake pedal. Adjust the switch so that the stoplight goes on just before braking action occurs. Move the switch body up or down as required for adjustment. Tighten the clamp nut after adjustment.

Turn Signals

Kawasaki bikes are equipped with 2 different types of turn signal flasher relays. Most F series models use one type; the G series uses another. If replacement becomes necessary, be sure you replace with the proper type.

If any turn signal bulb burns out, be sure to replace it with the same type. Improper action of the flasher relay, or even failure to operate may result from use of the wrong bulbs.

HORN

Current for the horn is supplied by the battery. One horn terminal is connected to the battery through the main switch. The other terminal is connected to the horn button. When the rider presses the button, current flows through the horn.

Figure 22 illustrates horn construction. As current flows through the coil, the core becomes magnetized and attracts the armature. As the armature moves, it opens the contacts, cutting off the current. The diaphragm spring then returns the armature to its original position. This process repeats rapidly until the rider releases the horn button. The action of the armature striking the end of the core produces the sound, which is amplified by the resonator.

MAIN SWITCH

Service on the main switch is limited to checking continuity between the various circuits.

BATTERY

Most Kawasaki bikes are equipped with lead-acid storage batteries, smaller in size but similar in construction to those found in automobiles.

WARNING
Read and thoroughly understand the section on safety precautions before doing any battery service.

Safety Precautions

When working with batteries, use extreme care to avoid spilling or splashing electrolyte.

This electrolyte is sulfuric acid, which can destroy clothing and cause serious chemical burns. If any electrolyte is spilled or splashed on clothing or body, it should immediately be neutralized with a solution of baking soda and water, then flushed with plenty of clean water.

Electrolyte splashed into the eyes is extremely dangerous. Safety glasses should always be worn when working with batteries. If electrolyte is splashed into the eye, force the eye open, flood with cool clean water for about 5 minutes, and call a physician immediately.

If electrolyte is spilled or splashed onto painted or unpainted surfaces, it should be neutralized immediately with baking soda solution and then rinsed with clean water.

When batteries are being charged, highly explosive hydrogen gas forms in each cell. Some of this gas escapes through the filler openings and may form an explosive atmosphere around the battery. *This explosive atmosphere may exist for hours.* Sparks, open flames, or a lighted cigarette can ignite this gas, causing an internal explosion and possible serious personal injury. The following precautions should be taken to prevent an explosion.

1. Do not smoke or permit any open flame near any battery being charged or which has been recently charged.

2. Do not disconnect live circuits at battery terminals, because a spark usually occurs where

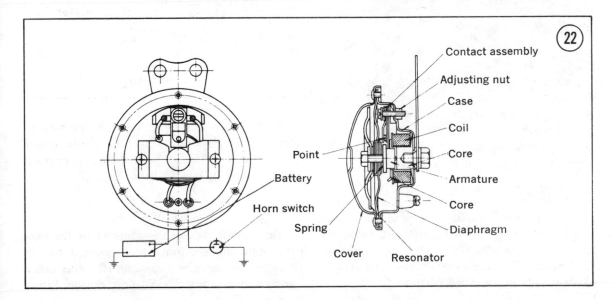

Point
Battery
Horn switch
Spring

Contact assembly
Adjusting nut
Case
Coil
Core
Armature
Core
Diaphragm
Cover   Resonator

a live circuit is broken. Care must always be taken when connecting or disconnecting any battery charger; be sure its power switch is off before making or breaking connections. Poor connections are a common cause of electrical arcs which cause explosions.

Electrolyte Level

Battery electrolyte level should be checked regularly, particularly during hot weather. Most batteries are marked with electrolyte level limit lines (**Figure 23**). Always maintain the fluid level between the 2 lines, using distilled water as required for replenishment. Distilled water is available at most supermarkets. It is sold for use in steam irons and is quite inexpensive.

Overfilling leads to loss of electrolyte, resulting in poor battery performance, short life, and excessive corrosion. Never allow the electrolyte level to drop below the top of the plates. That portion of the plates exposed to air may be permanently damaged, resulting in the loss of battery performance and shortened life.

Excessive use of water is an indication that the battery is being overcharged. The two most common causes of overcharging are high battery temperature or high voltage regulator setting. It is advisable to check the voltage regulator, on machines so equipped, if this situation exists.

Cleaning

Check the battery occasionally for presence of dirt or corrosion. The top of the battery, in particular, should be kept clean. Acid film and dirt permit current to flow between terminals, which will slowly discharge the battery.

For best results when cleaning, wash first with dilute ammonia or baking soda solution, then flush with plenty of clean water. Take care to keep filler plugs tight so that no cleaning solution enters the cells.

Battery Cables

To ensure good electrical contact, cables must be clean and tight on battery terminals. If the battery or cable terminals are corroded, the cables should be disconnected and cleaned separately with a wire brush and baking soda solution. After cleaning, apply a very thin coating of petroleum jelly to the battery terminals before installed the cables. After connecting the cables, apply a light coating to the connection. This procedure will help to prevent future corrosion.

Battery Charging

> WARNING
> *Do not smoke or permit any open flame in any area where batteries are being charged, or immediately after charging. Highly explosive hydrogen gas is formed during the charging process. Be sure to reread* Safety Precautions *in the beginning of this section.*

Motorcycle batteries are not designed for high charge or discharge rates. For this reason, it is recommended that a motorcycle battery be charged at a rate not exceeding 10 percent of its ampere-hour capacity. That is, do not exceed

0.5-ampere charging rate for a 5 ampere-hour battery. This charge rate should continue for 10 hours if the battery is completely discharged, or until specific gravity of each cell is up to 1.260-1.280, corrected for temperature. If after prolonged charging, specific gravity of one or more cells does not come up to at least 1.230, the battery will not perform as well as it should, but it may continue to provide satisfactory service for a time.

Some temperature rise is normal as a battery is being charged. Do not allow the electrolyte temperature to exceed 110°F. Should temperature reach that figure, discontinue charging until the battery cools, then resume charging at a lower rate.

Testing State of Charge

Although sophisticated battery testing devices are on the market, they are not available to the average motorcycle owner, and their use is beyond the scope of this book. A hydrometer, however, is an inexpensive tool, and will tell much about battery condition.

To use a hydrometer, place the suction tube into the filler opening and draw in just enough electrolyte to lift the float. Hold the instrument in a vertical position and read specific gravity on the scale, where the float stem emerges from the electrolyte (**Figure 24**).

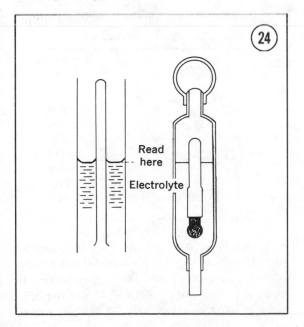

Specific gravity of the electrolyte varies with temperature, so it is necessary to apply a temperature correction to the reading so obtained. For each 10 degrees that battery temperature exceeds 80°F, add 0.004 to the indicated specific gravity. Likewise, subtract 0.004 from the indicated value for each 10 degrees that battery temperature is below 80°F.

Repeat this measurement for each battery cell. If there is more than 0.050 difference (50 points) between cells, battery condition is questionable.

State of charge may be determined from **Table 3**.

Table 3   STATE OF CHARGE

Specific Gravity	State of Charge
1.110 - 1.130	Discharged
1.140 - 1.160	Almost discharged
1.170 - 1.190	One-quarter charged
1.200 - 1.220	One-half charged
1.230 - 1.250	Three-quarters charged
1.260 - 1.280	Fully charged

Don't measure specific gravity immediately after adding water. Ride the machine a few miles to ensure thorough mixing of the electrolyte.

It is most important to maintain batteries fully charged during cold weather. A fully charged battery freezes at a much lower temperature than does one which is partially discharged. Freezing temperature depends on specific gravity (see **Table 4**).

Table 4   BATTERY FREEZING TEMPERATURE

Specific Gravity	Freezing Temperature Degrees F
1.100	18
1.120	13
1.140	8
1.160	1
1.180	—6
1.200	—17
1.220	—31
1.240	—50
1.260	—75
1.280	—92

CHAPTER FIVE

CARBURETION

For proper operation, a gasoline engine must be supplied with fuel and air, mixed in the proper proportions by weight. A mixture in which there is an excess of fuel is said to be rich. A lean mixture is one which contains insufficient fuel. It is the function of the carburetors to supply the proper mixture to the engine under all operating conditions.

Kawasaki machines are equipped with Mikuni carburetors. Service procedures are similar for the various carburetors. Differences are pointed out where they exist. Carburetors may be of either independent float or twin float type.

CARBURETOR OPERATION

The essential functional parts of Kawasaki carburetors are a float and float valve mechanism for maintaining a constant fuel level in the float bowl, a pilot system for supplying fuel at low speeds, a main fuel system which supplies the engine at medium and high speeds, and a starter system, which supplies the very rich mixture needed to start a cold engine. The operation of each system is discussed in the following paragraphs.

Float Mechanism

Figure 1 illustrates a typical float mechanism. Proper operation of the carburetor is dependent

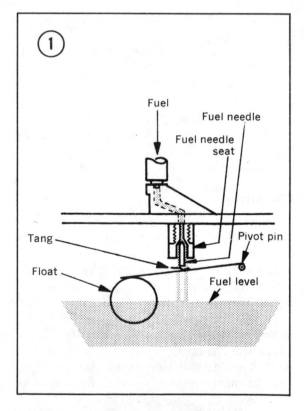

on maintaining a constant fuel level in the carburetor bowl. As fuel is drawn from the float bowl, the float level drops. When the float drops, the float needle valve moves away from its seat and allows fuel to flow past the valve and seat into the float bowl. As this occurs, the float is then raised, pressing the needle valve against its seat, thereby shutting off fuel flow. It can be seen from this discussion that a small piece of dirt can be trapped between the valve and seat, preventing the valve from closing and allowing fuel to rise beyond the normal level, resulting in flooding. **Figure 2** illustrates this condition.

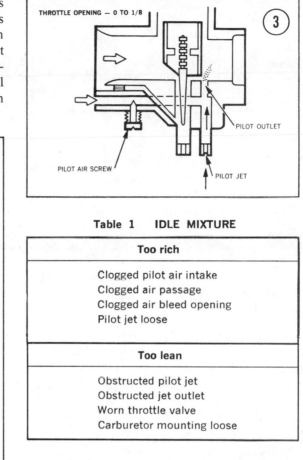

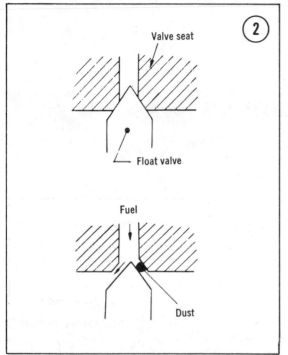

Table 1   IDLE MIXTURE
Too rich
Clogged pilot air intake Clogged air passage Clogged air bleed opening Pilot jet loose
Too lean
Obstructed pilot jet Obstructed jet outlet Worn throttle valve Carburetor mounting loose

Pilot System

Under idle or low speed conditions, at less than one-eighth throttle, the engine doesn't require much fuel or air, and the throttle valve is almost closed. A separate pilot system is required for operation under such conditions. **Figure 3** illustrates operation of the pilot system. Air is drawn through the pilot air inlet and controlled by the pilot air screw. This air is then mixed with fuel drawn through the pilot jet. The air/fuel mixture then travels from the pilot outlet into the main air passage, where it is further mixed with air prior to being drawn into the engine. The pilot air screw controls the idle mixture.

If proper idle and low speed mixture cannot be obtained within the normal adjustment range of the idle mixture screw, refer to **Table 1**.

Main Fuel System

As the throttle is opened still more, up to about one-quarter open, the pilot circuit begins to supply less of the mixture to the engine, as the main fuel system, illustrated in **Figure 4**, begins to function. The main jet, the needle jet, the jet needle, and the air jet make up the main fuel circuit. As the throttle valve opens more than about one-eighth of its travel, air is drawn through the main port, and passes under the throttle valve in the main bore. The velocity of the air stream results in reduced pressure around the jet needle. Fuel then passes through the main jet, past the needle jet and jet needle, and into the air stream where it is atomized and sent to the carburetor. As the throttle valve opens, more air flows through the carburetor, and the jet needle, which is attached to the throttle slide, rises to permit more fuel to flow.

A portion of the air bled past the air jet passes through the needle jet bleed air inlet into the

5

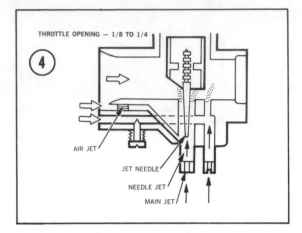

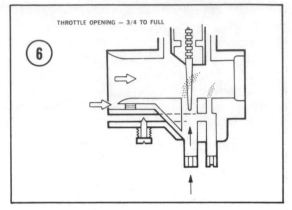

needle jet, where the air is mixed with the main air stream and atomized.

Airflow at small throttle openings is controlled primarily by the cutaway on the throttle slide.

As the throttle is opened wider, up to about three-quarters open, the circuit draws air from two sources, as shown in **Figure 5**. The first source is air passing through the venturi; the second source is through the air jet. Air passing through the venturi draws fuel through the needle jet. The jet needle is tapered, and therefore allows more fuel to pass. Air passing through the air jet passes to the needle jet to aid atomization of the fuel there.

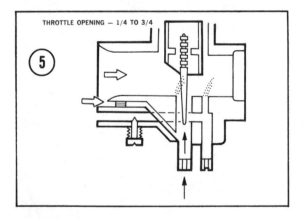

Figure 6 illustrates the circuit at high speeds. The jet needle is withdrawn almost completely from the needle jet. Fuel flow is then controlled by the main jet. Air passing through the air jet continues to aid atomization of the fuel as described in the previous paragraphs.

Any dirt which collects in the main jet or in the needle jet obstructs fuel flow and causes a lean mixture. Any clogged air passage, such as the air bleed opening or air jet, may result in an overrich mixture. Other causes of a rich mixture are a worn needle jet, loose needle jet, or loose main jet. If the jet needle is worn, it should be replaced, however it may be possible to effect a temporary repair by placing the needle jet clip in a higher groove.

Starter System

A cold engine requires a mixture which is far richer than normal. **Figure 7** illustrates the starter system. When the rider operates the lever, the starter plunger (13) is pulled upward. As the engine is cranked, suction from the engine draws fuel through the starter jet (10). This fuel is then mixed with air from the bleed air port (11) in the float chamber (12). This mixture is further mixed with primary air coming through the air passage (14), and is then delivered to the engine through the port (15) behind the throttle valve. Note that the mixture from the starter system is mixed with that from the pilot system.

CARBURETOR OVERHAUL

There is no set rule regarding frequency of carburetor overhaul. A carburetor used on a machine used primarily for street riding may go 5,000 miles without attention. If the machine is used in dirt, the carburetor might need an overhaul in less than 1,000 miles. Poor engine performance, hesitation, and little response to idle

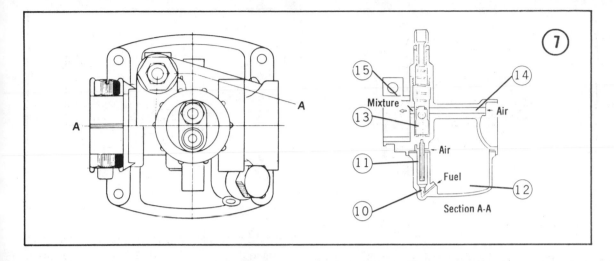

mixture adjustment are all symptoms of possible carburetor malfunctions. As a general rule, it is good practice to overhaul the carburetor each time you perform a routine decarbonization of the engine.

Disassembly, Independent Float Carburetors

Figure 8 (next page) is an exploded view of a typical independent float carburetor. Refer to this illustration during disassembly.

1. Remove the mixing chamber cap (**Figure 9**), if this step was not done previously.

2. Remove the spring, then pull out the throttle slide (**Figure 10**).

3. Remove both vent tubes (**Figure 11**).

4. Remove four retaining screws, then pull off the float bowl (**Figure 12**). Note carefully how each float is installed (**Figure 13**).

5. Pull out the float lever pivot pin (**Figure 14**). Note carefully how the float lever is installed; it is possible to put it back in upside-down.

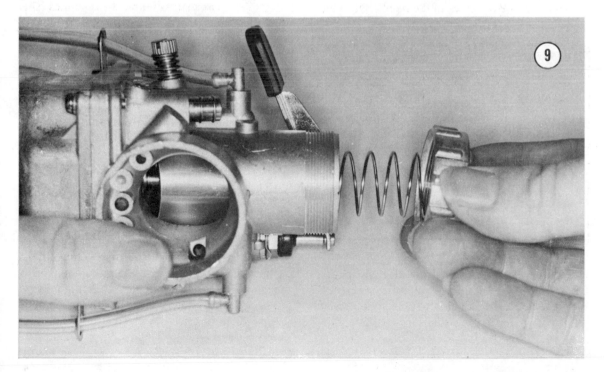

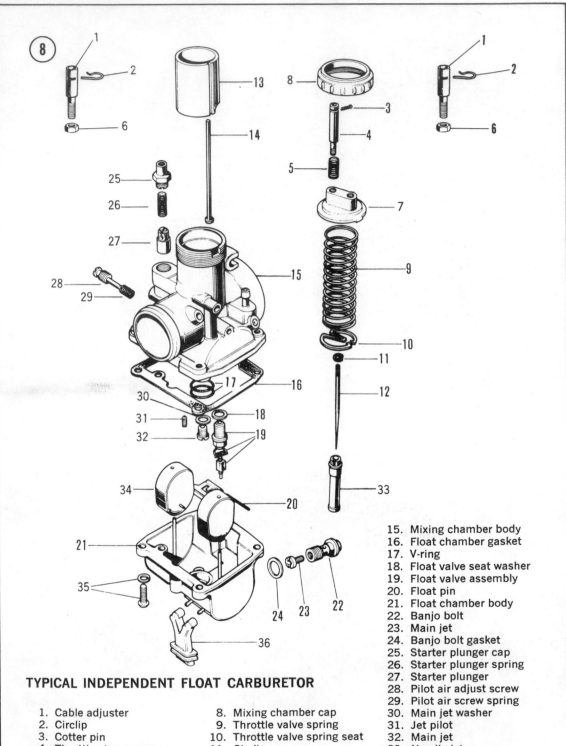

TYPICAL INDEPENDENT FLOAT CARBURETOR

15. Mixing chamber body
16. Float chamber gasket
17. V-ring
18. Float valve seat washer
19. Float valve assembly
20. Float pin
21. Float chamber body
22. Banjo bolt
23. Main jet
24. Banjo bolt gasket
25. Starter plunger cap
26. Starter plunger spring
27. Starter plunger
28. Pilot air adjust screw
29. Pilot air screw spring
30. Main jet washer
31. Jet pilot
32. Main jet
33. Needle jet
34. Float
35. Float chamber screw
36. Overflow pipe grommet

1. Cable adjuster
2. Circlip
3. Cotter pin
4. Throttle stop screw
5. Throttle stop screw spring
6. Cable adjuster lock nut
7. Mixing chamber top

8. Mixing chamber cap
9. Throttle valve spring
10. Throttle valve spring seat
11. Circlip
12. Jet needle 5EH7
13. Throttle valve
14. Throttle valve stop rod

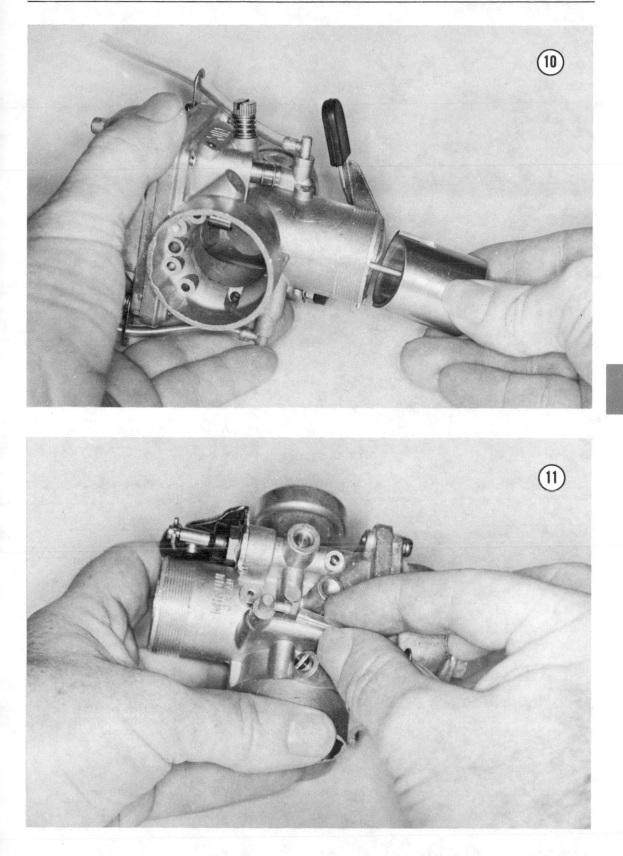

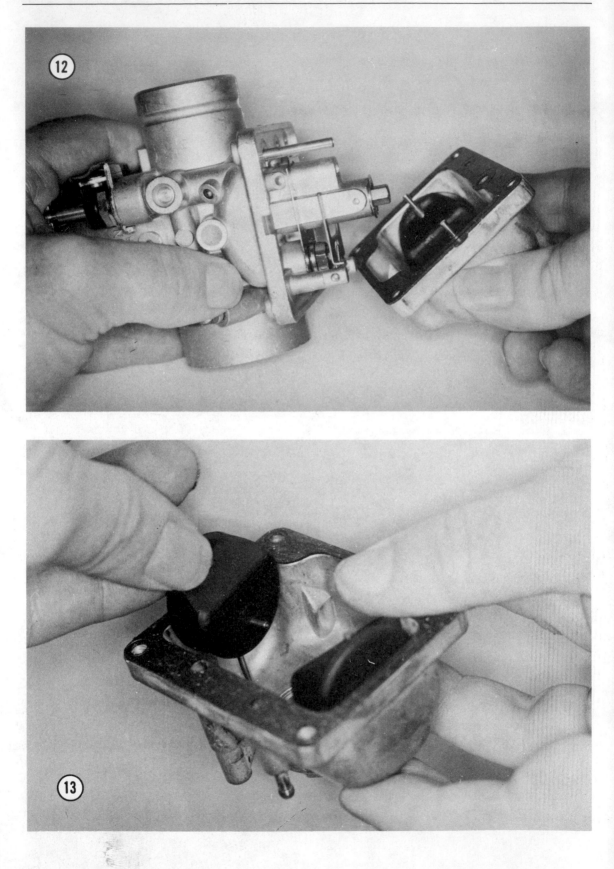

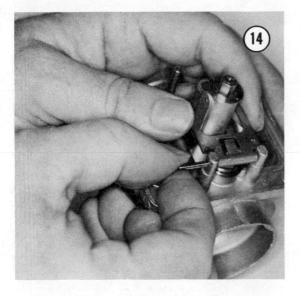

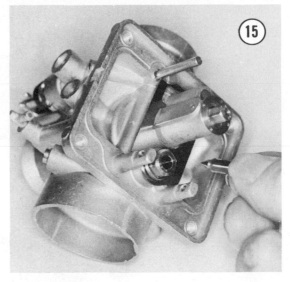

6. Pull out the float needle valve (**Figure 15**), then its seat (**Figure 16**). Note the location of each fiber washer as it is removed.

7. Remove the main jet (**Figure 17**), and with it, the needle jet retaining washer. Note which side of the washer goes up.

8. Turn the carburetor so that the needle jet falls out (**Figure 18**). Be sure to catch it as it falls; it is of soft brass and may be damaged otherwise. Note that there is a locating groove on the needle jet.

9. Remove the pilot jet (**Figure 19**).

5

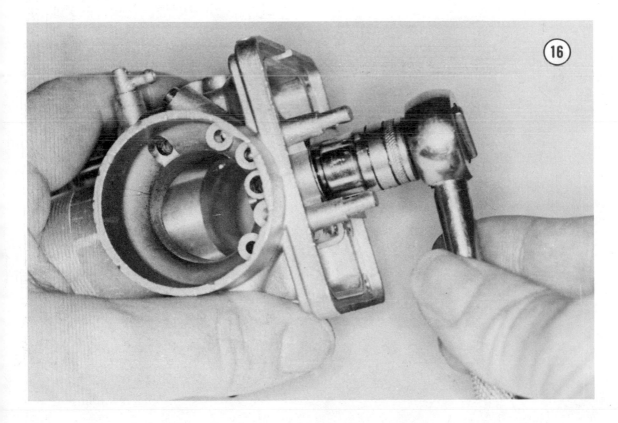

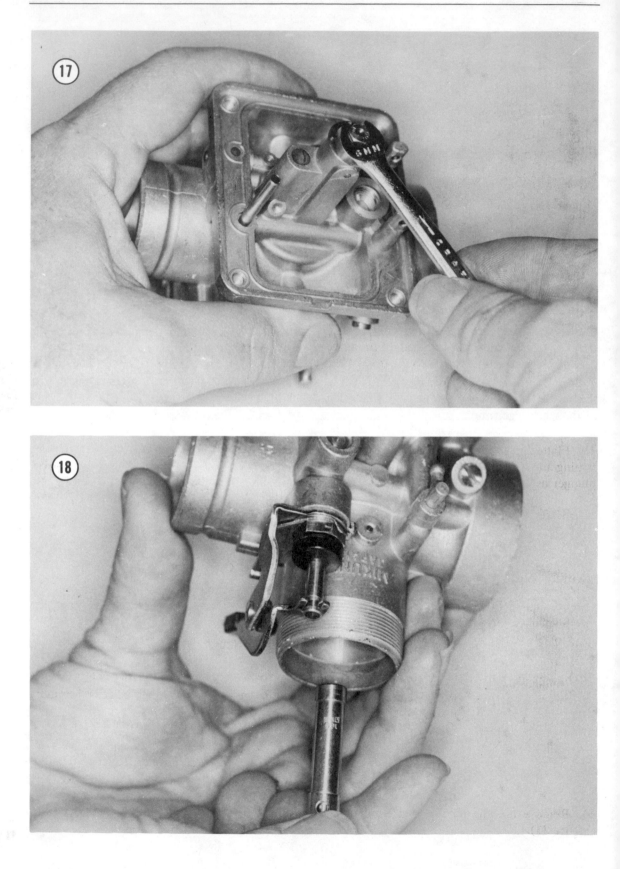

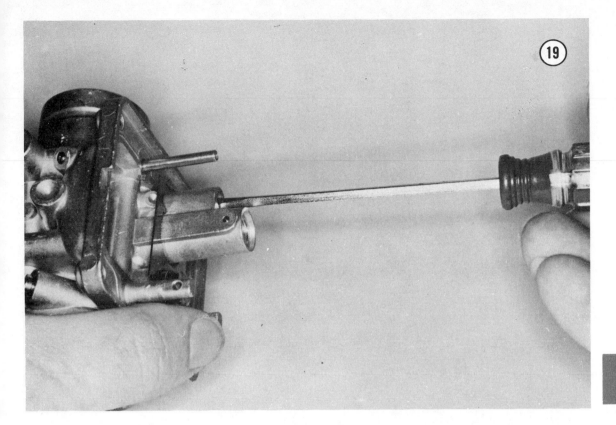

10. Flatten the lock tab, then remove the retaining nut (**Figure 20**) to remove the starter plunger assembly.

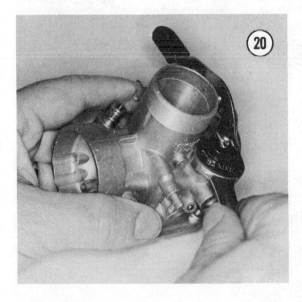

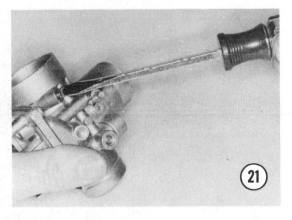

12. Remove the idle speed screw (**Figure 22**).

13. Reverse Steps 1 through 12 for reassembly.

Twin Float Carburetor Disassembly

Figure 23 (page 123) is an exploded view of a typical twin float carburetor. Refer to this illustration during disassembly.

1. Remove the ring nut from the mixing chamber (**Figure 24**) if this step was not done previously.

11. Remove the idle mixture (pilot air) screw (**Figure 21**).

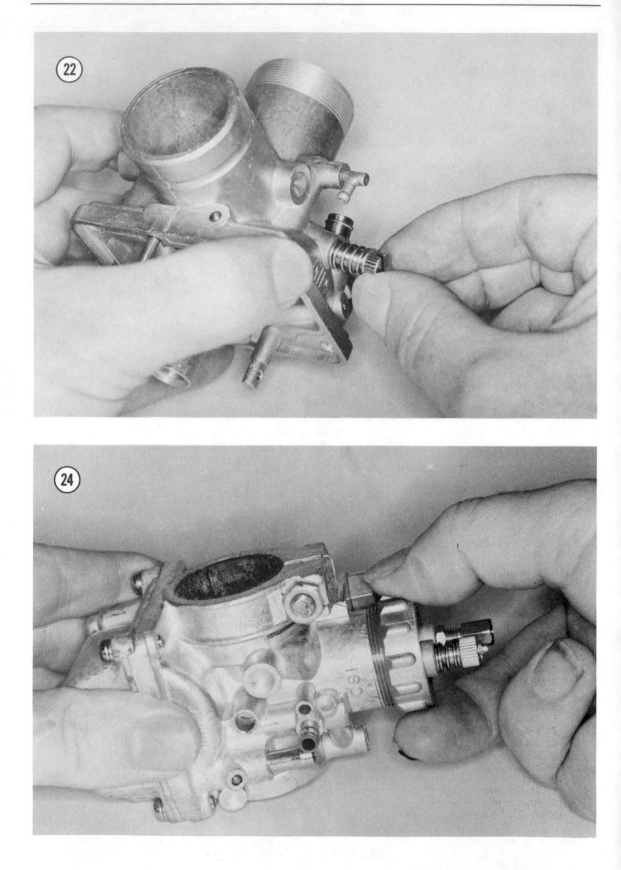

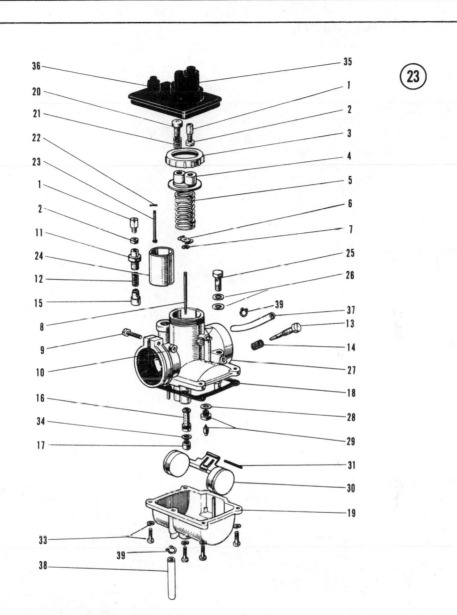

TYPICAL TWIN FLOAT CARBURETOR

1. Cable adjuster
2. Cable adjuster lock nut
3. Mixing chamber cap
4. Mixing chamber top
5. Throttle valve spring
6. Throttle valve spring seat
7. Needle clip
8. Jet needle
9. Carburetor mounting clamp screw
10. Nut
11. Starter plunger cap
12. Starter plunger spring
13. Pilot air adjusting screw

14. Pilot air adjusting screw spring
15. Starter plunger
16. Needle jet
17. Main jet
18. Float chamber gasket
19. Float chamber body
20. Throttle adjuster
21. Throttle adjuster spring
22. Cotter pin
23. Throttle valve stop rod
24. Throttle valve
25. Banjo bolt
26. Gasket

27. Mixing chamber body
28. Float valve seat washer
29. Float valve complete
30. Float
31. Float pin
33. Float chamber fitting screw
34. Main jet washer
35. Carburetor cap grommet
36. Carburetor cap
37. Fuel overflow pipe
38. Air vent pipe
39. Circlip

2. Remove the throttle slide (**Figure 25**).

3. Remove four retaining screws, then pull off the float bowl (**Figure 26**).

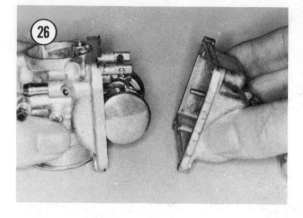

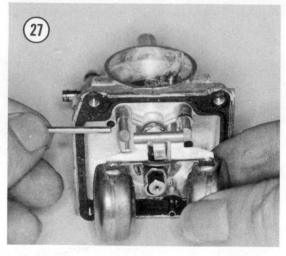

4. Pull out the float pivot shaft (**Figure 27**) to remove the float assembly. Handle this float gently to prevent bending.

5. Remove the main jet and needle jet as a unit (**Figure 28**), by unscrewing the needle jet from the carburetor body.

6. Separate the main jet from the needle jet (**Figure 29**).

7. Remove the pilot jet (**Figure 30**).

8. Remove the starter plunger assembly by loosening its spring cover (**Figure 31**). Be careful, since the spring is under compression.

9. Remove the pilot air screw (**Figure 32**).

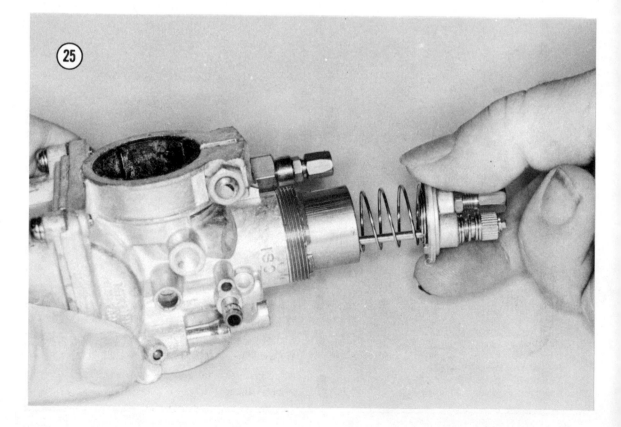

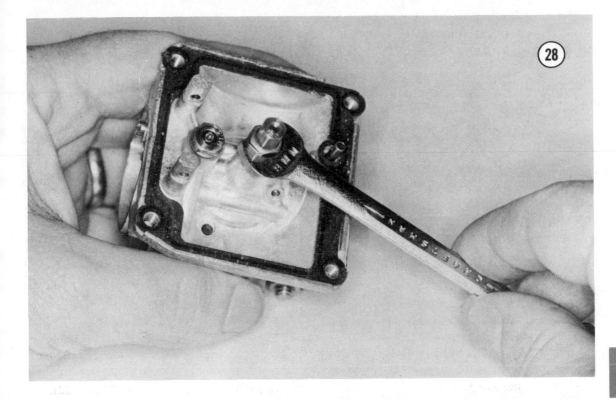

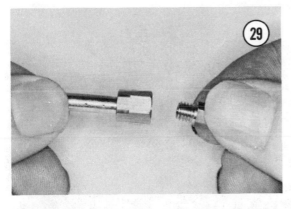

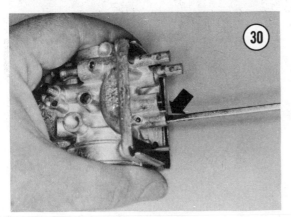

10. Remove the float needle valve assembly (**Figure 33**).

11. To disassemble the throttle slide assembly, remove the cotter pin (**Figure 34**).

12. Push the jet needle out from the throttle slide (**Figure 35**).

13. Reverse Steps 1 through 12 for reassembly.

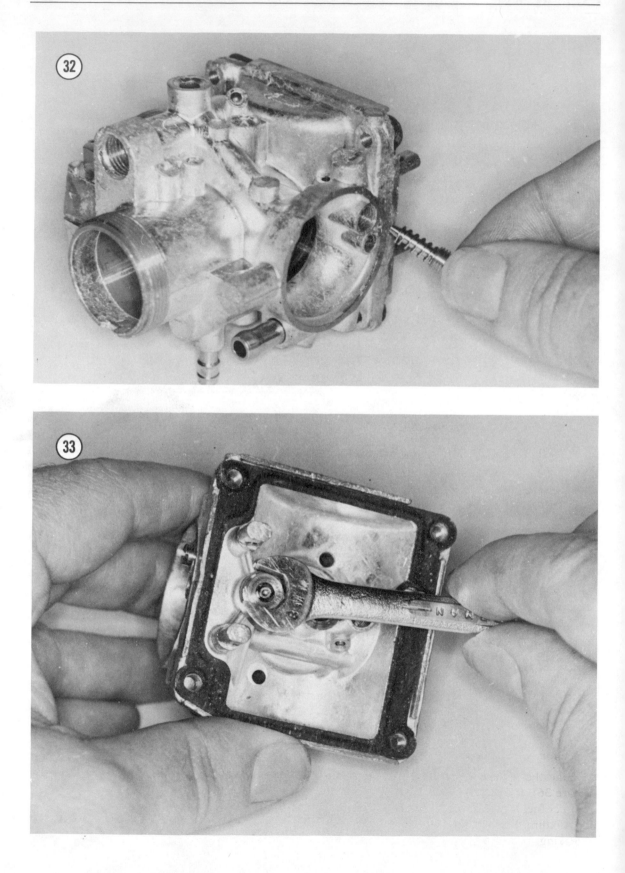

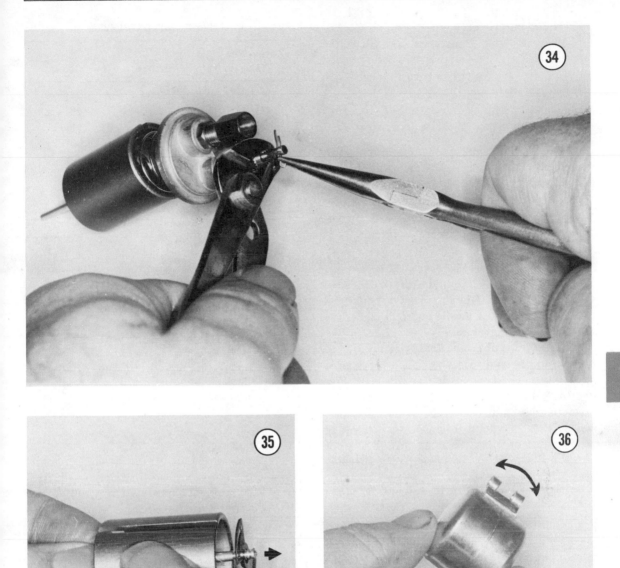

Inspection

Shake the float to check for gasoline inside (**Figure 36**). If fuel leaks into the float, the float chamber fuel level will rise, resulting in an over-rich mixture. Replace the float if it is deformed or leaking.

Replace the float valve if its seating end is scratched or worn. Depress the float valve gently with your finger and make sure that the valve seats properly. If the float valve spring is weak, fuel will overflow, causing an overrich mixture and flooding the float chamber whenever the fuel petcock is open.

Clean all parts in carburetor cleaning solvent. Dry the parts with compressed air. Clean the jets and other delicate parts with compressed air after the float bowl has been removed. Use new gaskets upon reassembly.

CARBURETOR ADJUSTMENT

Carburetor adjustment is not normally required except for occasional adjustment of idling speed (see Chapter Two), or at time of carburetor overhaul. The adjustments described here should only be undertaken if the rider has definite reason to believe they are required.

Float Level

The machine was delivered with the float level adjusted correctly. Rough riding, a bent float arm, or a worn float needle and seat can cause the float level to change.

Figure 37 illustrates the float level adjustment for all models with twin floats. The adjustment for independent float models is shown in **Figure 38**. Remove the carburetor, then remove the float chamber body. Invert the mixing chamber. Gently press the float downward until the tang on the float contacts the float needle. Do not press hard enough to compress the needle valve spring.

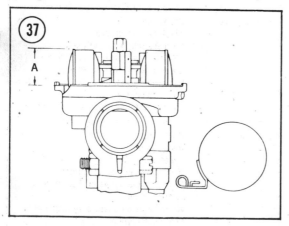

On all models except those with independent floats, measure distance (A) shown in Figure 37. **Table 2** lists float level for each model. If the float level is not correct, bend the tang on the float arm to make the adjustment. All float levels specified have a tolerance of plus or minus 0.04 inch (1.0 millimeter).

Table 2   FLOAT LEVEL

Carburetor Type	Inches	(Millimeters)
VM15SC	0.94	(24)
VM19SC	1.10	(28)
VM22SC	1.10	(28)
VM24SC	1.10	(28)
VM26SC	1.10	(28)
VM30SC	1.18	(30)
VM34SC	1.50	(38)

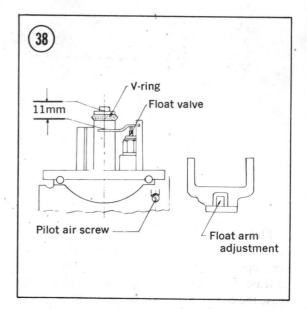

Speed Range Adjustments

The carburetor on your machine was designed to provide the proper mixture under all operating conditions. Little or no benefit will result from experimenting. However, unusual operating conditions such as sustained operation at high altitudes or unusually high or low temperatures may make modifications to the standard specifications desirable. The adjustments described in the following paragraphs should only be undertaken if the rider has definite reason to believe they are required. Make the tests and adjustments in the order specfied.

Figure 39 illustrates typical carburetor components which may be changed to meet individual operating conditions. Shown left to right are the main jet, needle jet, jet needle and clip, and throttle valve.

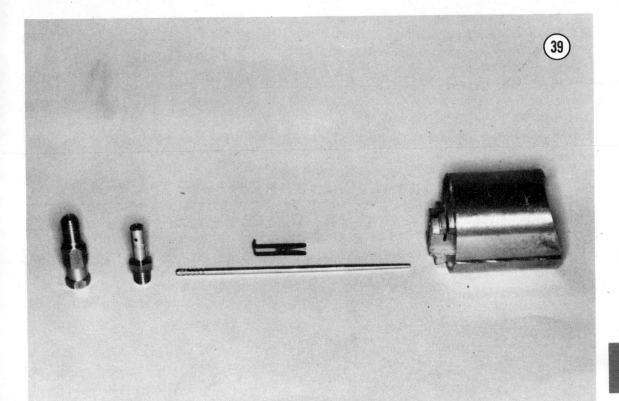

Make a road test at full throttle for final determination of main jet size. To make such a test, operate the motorcycle at full throttle for at least 2 minutes, then shut the engine off, release the clutch, and bring the machine to a stop.

If at full throttle, the engine runs "heavily", the main jet is too large. If the engine runs better by closing the throttle slightly, the main jet is too small. The engine will run at full throttle evenly and regularly if the main jet is of the correct size.

After each such test, remove and examine the spark plug. The insulator should have a light tan color. If the insulator has black sooty deposits, the mixture is too rich. If there are signs of intense heat, such as a blistered white appearance, the mixture is too lean.

As a general rule, main jet size should be reduced approximately 5 percent for each 3,000 feet (1,000 meters) above sea level.

Table 3 lists symptoms caused by rich and lean mixtures.

Table 3   IDLE MIXTURE TROUBLESHOOTING

Condition	Symptom
Rich Mixture	Rough idle
	Black exhaust smoke
	Hard starting, especially when hot
	"Blubbering" under acceleration
	Black deposits in exhaust pipe
	Gas-fouled spark plug
	Poor gas mileage
	Engine performs worse as it warms up
Lean Mixture	Backfiring
	Rough idle
	Overheating
	Hesitation upon acceleration
	Engine speed varies at fixed throttle
	Loss of power
	White color on spark plug insulator
	Poor acceleration

Adjust the pilot air screw as follows.

1. Turn the pilot air screw in until it seats lightly, then back it out about one and one-half turns.

2. Start the engine and warm it to normal operating temperature.

3. Turn the idle speed screw until the engine runs slower and begins to falter.

4. Adjust the pilot air screw as required to make the engine run smoothly.

5. Repeat Steps 3 and 4 to achieve the lowest stable idle speed.

Next, determine the proper throttle valve cutaway size. With the engine running at idle, open the throttle. If the engine does not accelerate smoothly from idle, turn the pilot air screw in (clockwise) slightly to richen the mixture. If the condition still exists, return the air screw to its original position and replace the throttle valve with one which has a smaller cutaway. If engine operation is worsened by turning the air screw, replace the throttle valve with one which has a larger cutaway.

For operation at one- to three-quarters throttle opening, adjustment is made with the jet needle. Operate the engine at half throttle in a manner similar to that for full throttle tests described earlier. To richen the mixture, place the jet needle clip in a lower groove. Conversely, placing the clip in a higher groove leans the mixture.

A summary of carburetor adjustments is given in **Table 4**.

Table 4   CARBURETOR ADJUSTMENTS

Throttle Opening	Adjustment	If too Rich	If too Lean
0 - ⅛	Air screw	Turn out	Turn in
⅛ - ¼	Throttle valve cutaway	Use larger cutaway	Use smaller cutaway
¼ - ¾	Jet needle	Raise clip	Lower clip
¾ - full	Main jet	Use smaller number	Use larger number

CARBURETOR COMPONENTS

The following paragraphs describe the various components of the carburetor which may be changed to vary the performance characteristics.

Throttle Valve

The throttle valve cutaway controls airflow at small throttle openings. Cutaway sizes are numbered. Larger numbers permit more air to flow at a given throttle opening and result in a leaner mixture. Conversely, smaller numbers result in a richer mixture.

Jet Needle

The jet needle, together with the needle jet, controls the mixture at medium speeds. As the throttle valve rises to increase airflow through the carburetor, the jet needle rises with it. The tapered portion of the jet needle rises from the needle jet and allows more fuel to flow, thereby providing the engine with the proper mixture at up to about three-quarters throttle opening. The grooves at the top of the jet needle permit adjustment of the mixture ratio in the medium speed range.

Needle Jet

The needle jet operates with the jet needle. Several holes are drilled through the side of the needle jet. These holes meter the airflow from the air jet. Air from the air jet is bled into the needle jet to assist in atomization of the fuel.

Main Jet

The main jet controls the mixture at full throttle, and has some effect at lesser throttle openings. Each main jet is stamped with a number. Fuel flow is approximately proportional to the number. Larger numbers provide a richer mixture.

MISCELLANEOUS CARBURETOR PROBLEMS

Water in the carburetor float bowl and sticking carburetor slide valves can result from careless washing of the motorcycle. To remedy the problem, remove and clean the carburetor bowl, main jet, and any other affected parts. Be sure to cover the air intake when washing the machine.

Be sure that the ring nut on the top of the carburetor is secure. Also be sure that the carburetor mounting bolts are tight.

If gasoline leaks past the float bowl gasket, high speed fuel starvation may occur. Varnish deposits on the outside of the float bowl are evidence of this condition.

Dirt in the fuel may lodge in the float valve and cause an overrich mixture. As a temporary measure, tap the carburetor lightly with any convenient tool to dislodge the dirt. Clean the fuel tank, petcock, fuel line, and carburetor at the first opportunity, should this occur.

CHAPTER SIX

FRAME, SUSPENSION AND STEERING

HANDLEBARS

The handlebar is made from solid drawn steel tubing. Most of the manual controls (**Figure 1**) are mounted on the handlebar assembly. Wiring from the switches on the handlebar assembly is routed to the headlight assembly, where it is connected to the main wiring harness.

Disassembly

1. Loosen the clutch cable locknut (**Figure 2**), then rotate the adjustment nut to provide the inner clutch cable with sufficient slack to remove the clutch cable from the lever.

2. Loosen the front brake adjustment nut (**Figure 3**), then remove the brake cable (**Figure 4**)

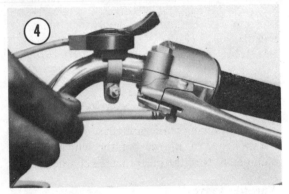

from the brake lever on the handlebar. On F series models, the front brake stop lamp switch is built into the front brake cable. Disconnect the switch lead (**Figure 5**) from the main wire harness before you remove the cable.

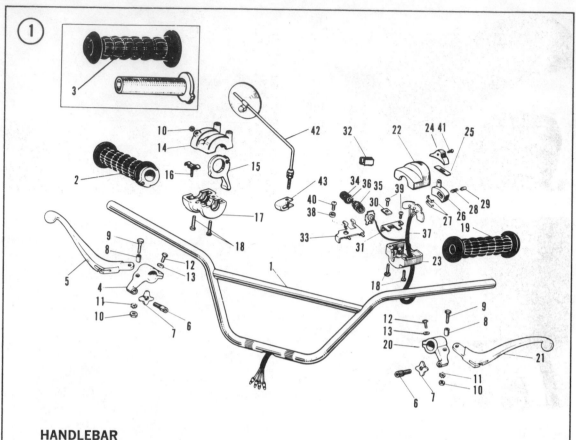

HANDLEBAR
AND CONTROLS

1. Handlebar
2. Throttle grip
3. Grip rubber
4. Brake lever holder
5. Lever
6. Screw
7. Nut
8. Collar
9. Bolt

10. Nut
11. Lockwasher
12. Bolt
13. Washer
14. Upper case
15. Lever
16. Spring
17. Lower case
18. Screw

19. Grip rubber
20. Lever holder
21. Lever
22. Upper case
23. Lower case
24. Knob
25. Spring
26. Switch
27. Contact plate

28. Spring
29. Contact
30. Switch holder
31. Switch holder
32. Cap
33. Switch holder
34. Horn button
35. Spring

36. Contact
37. Wiring harness
38. Washer
39. Screw
40. Screw
41. Screw
42. Mirror
43. Bracket

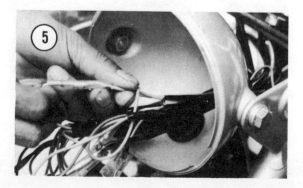

3. Disassemble the throttle grip assembly (**Figure 6**), then remove the control cable.

4. Disassemble the starter lever (**Figure 7**), then remove the starter cable. On F series and G4TR models, the throttle and starter cables are built into the throttle grip assembly.

5. Remove the horn, turn signal, and headlight leads from the wire harness inside the headlight assembly, then disassemble the left-hand grip assembly (**Figure 8**).

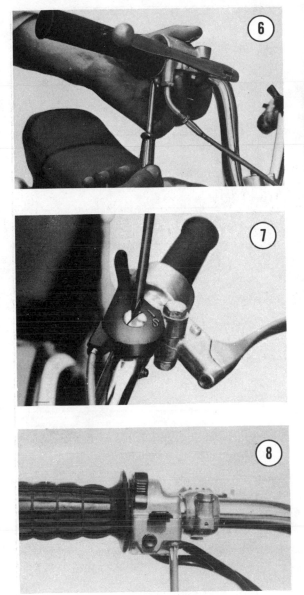

bar tubing and through the cord protector in the headlight. After installation, adjust the play in the throttle, clutch, and starter lever cables. Adjust the play in the front brake lever to 0.8-1.2 in. (20-30mm) by means of the brake adjusting nut on the brake.

WHEELS AND TIRES

Tires

Figure 10 is a cutaway view of a typical wheel and tire assembly. **Figure 11** is a sectional view of a tire mounted on its rim. Various tire sizes are fitted to Kawasaki machines. Refer to the specifications for tire sizes for your machine. Tires are available in different tread types to suit the different requirements of the rider. **Table 1** lists the normal tire pressures for the various models, measured with the tires cold. It is normal for tire pressure to increase after prolonged operation. Do not bleed air from a hot tire to decrease the pressure.

6. Remove the clamp bolts (**Figure 9**), then remove the handlebar from the bracket.

Inspection

Examine the handlebar for cracking or bending. Minor bends may be straightened. Replace the handlebar if any cracks exist, or in the event of major bending.

Installation

Reverse the removal procedure to install the handlebar. Pass the wiring through the handle-

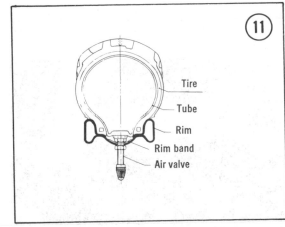

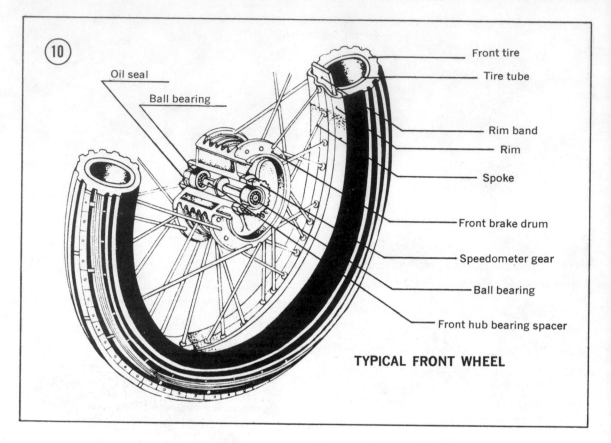

⑩

Oil seal

Ball bearing

Front tire

Tire tube

Rim band

Rim

Spoke

Front brake drum

Speedometer gear

Ball bearing

Front hub bearing spacer

TYPICAL FRONT WHEEL

Table 1   TIRE PRESSURE

Tire Size	Tire Pressure Pounds per Square Inch	
	Front	Rear
3.00-16	23	28
2.50-18	23	28
2.75-18	23	28
3.00-18	23	28
3.25-18	14*	14*
3.25-18	23	28
3.50-18	23	28
4.00-18	23	28
3.00-19	23	28
3.00-21	14*	14*

*Tire pressure for moto cross racing

Check the tires periodically for wear, bruises, cuts, or other damage. Remove any small stones which may lodge in the tread with a small screwdriver or similar tool.

Rims

The rim supports the tire and provides rigidity to the wheel assembly. A rim band protects the inner tube from abrasion. Rims on model F5 are of aluminum for light weight.

Spokes

The spokes support the weight of the motorcycle and rider, and transmit tractive and braking forces, as shown in **Figure 12**. Diagram A illustrates action of the spokes as they support the machine. Tractive forces are shown in diagram B. Braking forces are shown in diagram C.

Check the spokes periodically for looseness or bending. A bent or otherwise faulty spoke will adversely affect neighboring spokes, and should therefore be replaced immediately. To remove the spoke, completely unscrew the threaded portion, then remove the bent end from the hub.

Spokes tend to loosen as the machine is used. Retighten each spoke one turn, beginning with those on one side of the hub, then those on the other side. Tighten the spokes on a new machine after the first 50 miles of operation, then at 50-mile intervals until they no longer loosen.

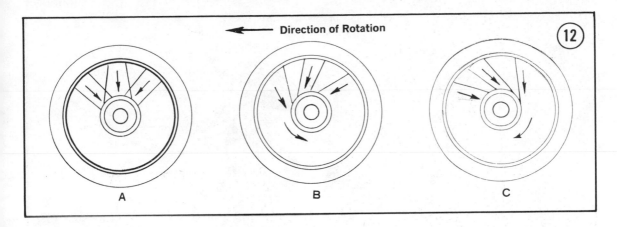

Direction of Rotation

A   B   C

If the machine is subjected to particularly severe service, as in off-road or competition riding, check the spokes frequently.

Bead Protector

Some F series machines are equipped with bead protectors (**Figure 13**) on each wheel. The bead protector prevents the tire from slipping on the rim, especially during maximum effort braking at high speeds, and thereby prevents damage to the valve stem.

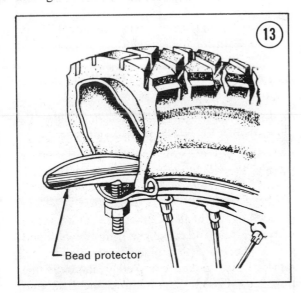

Bead protector

Wheel Balance

An unbalanced wheel results in unsafe riding conditions. Depending on the degree of unbalance and the speed of the motorcycle, the rider may experience anything from a mild vibration to a violent shimmy which may even result in loss of control. Balance weights (**Figure 14**) are applied to the spokes on the light side of the wheel to correct this condition.

Mark
Balance weight

Before you attempt to balance the wheel, check to be sure that the wheel bearings are in good condition and properly lubricated. Also make sure that the brakes don't drag, so that the wheel rotates freely. With the wheel free of the ground, spin it slowly and allow it to come to rest by itself. Add balance weights to the spokes on the light side as required, so that the wheel comes to rest at a different position each time it is spun. Balance weights are available in weights of 10, 20, and 30 grams. Remove the drive chain when you balance the rear wheel.

Front Hub

Figure 15 is an exploded view of a typical front hub. The entire hub assembly rotates on 2 ball bearings. The speedometer gears transmit the front wheel rotation to the speedometer. The brake panel supports the brake mechanism.

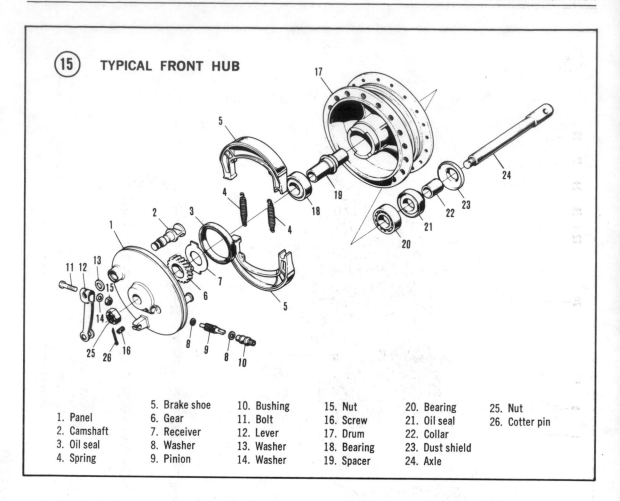

(15) TYPICAL FRONT HUB

1. Panel	5. Brake shoe	10. Bushing	15. Nut	20. Bearing	25. Nut
2. Camshaft	6. Gear	11. Bolt	16. Screw	21. Oil seal	26. Cotter pin
3. Oil seal	7. Receiver	12. Lever	17. Drum	22. Collar	
4. Spring	8. Washer	13. Washer	18. Bearing	23. Dust shield	
	9. Pinion	14. Washer	19. Spacer	24. Axle	

Rear Hub

An exploded view of the rear hub on most models is shown in **Figure 16**. The rear hub consists of 4 major parts: brake drum, brake panel, sprocket coupling, and rear sprocket. The rear wheel bearings are mounted in the brake drum. The brake panel supports the brake mechanism, except for the brake drum. The sprocket coupling absorbs shocks throughout the entire drive train. The sprocket transmits engine power to the rear wheel through the sprocket coupling.

On some models, the sprocket is bolted directly to the hub; no shock damper is used. Such an undamped hub is shown in **Figure 17**. The rear sprocket on model F5 is made from aluminum to further reduce weight.

Front Wheel Removal

Front wheel removal is similar for all models. Proceed as follows:

1. Loosen the front brake adjustment nut, then remove the brake cable at the front hub.

2. Loosen speedometer cable nut (**Figure 18**), then remove the speedometer cable.

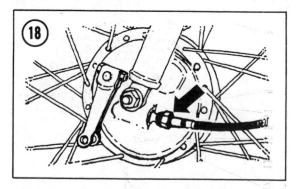

3. Raise the front of the motorcycle and support it on a box or stand placed under the engine.

4. Remove the front hub shaft nut (**Figure 19**) on the side of the front brake panel.

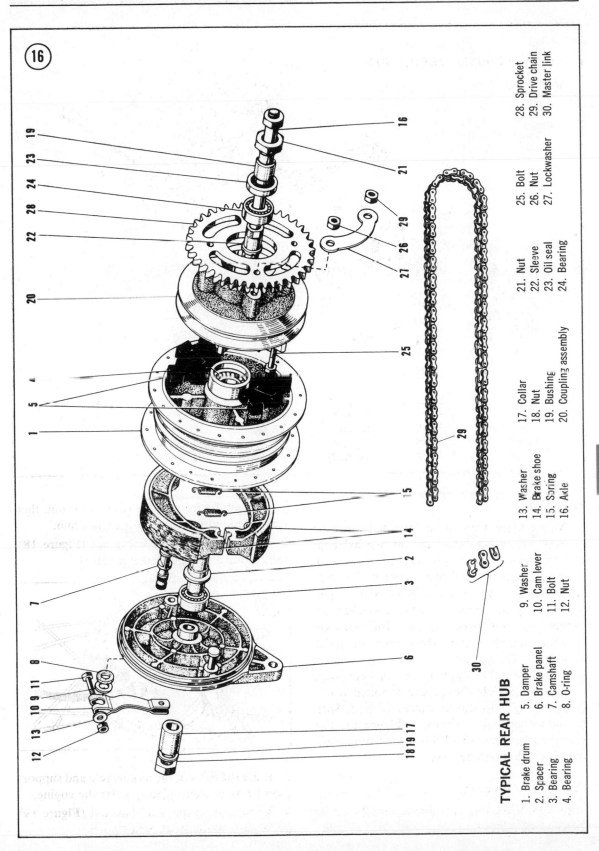

TYPICAL REAR HUB

1. Brake drum
2. Spacer
3. Bearing
4. Bearing
5. Damper
6. Brake panel
7. Camshaft
8. O-ring
9. Washer
10. Cam lever
11. Bolt
12. Nut
13. Washer
14. Brake shoe
15. Spring
16. Axle
17. Collar
18. Nut
19. Bushing
20. Coupling assembly
21. Nut
22. Sleeve
23. Oil seal
24. Bearing
25. Bolt
26. Nut
27. Lockwasher
28. Sprocket
29. Drive chain
30. Master link

6

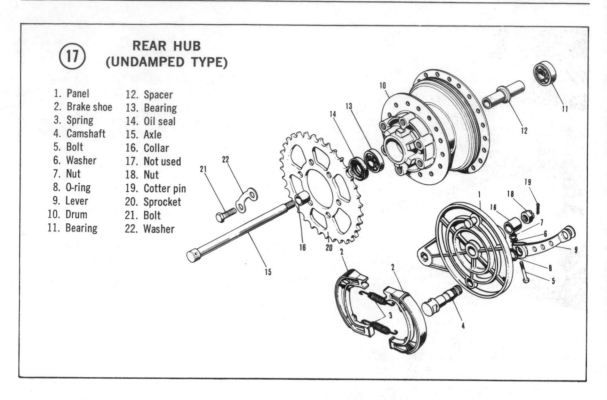

REAR HUB (UNDAMPED TYPE)

1. Panel
2. Brake shoe
3. Spring
4. Camshaft
5. Bolt
6. Washer
7. Nut
8. O-ring
9. Lever
10. Drum
11. Bearing

12. Spacer
13. Bearing
14. Oil seal
15. Axle
16. Collar
17. Not used
18. Nut
19. Cotter pin
20. Sprocket
21. Bolt
22. Washer

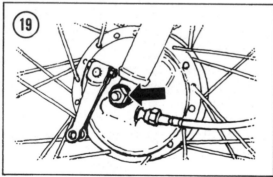

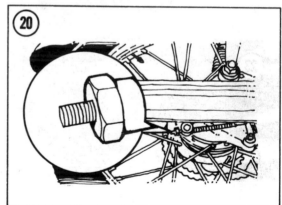

CAUTION

Do not attempt to loosen the nut on the other end of the shaft.

5. On Models F5, F8, F9, and F81M, separate the brake torque link from the front fork.

6. Pull out the shaft and remove the wheel from the motorcycle.

Rear Wheel Removal

1. Remove the rear brake adjustment nut (**Figure 20**), then remove the inner brake cable from the brake lever. Apply pressure to the brake pedal when you remove the brake cable.

2. Remove the torque link.

3. Remove the chain cover (**Figure 21**).

4. Remove the clip from the master link (**Figure 22**), then remove the chain. It may be necessary to rotate the rear wheel to position the master link for convenient removal. Then remove the drive chain.

5. Remove the axle shaft nut on the sprocket side (**Figure 23**).

CAUTION

Do not attempt to remove the nut on the other end of the shaft.

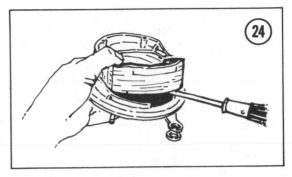

race of the wheel bearing on the opposite side. Drive out the bearing and oil seal together. Be sure to re-position the drift punch after each hammer blow so that the bearing is not cocked in its bore.

3. Insert the drift punch from the other side of the brake drum, then repeat Step 2 to drive out the other bearing.

Inspection

1. Support each wheel shaft in a lathe, V-blocks, or other suitable centering device. Rotate the shaft through a complete revolution. Straighten or replace the shaft if it is bent more than 0.016 in. (0.4mm).

2. Check the inner and outer races of the wheel bearings for cracks, galling, or pitting. Rotate the bearings by hand, and check for roughness. Measure the bearings for wear as shown in **Figure 25**. Replace the bearings if wear exceeds the limits shown.

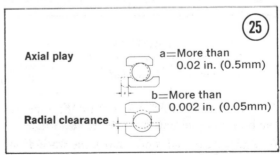

6. Pull out the shaft.

7. Remove the spacer, then lean the machine to one side and remove the wheel and brake mechanism together.

Wheel Disassembly

1. Pry each brake shoe from the brake panel (**Figure 24**), using a large screwdriver or similar tool.

2. Insert a long drift punch from the inner side of the brake drum, with its end against the inner

3. Inspect the main and auxiliary lips of the coil seal (**Figure 26**) for wear or damage. Replace oil seal if there is any doubt about its condition.

4. On machines so equipped, inspect the rubber shock dampers in the rear hub (**Figure 27**). Replace the dampers if worn or damaged.

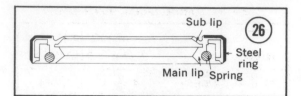

Sub lip

Steel ring

Main lip Spring

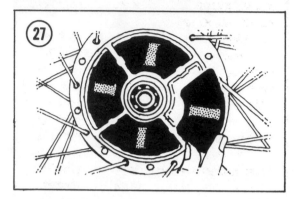

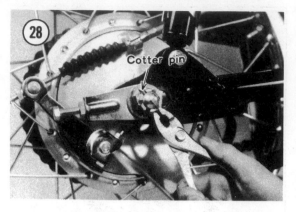

Cotter pin

Wheel Reassembly

Reverse the disassembly procedure to re-assemble the wheels. Observe the following notes as you reassemble the wheel.

1. Clean the wheel bearings carefully, then lubricate them before installation.

2. Use an arbor press to install the bearings and oil seals. Be sure that the bearings and seals are seated squarely in their bores.

3. Be sure that there are no scratches, oil, or grease on the inner surface of the brake drum, or on the friction surfaces of the brake shoes. Clean the contact surfaces thoroughly with lacquer thinner before assembly.

4. Torque the shaft and torque link nuts as given in **Table 2**.

Table 2   SHAFT AND LINK NUT TORQUES

	Front	Rear
Shaft nut	48-61 ft-lbs (6.7-8.5 kg-m)	55-68 ft-lbs (7.7-9.8 kg-m)
Torque link	8.5-11 ft-lbs (1.2-1.5 kg-m)	16-22 ft-lbs (2.2-3.1 kg-m)

5. Secure the axle and torque link nuts with cotter pins (**Figure 28**) after the nuts are tightened.

6. Check the wheels for runout after assembly.

Checking Wheel Runout

To measure runout of the wheel rim, support the wheel so it is free to rotate. Position a dial indicator as shown in **Figure 29**. Observe the dial indicator as you rotate the wheel through a complete revolution. The runout limit for all models is 0.04 in. (1.0mm). Excessive runout may be caused by a bent rim or loose spokes. Repair or replace as required.

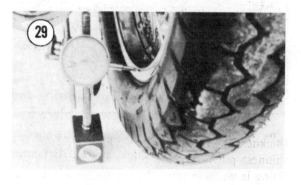

BRAKES

Figure 30 illustrates the major parts of the brakes. Operation of the brake pedal or lever rotates a camshaft, which in turn forces the brake shoes into contact with the brake drum.

Brake Inspection

Measure the inner diameter of the brake drum, as shown in **Figure 31**. Brake drum wear limits are listed in **Table 3**.

Examine the brake lining for oil or other foreign material. Replace any oil-soaked lining immediately. Dirt imbedded in the brake lining may be removed with a wire brush. Measure the

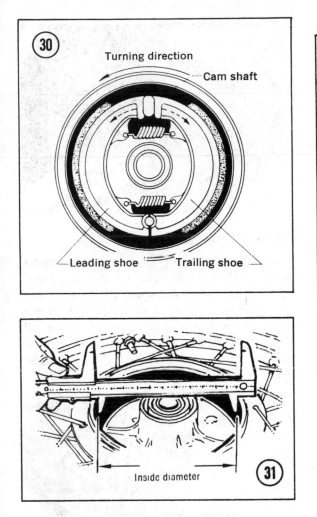

Turning direction
Cam shaft
Leading shoe   Trailing shoe

30

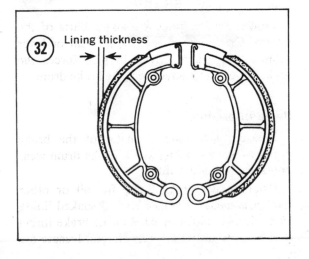

Inside diameter

31

thickness of the brake lining (**Figure 32**) at the thinnest part. Replace the brake shoes if the lining is worn beyond the repair limit given in **Table 4**.

Lining thickness

32

Table 3   DRUM BRAKE WEAR LIMITS

Model	Repair Limit	
	Inches	(Millimeters)
J1, G, M, C2 Series	4.36	(110.75)
G31M-A, C1D, F6, F7	5.15	(130.75)
KE, KH, KV100	4.36	(110.75)
KD, KE, KS, KX125		
(front)	4.75	(120.75)
(rear)	5.15	(130.75)
B1 Series	5.94	(150.75)
F2, F3, F4, F5, F8, F9	5.94	(150.75)
KE175 (front)	4.75	(120.75)
(rear)	5.15	(130.75)
KT250 (front)	4.75	(120.75)
(rear)	5.15	(130.75)
F21M, KX250 (front)	5.15	(130.75)
(rear)	5.94	(150.75)
F81M	5.94	(150.75)
KX400, KX450 (front)	5.15	(130.75)
(rear)	5.94	(150.75)

Table 4   BRAKE LINING THICKNESS

Model	Repair Limit	
	Inch	(Millimeters)
J1, G1L, G1M	0.06	(1.5)
GA1, GA2, G3TR	0.06	(1.5)
GA1-A, GA2-A, G3SS	0.08	(2.0)
G3TR-A, G4TR, G5, G31M-A	0.08	(2.0)
C1D	0.07	(1.8)
C2SS, M Series	0.06	(1.5)
KE, KH, KV100	0.06	(1.5)
B1L, F2, F3, F4	0.10	(2.5)
KD, KE, KS, KX125	0.08	(2.0)
KE175	0.08	(2.0)
F6, F7	0.08	(2.0)
F21M (front)	0.07	(1.8)
(rear)	0.10	(2.5)
B1L-A, F5, F8, F9	0.12	(3.0)
KT250	0.08	(2.0)
F81M	0.12	(3.0)
KX250, 400, 450 (front)	0.08	(2.0)
(rear)	0.12	(3.0)

6

If the brake shoe return spring is worn or stretched, the brake shoes will not retract fully and the brakes may drag. Measure the free length (**Figure 33**) of the return spring. Replace spring if it is stretched beyond repair limit. See **Table 5**.

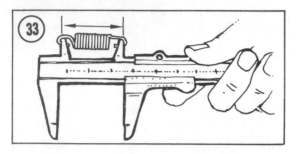

Table 5   RETURN SPRING WEAR LIMIT

Model	Wear Limit Inches	(Millimeters)
J1, G1, GA Series	1.30	(33.0)
G3TR, C1D, C2SS	1.30	(33.0)
G4TR, G5, G31M-A	1.34	(34.0)
M Series	1.34	(34.0)
KE, KH, KV100	1.34	(34.0)
F6, F7	1.34	(34.0)
F2, F3, F4	1.97	(50.0)
B1 Series	1.97	(50.0)
KD, KE, KS, KX125 (short)	1.34	(34.0)
(long)	1.89	(48.0)
KE175 (short)	1.34	(34.0)
(long)	1.89	(48.0)
F5, F8, F81M	2.01	(51.0)
KT250 (short)	1.34	(34.0)
(long)	1.89	(48.0)
KX250	2.09	(53.0)
F21M (front)	1.34	(34.0)
(rear)	1.57	(50.0)
KX400, KX450	2.09	(53.0)

Measure the clearance between the brake camshaft and the bushing in the brake panel. Standard clearance for all models is 0.0008-0.0028 in. (0.02-0.07mm). Replace the camshaft and/or the brake panel if the clearance exceeds 0.02 in. (0.5mm).

To reassemble the brake mechanism, reverse the disassembly procedure. Be sure that the front

brake cable is approximately perpendicular to the brake cam lever (**Figure 34**). Grease the brake pedal bearing, brake lever, and brake cam bearings in the brake panel.

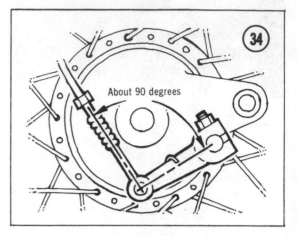

About 90 degrees

Brake Adjustment

Adjust the front brake by turning the adjustment nut at the front brake cam lever. The adjustment is correct if braking action begins when the front brake lever (**Figure 35**) is pulled approximately one inch (25mm). Since the front brake stop lamp switch is built into the cable, no adjustment on it is required.

1 inch

Adjust the rear brake by turning the adjustment nut until braking action begins at 1.0-1.4 in. (25-35mm) travel of the brake pedal (**Figure 36**). Adjust the rear brake stop lamp switch (**Figure 37**) so that the stop lamp lights when the brake pedal has traveled 0.6-0.8 in. (15-20mm).

FRONT FORKS

Two basic types of front forks are used on these machines. Early model machines are

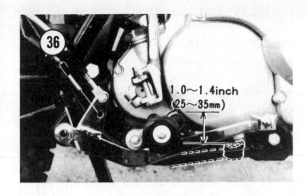

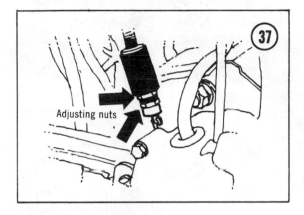

Adjusting nuts

2. Remove the headlight assembly (**Figure 41**).

3. Remove the speedometer and tachometer, as shown in **Figures 42 and 43**.

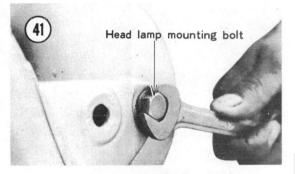

Head lamp mounting bolt

equipped with forks identified by a large tube nut securing the fork assembly (3, **Figure 38**, and 13, **Figure 39**). There are 2 categories of early model forks, one for smaller models (Figure 38) and one for larger models (Figure 39).

Forks on later model machines can be identified by the Allen bolt in the bottom of each fork leg (31, Figure 55, page 149).

CAUTION
Be sure that you correctly identify your forks and use the right procedures or serious damage may result.

Some F5, F7, F8, and F9 models feature Hatta forks which allow the rider to adjust trail, caster, and stroke to suit various riding conditions.

Removal (Early Models)

The initial steps for fork removal are similar for all models. Proceed as follows.

1. Remove all connectors in the headlight assembly from the main wire harness, as shown in **Figure 40**.

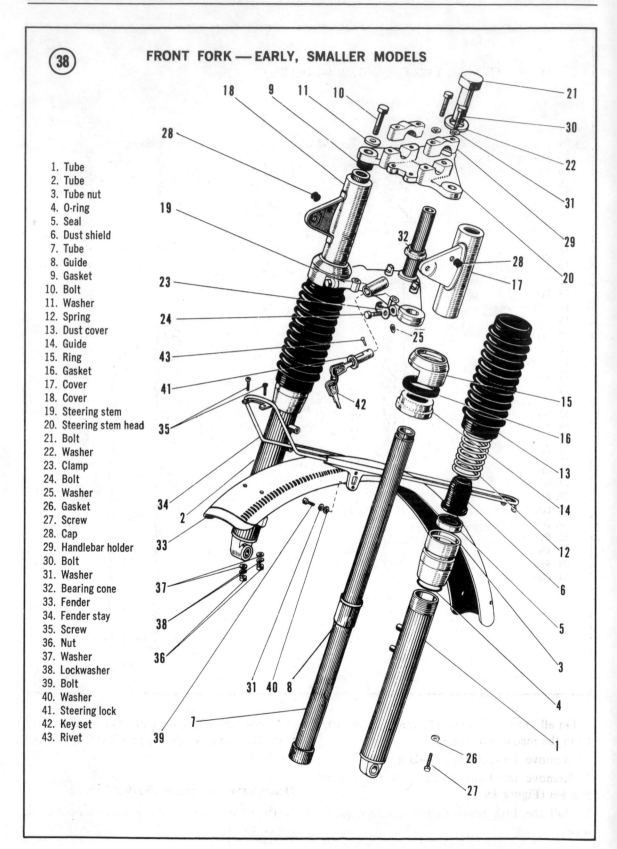

FRONT FORK — EARLY, SMALLER MODELS

38

1. Tube
2. Tube
3. Tube nut
4. O-ring
5. Seal
6. Dust shield
7. Tube
8. Guide
9. Gasket
10. Bolt
11. Washer
12. Spring
13. Dust cover
14. Guide
15. Ring
16. Gasket
17. Cover
18. Cover
19. Steering stem
20. Steering stem head
21. Bolt
22. Washer
23. Clamp
24. Bolt
25. Washer
26. Gasket
27. Screw
28. Cap
29. Handlebar holder
30. Bolt
31. Washer
32. Bearing cone
33. Fender
34. Fender stay
35. Screw
36. Nut
37. Washer
38. Lockwasher
39. Bolt
40. Washer
41. Steering lock
42. Key set
43. Rivet

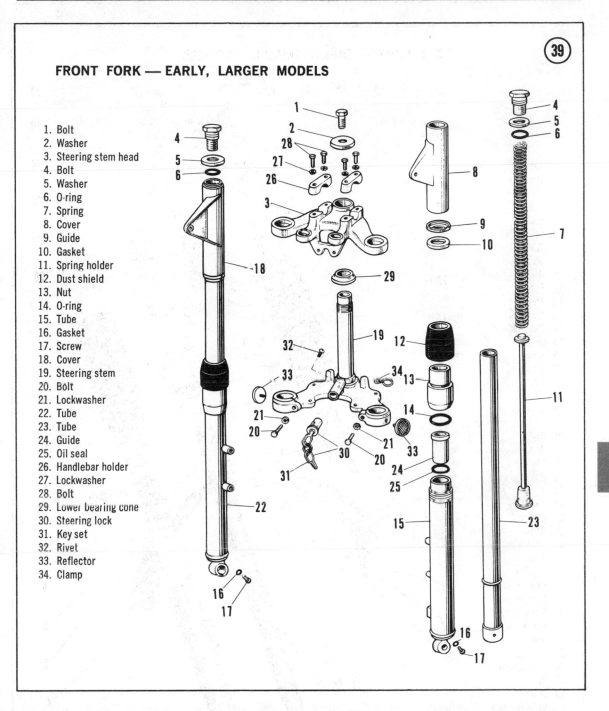

FRONT FORK — EARLY, LARGER MODELS

39

1. Bolt
2. Washer
3. Steering stem head
4. Bolt
5. Washer
6. O-ring
7. Spring
8. Cover
9. Guide
10. Gasket
11. Spring holder
12. Dust shield
13. Nut
14. O-ring
15. Tube
16. Gasket
17. Screw
18. Cover
19. Steering stem
20. Bolt
21. Lockwasher
22. Tube
23. Tube
24. Guide
25. Oil seal
26. Handlebar holder
27. Lockwasher
28. Bolt
29. Lower bearing cone
30. Steering lock
31. Key set
32. Rivet
33. Reflector
34. Clamp

On all but F series models, remove the forks from the machine as follows.

1. Remove the upper bolts (**Figure 44**).

2. Remove the lower bolts from the under-bracket (**Figure 45**).

3. Pull the fork tubes downward to remove them.

F series models require that the oil be drained from the forks, as shown in **Figure 46**, before removal.

Disassembly/Assembly (Early Models)

1. Remove the dust seal, spring, dust boots, and spring guide.

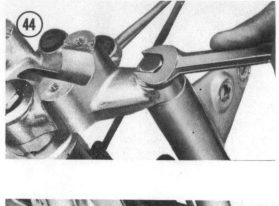

Inspection

1. Assemble inner and outer tubes (**Figure 49**), then slide them together. Check for looseness, noise, or binding. Replace defective parts.

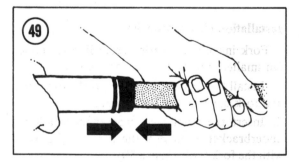

2. Invert the fork and drain the oil.

3. Wrap a piece of rubber sheeting or a section of inner tube around the outer tube nut, and clamp the nut in a vise (**Figure 47**). Be careful that you do not deform the tube by clamping the vise too tightly.

4. Turn the outer tube counterclockwise to separate the tubes. The outer tube may be turned easily by using the front axle shaft as a lever, as shown in **Figure 48**.

5. Assembly is the reverse of these steps. Replace oil seal and O-ring attached to outer tube.

2. Any scratches or roughness on the inner tube in the area where it passes through the oil seal will damage the oil seal. Examine this area carefully.

3. Inspect the dust seal carefully. If this seal is damaged, foreign material will enter the fork.

4. Measure the free length of each fork spring. Replace any spring which is shorter than the repair limit. See **Table 6**.

Table 6   FORK SPRING FREE LENGTH

Model	Repair Limit Inches	(Millimeters)
J1, G1, G1M	5.04	(127)
GA, G3 Series	6.06	(154)
G4TR	11.65	(296)
G5	15.55	(395)
G31M-A*, F7*	4.76	(121)
	13.23	(336)
C1D	6.06	(154)
M Series	13.31	(338)
KE, KH, KV100	15.55	(395)
C-3SS	5.31	(135)
B1 Series, F2	6.85	(174)
KD, KE, KS, KX125	19.30	(490)
F6	18.90	(480)
F3	6.69	(170)
F4	14.96	(380)
F5, F8, F9, F81M	18.27	(464)
F21M	14.09	(358)
KE175	18.70	(475)
KT250 (long)	9.88	(251)
(short)	4.09	(104)
KX250	18.50	(470)
KX400, KX450	17.59	(447)

*Two springs in each fork leg.

tube upward until the end of the inner tube reaches the stepped portion of the steering stem head, then secure it with the upper bolt. Finally, tighten the steering stem bolt.

9. On larger models, place the left and right lamp bracket and the rubber damper in position between the upper and lower brackets. Insert the fork from below, then tighten the bolts. Adjust the fork as desired after installation as outlined in the following steps:

   a. Refer to **Figures 51 and 52**. (A) is the standard position, (B) is the off-road position, and (C) is the position for high speed riding.

Installation (Early Models)

Fork installation varies according to model. On smaller models, proceed as follows.

1. Install the fork cover gasket, fork cover ring, and fork cover to the underbracket.

2. Insert the front fork from underneath the underbracket, then pull the fork fully upward with the fork tool (**Figure 50**).

3. Hold the fork in position by clamping the inner tube clamp bolt.

4. Remove the fork tool.

5. Partially tighten the top bolt.

6. Temporarily loosen inner tube clamp bolt.

7. Tighten the top bolt fully.

8. Tighten the inner tube clamp bolt fully.

On model G4TR, insert the front fork from the bottom of the steering stem. Push the inner

b. To adjust the position of the steering stem, refer to **Figure 53**. (D) is the standard riding position. Positions (E) and (F) are used as desired for high speed riding. Loosen the 4 clamp bolts on the steering stem, slide the tubes into the desired position, then tighten the 4 clamp bolts.

c. Refer to **Figure 54** for fork spring adjustment. The spring tension is varied by removing the rubber cap, then turning the rod to position (A), (B), or (C), as required.

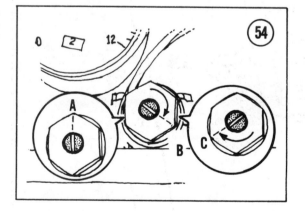

Removal/Installation (Later Models)

Refer to **Figure 55** for this procedure.

1. Remove front wheel. If fork tube is to be disassembled, loosen top bolt (**Figure 56**).

2. Using an Allen wrench, loosen upper and lower clamp bolts (**Figure 57**). Using a twisting motion, work fork tube down and out.

> NOTE: *If fork tube cannot be removed by twisting, remove fork cover and damper rubbers* (**Figure 58**).

FRONT FORK
(LATER MODELS)

1. Stem head bolt
2. Washer
3. Bolt
4. Top bolt
5. O-ring
6. Stem head
7. Clamp bolt
8. Stem head clamp bolt
9. Washer
10. Rubber damper
11. Outer race
12. Outer race
13. Fork cover
14. Steering stem shaft
15. Steering stem base
16. Clamp bolt
17. Steering stem base clamp bolt
18. Spring
19. Inner tube
20. Cylinder assembly
21. Cylinder base
22. Lockwasher
23. Spring
24. Dust seal
25. Circlip
26. Oil seal
27. Outer tube
28. Gasket
29. Drain screw
30. Washer
31. Allen bolt
32. Stud bolt
33. Axle clamp
34. Lockwasher
35. Nut

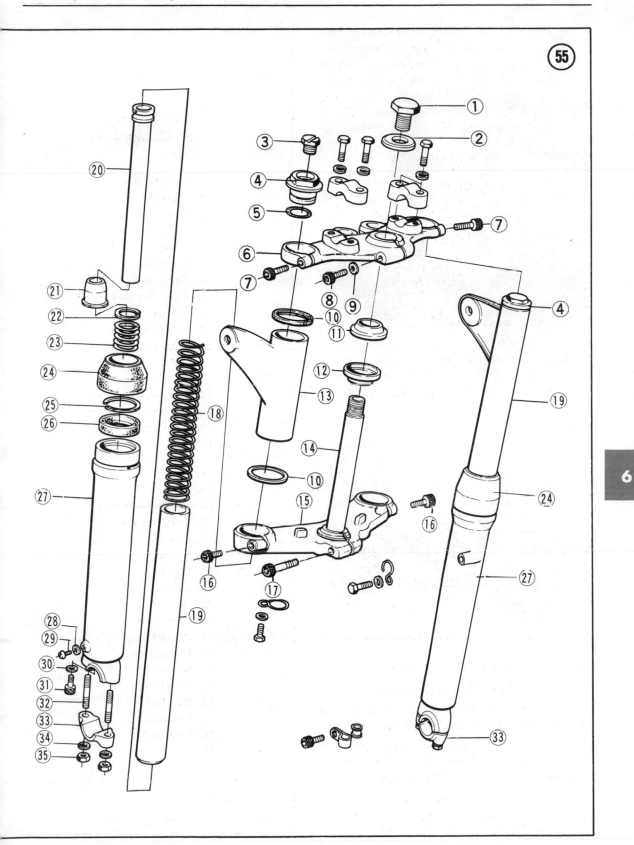

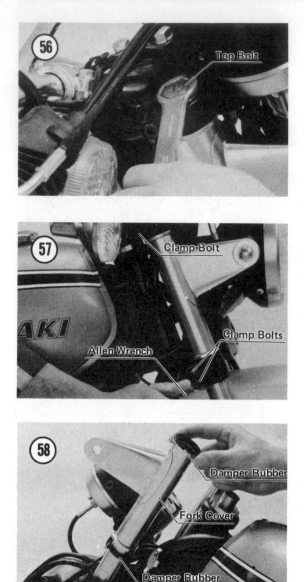

Disassembly (Later Models)

Refer to Figure 55 for this procedure.

1. Remove top bolt and remove spring (**Figure 59**).

2. Pour out oil. Pump fork if necessary to remove all oil.

3. Slide dust seal off inner tube.

4. Using special tools and Allen wrench, remove Allen bolt from bottom of outer tube (**Figure 60**) and pull inner tube from outer tube.

> NOTE: *If special tools are unavailable, take the fork tubes to your local Kawasaki dealer. He can disassemble them and replace the seals in much less time than it would take to fabricate the necessary special tools.*

3. Installation is the reverse of these steps. Keep the following points in mind:

    a. Smear a small amount of oil on inside of damper rubbers at the end of fork covers.

    b. Slide fork tube up through lower and upper clamps until upper surface of top bolt flange is even with upper edge of stem head.

    c. Torque upper and lower clamp bolts to 11-16.5 ft.-lb. (1.5-2.3 mkg).

    d. Torque top bolt to 11-14.5 ft.-lb. (1.5-2.0 mkg).

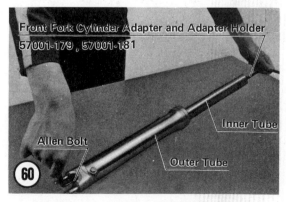

5. Slide cylinder, piston unit, and spring out of the top of the inner tube (**Figure 61**).

6. Remove circlip from outer tube and remove oil seal (**Figure 62**). It may be necessary to heat

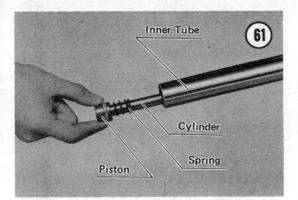

6. Fill fork tube with proper amount of oil (**Table 7**).

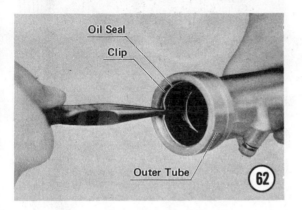

Table 7   FORK OIL QUANTITY

Model	Quantity Quart	(Milliliters)
J1, G1 Series	0.14	(135)
M Series	0.09	(90)
GA, G3 Series	0.14	(130)
G4TR, G5	0.18	(170)
F21M	0.18	(170)
KD, KE, KS125	0.16	(150)
KX125	0.13	(120)
KE175	0.16	(150)
G31M-A, F7	0.12	(115)
C1D, F2, B1 Series	0.18	(175)
C2SS (early)	0.13	(120)
C2SS (late), F6	0.18	(175)
F3	0.19	(180)
F4	0.21	(195)
F5, F8, F9, F81M	0.18	(175)
KT250	0.18	(170)
KX250	0.21	(200)
KX400, KX450	0.19	(180)

outer tube around the oil seal to facilitate seal removal.

7. Remove cylinder base from top of outer tube.

Inspection

Refer to inspection procedure for early model forks.

Assembly (Later Models)

Refer to Figure 55 for this procedure.

1. Install cylinder base into outer tube.

2. Install oil seal into outer tube using oil seal driver (**Figure 63**). Install circlip.

3. Install cylinder and piston unit with spring into inner tube. Fit bottom of cylinder into cylinder base and push inner tube fully into outer tube.

4. Apply a non-permanent locking compound (such as Loctite Lock N' Seal) to Allen bolt. Install and tighten Allen bolt.

5. Slide dust seal into place.

7. Install spring with relatively concentrated end at top and replace top bolt. Torque top bolt to 11-14.5 ft.-lb. (1.5-2.0 mkg).

Fork Oil

Change front fork oil initially at 300 miles (500 km) and every 3,000 miles (5,000 km) thereafter. Table 7 lists the proper oil quantity for each fork leg.

6

STEERING SYSTEM

Figure 64 is a sectional view of a typical steering stem. The frame head pipe and the underbracket are provided with ball bearings for smooth action.

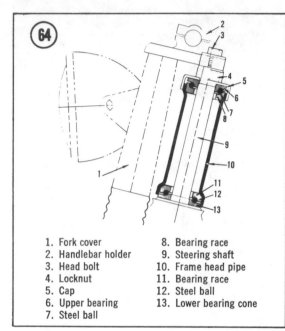

1. Fork cover
2. Handlebar holder
3. Head bolt
4. Locknut
5. Cap
6. Upper bearing
7. Steel ball
8. Bearing race
9. Steering shaft
10. Frame head pipe
11. Bearing race
12. Steel ball
13. Lower bearing cone

Disassembly

1. Remove the handlebar, tachometer, speedometer, and front fork. Refer to the applicable sections in this chapter.

2. Remove the steering stem head (**Figure 65**).

3. Remove the locknut (**Figure 66**).

4. Pull the underbracket downward to remove it from the machine. Take care that you do not drop the ball bearings during this step.

5. If it is necessary to remove the ball races, tap them out with a hammer and long punch, as shown in **Figure 67**.

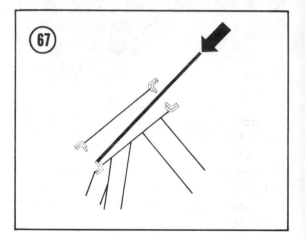

6. Remove the lower race from the steering stem with a hammer and chisel (**Figure 68**).

Inspection

Examine the underbracket shaft carefully. Replace it if the shaft is bent. Check the balls and races for cracks, wear, or other damage. Do not use a combination of new and used parts in the bearings. Replace the entire bearing assembly if any defects are found.

Assembly

1. Press in the upper and lower races.

2. Grease balls liberally, then attach them to the upper and lower races, as shown in **Figure 69**.

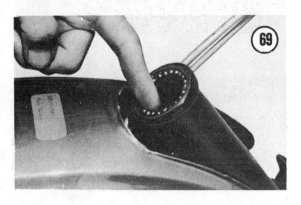

3. Insert the underbracket shaft from below, install the upper bearing race, and temporarily tighten the locknut.

4. Turn the underbracket to the left and right, and as you do so, tighten the locknut until the underbracket turns smoothly, with no looseness or binding.

5. Install the steering stem head.

6. Install the front forks.

7. Recheck the adjustment of the locknut by grasping the tips of the forks and checking for any play.

SHOCK ABSORBERS

Figure 70 is a sectional view of a typical rear shock absorber. The major parts of the shock absorber are a spring and hydraulic damping mechanism encased within the inner and outer shells. The shock absorbers may be adjusted to suit various riding conditions, as shown in **Figure 71**. Adjust both sides equally.

To remove the shock absorbers, remove the mounting bolts. Do not damage the rubber bushings as you remove and replace the bolts. See **Figure 72**.

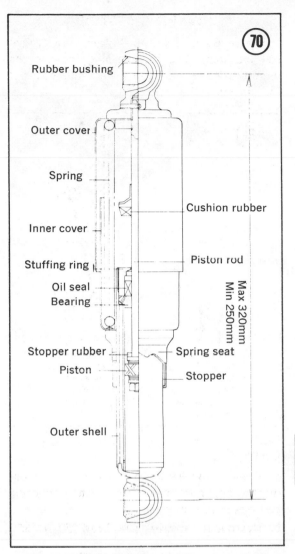

Check the damping force by attempting to compress and extend the units quickly. If there is no marked difference between the effort

required to operate the unit quickly or slowly, or if there are any oil leaks, replace the shock absorber.

FENDERS

Figure 73 illustrates typical fenders and their attaching hardware. Fenders on some models are of aluminum. Front and rear fenders may be taken off easily after the wheels are removed, merely by removing their attaching hardware (**Figures 74 and 75**).

SWINGING ARM

Figure 76 illustrates a typical swinging arm assembly. The entire assembly pivots up and down on the pivot shaft. The rear part of the swinging arm is attached to the motorcycle frame through the shock absorbers.

Disassembly

1. Remove the drive chain.
2. Remove the rear sprocket (**Figure 77**).
3. Remove the pivot shaft (**Figure 78**).
4. Remove the swinging arm (**Figure 79**).

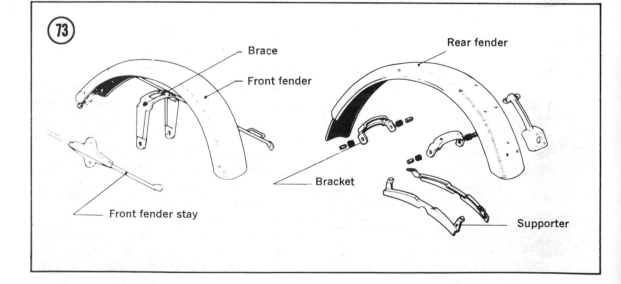

Brace

Front fender

Rear fender

Bracket

Front fender stay

Supporter

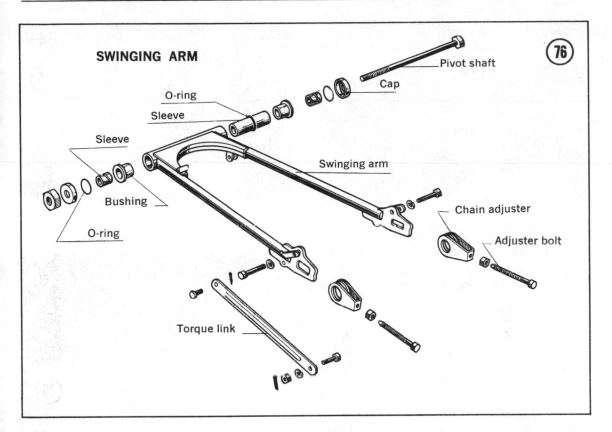

SWINGING ARM

Pivot shaft

Cap

O-ring

Sleeve

Sleeve

Bushing

O-ring

Swinging arm

Chain adjuster

Adjuster bolt

Torque link

76

77

78

79

Inspection

The pivot section is susceptible to wear, especially in the bushings and shaft. Examine these parts carefully. Replace the pivot shaft if it is bent more than 0.02 in. (0.5mm). Replace the bushings and/or the shaft if the clearance between the shaft and the bushings exceeds 0.014 in. (0.35mm). Shimmy wander, and wheel hop are common symptoms of worn swinging arm bushings. If either of the arms is bent, the rear wheel will be out of alignment. Examine the weld carefully. Replace the entire swinging arm assembly if the weld is cracked.

6

REAR SPROCKET

To remove the rear sprocket, use a hammer and chisel (**Figure 80**) to remove the lockwashers, then remove the nuts which attach the sprocket to the sprocket coupling.

Any bending of the sprocket will make drive chain adjustment difficult, and may result in chain breakage. To check for bending, place the sprocket on a flat surface, then check the gap between the surface and the sprocket. Replace the sprocket if the gap exceeds 0.02 in. (0.5mm) at any point.

The drive chain may slip from the sprocket if the sprocket is worn. Measure the diameter (**Figure 81**) of the sprocket at the base of the teeth. Replace any sprocket worn beyond the replacement limit. See **Table 8**.

FUEL AND OIL TANK

Figure 82 illustrates a typical fuel tank. The tank is made from corrosion resistant steel. A fuel cock is attached to the lower portion of the tank so that the fuel may be shut off when the machine is not running. Some models are equipped with an automatic fuel cock.

Table 8   SPROCKET WEAR

Model	Wear Limit Inches	(Millimeters)
J1, M Series	5.51	(140)
G1, GA1, GA1-A	5.31	(135)
GA2, GA2-A, G3TR	5.31	(135)
G3SS-A	5.47	(139)
G31M-A, G3TR-A, G4, G5	6.26	(159)
KE100	6.26	(159)
B1L, B1L-A, F2	6.26	(159)
KS125	7.56	(192)
F7	7.56	(192)
F6	8.35	(212)
F8, F81M	8.46	(215)
KE175	7.24	(184)
KT250	7.87	(200)
F5, F9	7.68	(195)

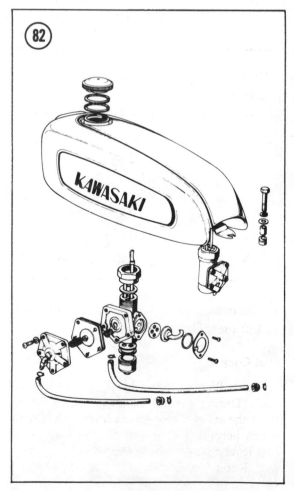

Fuel Tank Removal

WARNING

These operations, or any other operations which may result in spilled gasoline, are potentially hazardous. Do not smoke or permit any sparks or open flame within 50 feet of work area.

1. Turn the fuel cock to "O" (STOP). On models F5 and F7, turn the cock to ON or RES.
2. Remove the nut from the front of the tank (**Figure 83**).

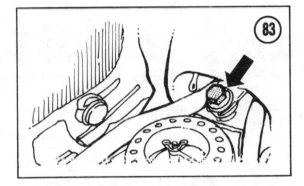

3. Remove the strap from the rear of the tank (**Figure 84**).

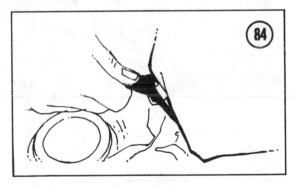

4. Disconnect the fuel line from the fuel cock.
5. Lift the tank from the machine.

Fuel Cock

Figure 85 is a sectional view of a typical fuel cock. During normal running, fuel is drawn from the main standpipe within the fuel tank, which permits fuel to flow only as long as the fuel level remains above the top of the standpipe. Reserve fuel is supplied from the auxiliary standpipe.

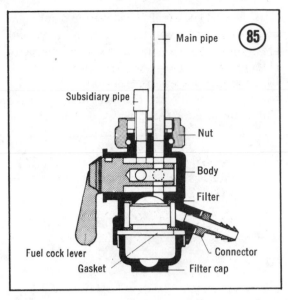

Inspect the fuel cock for leakage. Remove and clean the sediment bowl occasionally. Clean the fuel cock by blowing compressed air through it.

Automatic Fuel Cock

Models F5 and F7 are equipped with an automatic fuel cock (**Figure 86**). Negative pressure developed in the carburetor when the engine is running is transmitted through a tube to a diaphragm-actuated valve within the assembly.

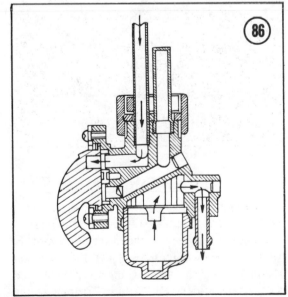

If the fuel cock leaks, remove the diaphragm cover and diaphragm, then clean the valve and seat. Be sure to assemble the valve correctly (**Figure 87**), with the vent holes aligned. Also, be sure that there are no leaks in the signal tube from the carburetor to the fuel cock. Air leaks will result in poor fuel flow.

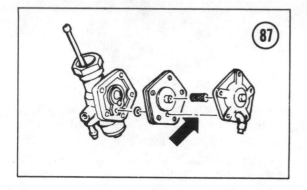

Oil Tank

The oil tank (**Figure 88**) is below the seat, on the right side of the machine. Service to the oil tank is limited to occasional cleaning. Remember to bleed oil pump after you clean the tank.

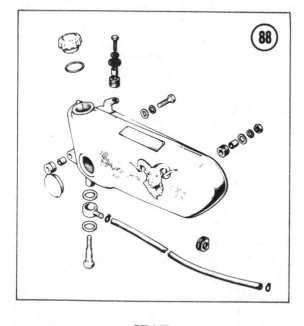

SEAT

Figure 89 illustrates a typical seat and its attaching hardware. On model B1L-A, the seat is attached with bolts; other models are attached with pivot holders and hooks. To remove the

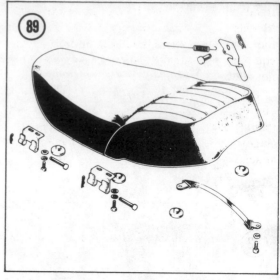

seat, remove the attaching hardware, as shown in **Figures 90 and 91**.

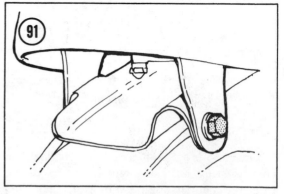

STANDS AND FOOTRESTS

These machines are equipped with various types of stands. Some models have both a center stand and a side, or kickstand (**Figure 92**). Models G4TR, F5, F6, F7, and F8 have only the side stand. Models G31M and F81M are equipped with only a portable stand which is not attached to the frame.

To remove the center stand (**Figure 93**), pull out the cotter pin, pull out the shaft, then remove the spring. To remove the side stand (**Figure 94**), remove the spring, then the attaching bolt.

EXHAUST PIPE AND MUFFLER

Disassembly

On models G31M-A, G4TR, and F series, remove the mounting bolts at the rear of the muffler (**Figure 95**), then remove the hook springs (**Figure 96**) which attach the exhaust pipe to the cylinder flange.

Muffler and exhaust pipe removal is accomplished on models GA-1-A, GA2-A, G3SS-A, and G3TR-A by first removing the cylinder

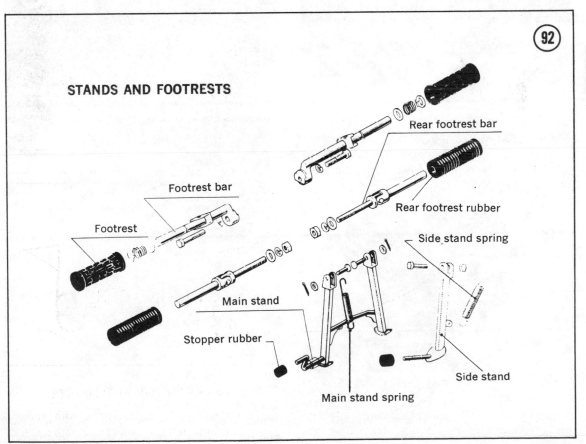

STANDS AND FOOTRESTS

Footrest bar

Footrest

Rear footrest bar

Rear footrest rubber

Side stand spring

Main stand

Stopper rubber

Main stand spring

Side stand

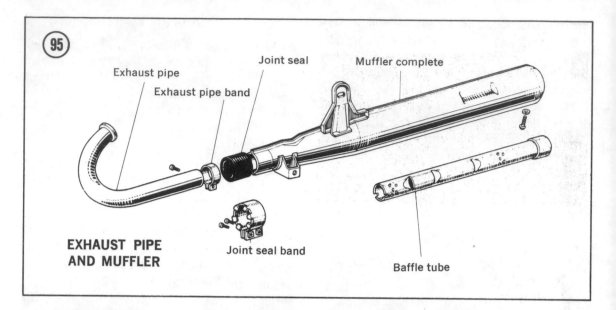

Joint seal

Muffler complete

Exhaust pipe

Exhaust pipe band

EXHAUST PIPE AND MUFFLER

Joint seal band

Baffle tube

flange (**Figure 97**) and the clamp where the exhaust pipe enters the muffler. Remove the exhaust pipe. The muffler may then be removed by removing the front and rear attaching bolts (**Figure 98**).

To remove the baffle tube, remove the screw at the back of the muffler (**Figure 99**), then pull out the baffle tube (**Figure 100**).

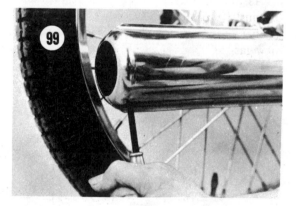

Inspection

Carbon deposits within the exhaust pipe and muffler cause the engine to lose power. Clean carbon from the baffle tube with a wire brush. If the deposits are too heavy to remove with a brush, heat baffle tube with a torch (**Figure 101**) and tap the tube lightly. Clean the carbon from

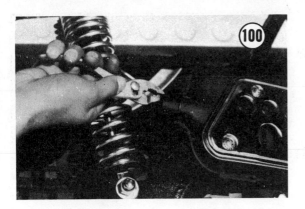

the exhaust pipe by running a used drive chain through the pipe.

As the machine ages, the joint between the exhaust pipe and muffler may leak. Replace the rubber connector if leakage occurs. Always use new gaskets upon reassembly.

DRIVE CHAIN

The drive chain (**Figure 102**) becomes worn after prolonged use. Wear in the pins, bushings, and rollers causes the chain to stretch. Sliding between the roller surface and sprocket teeth also contributes to wear.

Inspection

Inspect the drive chain periodically. Pay particular attention to cracks in the rollers and link plates, and replace the chain if there is any doubt about its condition.

Adjust the free play in the chain so that there is one inch (25mm) vertical play (**Figure 103**) in the center of the chain run with the machine on the ground. **Figure 104** illustrates the adjustment procedure. Be sure to adjust each side equally. The rear brake is affected by any chain adjustment. Be sure to adjust the rear brake after you adjust the chain (**Figure 105**).

6

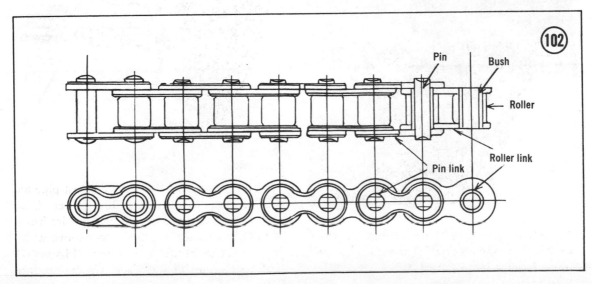

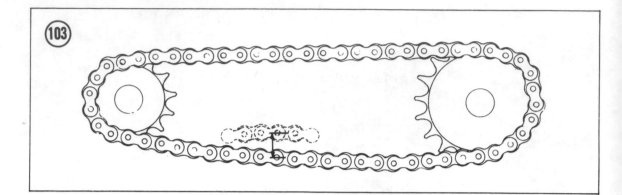

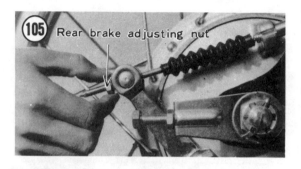

If the chain has become so worn that adjustment is not possible, use a chain breaker (**Figure 106**) or chisel (**Figure 107**) to shorten the chain by one link.

Install the master link so that the clip opening faces opposite to the direction of chain movement (**Figure 108**). Failure to do so may result in loss of the clip and resultant chain breakage.

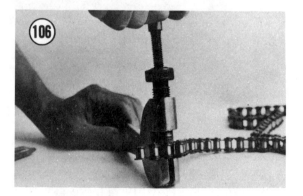

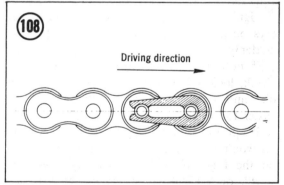

Driving direction

CHAPTER SEVEN

TROUBLESHOOTING

Diagnosing motorcycle ills is relatively simple if you use orderly procedures and keep a few basic principles in mind.

Never assume anything. Don't overlook the obvious. If you are riding along and the bike suddenly quits, check the easiest, most accessible problem spots first. Is there gasoline in the tank? Is the gas petcock in the ON or RESERVE position? Has the spark plug wire fallen off? Check the ignition switch. Sometimes the weight of keys on a key ring may turn the ignition off suddenly.

If nothing obvious turns up in a cursory check, look a little further. Learning to recognize and describe symptoms will make repairs easier for you or a mechanic at the shop. Describe problems accurately and fully. Saying that "it won't run" isn't the same as saying "it quit on the highway at high speed and wouldn't start", or that "it sat in my garage for three months and then wouldn't start".

Gather as many symptoms together as possible to aid in diagnosis. Note whether the engine lost power gradually or all at once, what color smoke (if any) came from the exhaust, and so on. Remember that the more complicated a machine is, the easier it is to troubleshoot because symptoms point to specific problems.

You don't need fancy equipment or complicated test gear to determine whether repairs can be attempted at home. A few simple checks could save a large repair bill and time lost while the bike sits in a dealer's service department. On the other hand, be realistic and don't attempt repairs beyond your abilities. Service departments tend to charge heavily for putting together a disassembled engine that may have been abused. Some won't even take on such a job—so use common sense; don't get in over your head.

OPERATING REQUIREMENTS

An engine needs 3 basics to run properly: correct gas/air mixture, compression, and a spark at the right time. If one or more are missing, the engine won't run. The electrical system is the weakest link of the three. More problems result from electrical breakdowns than from any other source. Keep that in mind before you begin tampering with carburetor adjustments and the like.

If a bike has been sitting for any length of time and refuses to start, check the battery (if the machine is so equipped) for a charged condition first, and then look to the gasoline delivery system. This includes the tank, fuel petcocks, lines, and the carburetor. Rust may have formed in the tank, obstructing fuel flow. Gasoline deposits may have gummed up carburetor jets and air passages. Gasoline tends to lose its potency after standing for long periods. Condensation may contaminate it with water. Drain old gas and try starting with a fresh tankful.

Compression, or the lack of it, usually enters the picture only in the case of older machines. Worn or broken pistons, rings, and cylinder bores could prevent starting. Generally a gradual power loss and harder and harder starting will be readily apparent in this case.

STARTING DIFFICULTIES

Check gas flow first. Remove the gas cap and look into the tank. If gas is present, pull off a fuel line at the carburetor and see if gas flows freely. If none comes out, the fuel tap may be shut off, blocked by rust or foreign matter, or the fuel line may be stopped up or kinked. If the carburetor is getting usable fuel, turn to the electrical system next.

Check that the battery is charged by turning on the lights or by beeping the horn. Refer to your owner's manual for starting procedures with a dead battery. Have the battery recharged if necessary.

Pull off the spark plug cap, remove the spark plug, and reconnect the cap. Lay the plug against the cylinder head so its base makes a good connection, and turn the engine over with the kick-starter. A fat, blue spark should jump across the electrodes. If there is no spark, or a weak one, there is electrical system trouble. Check for a defective plug by replacing it with a known good one. Don't assume a plug is good just because it's new.

Once the plug has been cleared of guilt, but there's still no spark, start backtracking through the system. If the contact at the end of the spark plug wire can be exposed, it can be held about ⅛ inch from the head while the engine is turned over to check for a spark. Remember to hold the wire only by its insulation to avoid a nasty shock. If the plug wires are dirty, greasy, or wet, wrap a rag around them so you don't get shocked. If you do feel a shock or see sparks along the wire, clean or replace the wire and/or its connections.

If there's no spark at the plug wire, look for loose connections at the coil and battery. If all

seems in order here, check next for oily or dirty contact points. Clean points with electrical contact cleaner, or a strip of paper. On battery ignition models, with the ignition switch turned on, open and close the points manually with a screwdriver.

No spark at the points with this test indicates a failure in the ignition system. Refer to Chapter Four (*Electrical System*) for checkout procedures for the entire system and individual components. Refer to Chapter Two for checking and setting ignition timing.

Note that spark plugs of the incorrect heat range (too cold) may cause hard starting. Set gap to specifications. If you have just ridden through a puddle or washed the bike and it won't start, dry off the plug and plug wire. Water may have entered the carburetor and fouled the fuel under these conditions, but a wet plug and wire are the more likely problem.

If a healthy spark occurs at the right time, and there is adequate gas flow to the carburetor, check the carburetor itself at this time. Make sure all jets and air passages are clean, check float level, and adjust if necessary. Shake the float to check for gasoline inside it, and replace or repair as indicated. Check that the carburetor is mounted snugly, and no air is leaking past the mounting flange. Check for a clogged air filter.

Compression may be checked in the field by turning the kickstarter by hand and noting that an adequate resistance is felt, or by removing the spark plug and placing a finger over the plug hole and feeling for pressure.

An accurate compression check gives a good idea of the condition of the basic working parts of the engine. To perform this test, you need a compression gauge. The motor should be warm.

1. Remove the plug from the cylinder to be tested and clean out any dirt or grease.

2. Insert the tip of the gauge into the hole, making sure it is seated correctly.

3. Open the throttle all the way.

4. Crank the engine several times and record the highest pressure reading on the gauge. Refer to Chapter Two (*Periodic Maintenance*) to interpret results.

POOR IDLING

Poor idling may be caused by incorrect carburetor adjustment, incorrect timing, or ignition system defects. Check the gas cap vent for an obstruction. Also check for loose carburetor mounting bolts or a poor carburetor flange gasket.

MISFIRING

Misfiring can be caused by a weak spark or dirty plugs. Check for fuel contamination. Run the machine at night or in a darkened garage to check for spark leaks along the plug wires and under the spark plug cap. If misfiring occurs only at certain throttle settings, refer to the carburetor chapter for the specific carburetor circuits involved. Misfiring under heavy load, as when climbing hills or accelerating, is usually caused by bad spark plugs.

FLAT SPOTS

If the engine seems to die momentarily when the throttle is opened and then recovers, check for a dirty main jet in the carburetor, water in the fuel, or an excessively lean mixture.

POWER LOSS

Poor condition of rings, pistons, or cylinders will cause a lack of power and speed. Ignition timing should be checked.

OVERHEATING

If the engine seems to run too hot all the time, be sure you are not idling it for long periods. Air-cooled engines are not designed to operate at a standstill for any length of time. Heavy stop and go traffic is hard on a motorcycle engine. Spark plugs of the wrong heat range can burn pistons. An excessively lean gas mixture may cause overheating. Check ignition timing. Don't ride in too high a gear. Broken or worn rings may permit compression gases to leak past them, heating heads and cylinders excessively. Check oil level and use the proper grade lubricants.

BACKFIRING

Check that the timing is not advanced too far. Check fuel for contamination.

ENGINE NOISES

Experience is needed to diagnose accurately in this area. Noises are hard to differentiate and harder yet to describe. Deep knocking noises usually mean main bearing failure. A slapping noise generally comes from loose pistons. A light knocking noise during acceleration may be a bad connecting rod bearing. Pinging, which sounds like marbles being shaken in a tin can, is caused by ignition advanced too far or gasoline with too low an octane rating. Pinging should be corrected immediately or damage to pistons will result. Compression leaks at the head/cylinder joint will sound like a rapid on and off squeal.

PISTON SEIZURE

Piston seizure is caused by incorrect piston clearances when fitted, fitting rings with improper end gap, too thin an oil being used, incorrect spark plug heat range, or incorrect ignition timing. Overheating from any cause may result in seizure.

EXCESSIVE VIBRATION

Excessive vibration may be caused by loose motor mounts, worn engine or transmission bearings, loose wheels, worn swinging arm bushings, a generally poor running engine, broken or cracked frame, or one that has been damaged in a collision. See also *Poor Handling*.

CLUTCH SLIP OR DRAG

Clutch slip may be due to worn plates, improper adjustment, or glazed plates. A dragging clutch could result from damaged or bent plates, improper adjustment, or even clutch spring pressure.

POOR HANDLING

Poor handling may be caused by improper tire pressures, a damaged frame or swinging arm, worn shocks or front forks, weak fork springs, a bent or broken steering stem, misaligned wheels, loose or missing spokes, worn tires, bent handlebars, worn wheel bearings, or dragging brakes.

7

BRAKE PROBLEMS

Sticking brakes may be caused by broken or weak return springs, improper cable or rod adjustment, or dry pivot and cam bushings. Grabbing brakes may be caused by greasy linings which must be replaced. Brake grab may also be due to out-of-round drums or linings which have broken loose from the brake shoes. Glazed linings will cause loss of stopping power.

LIGHTING PROBLEMS

Bulbs which continuously burn out may be caused by excessive vibration, loose connections that permit sudden current surges, poor battery connections, or installation of the wrong type bulb.

A dead battery or one which discharges quickly may be caused by a faulty generator or rectifier. Check for loose or corroded terminals. Shorted battery cells or broken terminals will keep a battery from charging. Low water level will decrease a battery's capacity. A battery left uncharged after installation will sulphate, rendering it useless.

A majority of light and horn or other electrical accessory problems are caused by loose or corroded ground connections. Check those first, and then substitute known good units for easier troubleshooting.

TROUBLESHOOTING GUIDE

The following quick reference guide (**Table 1**) summarizes part of the troubleshooting process. Use this table to outline possible problem areas, then refer to the specific chapter or section involved.

Table 1   TROUBLESHOOTING GUIDE

Item	Problem or Cause	Things to Check
Loss of power	Poor compression	Piston rings and cylinder Head gaskets Crankcase leaks
	Overheated engine	Lubricating oil supply Clogged cooling fins Ignition timing Slipping clutch Carbon in combustion chamber
	Improper mixture	Dirty air cleaner Restricted fuel flow Gas cap vent hole
	Miscellaneous	Dragging brakes Tight wheel bearings Defective chain Clogged exhaust system
Steering	Hard steering	Tire pressures Steering damper adjustment Steering stem head Steering head bearings

(continued)

Table 1   **TROUBLESHOOTING GUIDE**   (continued)

Item	Problem or Cause	Things to Check
Steering (continued)	Pulls to one side	Unbalanced shock absorbers Drive chain adjustment Front/rear wheel alignment Unbalanced tires Defective swing arm Defective steering head
	Shimmy	Drive chain adjustment Loose or missing spokes Deformed rims Worn wheel bearings Wheel balance
Gearshifting difficulties	Clutch	Adjustment Springs Friction plates Steel plates Oil quantity
	Transmission	Oil quantity Oil grade Return spring or pin Change lever or spring Drum position plate Change drum Change forks
Brakes	Poor brakes	Worn linings Brake adjustment Oil or water on brake linings Loose linkage or cables
	Noisy brakes	Worn or scratched lining Scratched brake drums Dirt in brakes
	Unadjustable brakes	Worn linings Worn drums Worn brake cams

7

CHAPTER EIGHT

PERFORMANCE IMPROVEMENT

Kawasaki has produced many excellent dual-purpose and off-road motorcycles to suit every need and taste. There are literally dozens of different models in the 80-450cc category. For this reason, we have limited the bikes specifically mentioned in this chapter to those which are best suited, and respond well, to performance improvement. Step-through models and strictly commuter bikes have been omitted but you will still find that much of the general information applies. Even specifics on engine modification will apply to some models which have the same engine as a more popular model. The specifications in the Appendix will help you to decide which bike is closest to yours in construction. For example, the MC1-M engine (mentioned in this chapter) is nearly identical in most major design areas as the GA-1. The tip-off is that the bore, stroke, displacement, and horsepower are the same. It would not hurt to double check your assumption but this will at least help you get started in the right direction.

Wherever possible we have tried to include procedures using components from other Kawasaki models. This will allow you to purchase parts from a dealer or wrecking yard. Often as not, you will find such factory parts available through classified ads.

For example, someone with an H-1 may want to sell the stock 28mm Mikuni carbs and buy a set of H-2 Mikunis. You will probably be able to pick one of these up for your F-7 at a fraction of the cost of a new one. Likewise, you can sell your old carb to defray the cost!

Performance modification is usually thought of as more horsepower and consequently this is the area that receives the most attention. However, increased engine output is just one factor in total performance improvement and can be detrimental if the motorcycle already has serious shortcomings in handling and braking.

Performance improvement, as discussed here, refers to total performance including engine, drive train, suspension, brakes, weight reduction, and reliability.

The recommended approach begins with chassis modification; most of the bikes covered produce more power in stock trim than can be used with the standard suspension anyway. So rather than begin with modification for more power, it is best to improve the handling and braking so that power which is already available can be used more efficiently.

Faster does not necessarily mean quicker. Excessive horsepower which will cause the motorcycle to accelerate rapidly will do little in helping the same motorcycle negotiate rough sections or sharp turns if the suspension is inadequate. Conversely, chassis improvement can help the motorcycle negotiate a course quicker without any power increase. In addition, chassis modification usually costs less than engine work. If for no other reason than economy, the chassis-first approach makes good sense.

The modifications described in this chapter are not intended for the professional racer who would be better off to purchase the latest "trick" racer. These modifications are intended for the off-road rider who wants better performance without spending a fortune on parts. **Table 1** (found at the end of the chapter) lists major manufacturers and suppliers of Kawasaki hop-up equipment. **Table 2** lists specifications for modifying the more popular engines.

WHAT DO YOU WANT?

Before beginning work on the motorcycle, consider first what you want as an end product by answering these few questions:

1. What will be the motorcycle's use?
   a. Motocross
   b. Enduro
   c. Trail riding
   d. Play
2. What is your riding ability?
3. How much do you wish to spend—time and money?
4. How much of the required work can you perform?

Consider these questions seriously and answer them honestly; no one is looking over your shoulder so there is no shame involved in admitting that you are only a moderately experienced rider on a budget. If you fail to carefully and accurately assess what you want from the motorcycle there is little chance that the bike will suit your needs.

Before modifying the engine, decide if you want more low end torque or more peak horsepower. It is often impossible to obtain both. Increased torque will be more desirable for trail-riding, while increased horsepower will be needed for competition. Beyond initial stages of modification the engine may become too inflexible and will idle poorly or bog at low speeds. It is rarely practical to go "all out" on performance modifications in one large step.

Perform one or two simple changes, evaluate them fully, then go on to a few more changes.

One of the first procedures you should consider may add up to 10% horsepower to a stock engine, improve gas mileage, make the engine run smoother, and quieter, and will cost less than $5.00! It is a simple tune-up. The steps involved in a thorough tune-up are described in Chapter Two. Once the engine is running properly in stock form, it will be easier to evaluate other changes to improve power. The items discussed in this chapter will produce a satisfying, strong street machine but not an all-out, unreliable racer.

The term "bolt-on" can be misleading. It can mean something you can add in 10 minutes with ordinary hand tools. In this manual, it is any component which can be added by anyone who can do similar work on a stock engine. Very little, if any, machine work is necessary. Bolt-on equipment designs and materials change frequently. We cannot control how the equipment will be installed nor how the bike will be used. Good judgment and common sense will help you avoid disappointment.

CAUTION
Clymer Publications cannot guarantee or be responsible for performance, damage to the motorcycle, or personal injury resulting from the performance modification procedures given in this manual. In addition, any modification you make may void all warranties regardless of the motorcycle's age or mileage.

Finally, be wary of performance improvement claims by aftermarket equipment manufacturers. For the most part, they are honest and sincere and their products are generally what they claim to be. But be sure to assess what they are offering in terms of your own needs, ability, and budget.

RESTORATION

In its strictest sense, restoration means to rebuild something back to its original "as-new" condition. This may be necessary for an antique or classic motorcycle to retain its collector value but is a waste of time and energy for the

Table 2   ENGINE PERFORMANCE SPECIFICATIONS

Model	MC-1 (90cc)		F-6 (124cc)		F-7 (174cc)	
Degree of Modification	Mild	Wild	Mild	Wild	Mild	Wild
Raise exhaust port by	0.080 in. (2.0mm)	0.100 in. (2.5mm)	0.040 in. (1.0mm)	0.080 in. (2.0mm)	0.060 in. (1.5mm)	0.080 in. (2.0mm)
Raise transfer port by	——	——	——	——	——	——
Lower bottom of intake port by	——	——	——	——	——	——
Cut rotary valve to open at	135° BTDC	140° BTDC	130° BTDC	140° BTDC	130° BTDC	140° BTDC
Cut rotary valve to close at	65° ATDC	70° ATDC	65° ATDC	70° ATDC	65° ATDC	70° ATDC
Ignition modification	——	——	——	Install G31M magneto	——	——
Set ignition timing to read	Stock	Stock	3.0mm BTDC	2.5mm BTDC	Stock	Stock
Cut off top of piston by (refer to text)	0.050 in. (1.3mm)	0.080 in. (2.0mm)	——	——	0.080 in. (2.0mm)	0.080 in. (2.0mm)
Cut off intake skirt of piston	——	——	——	——	——	——
Cut off top of cylinder**	——	——	——	——	0.080 in. (2.0mm)	0.080 in. (2.0mm)
Main jet size change	+ 1 jet size	+ 2 jet sizes	+ 2 jet sizes	+ 2 jet sizes	+ 2 jet sizes	+ 2 jet sizes
Carburetion change	——	——	——	Install F-7 carburetor and ream venturi 0.025 in. (0.6mm)	Ream venturi by 0.060 in. (1.5mm)	Use H-1 22mm Mikuni*
Miscellaneous	Cut 0.10 in. (2.5mm) off cylinder head and recut squish area**	Cut 0.10 in. (2.5mm) off cylinder head and recut squish area**	——	By 0.060 in. (1.5mm)	——	——
Adjust compression to read	——	——	——	——	——	——

(continued)

Table 2   ENGINE PERFORMANCE SPECIFICATIONS (continued)

Model	F-11 (247cc)		F-5/F-9 (346cc)	
Degree of Modification	Mild	Wild	Mild	Wild
Raise exhaust port by	0.020 in. (0.5mm)	0.020 in. (0.5mm)	0.080 in. (2.0mm)	0.120 in. (3.0mm)
Raise transfer port by	——	0.020 in. (0.5mm)	——	——
Lower bottom of intake port by	——	0.120 in. (3.0mm)	——	——
Cut rotary valve to open at	——	——	135° BTDC	140° BTDC
Cut rotary valve to close at	——	——	65° ATDC	70° ATDC
Ignition modification	——	Install F81M magneto	——	——
Set ignition timing to read	2.6mm BTDC	3.0mm BTDC	Stock	Stock
Cut off top of piston by (refer to text)	0.080 in. (2.0mm)	0.020 in. (2.0mm)	——	——
Cut off intake skirt of piston	0.150 in. (3.8mm)	0.080 in. (2.0mm)	——	——
Cut off top of cylinder**	0.100 in. (2.5mm)	0.100 in. (2.5mm)	——	——
Main jet size change	+ 2 jet sizes	+ 2 jet sizes	+ 2 jet sizes	+ 2 jet sizes
Carburetion change	Ream carburetor by 0.025 in. (0.6mm)	Install 34mm Mikuni	——	Install 35mm Mikuni
Miscellaneous	——	——	——	——
Adjust compression to read	165 psi	160 psi	——	——

* Some slight modification will be required to adapt.
** Refer such work to a competent machine shop.

8

average rider. As discussed in this chapter, restoration means to renew the motorcycle's appearance and to update its total performance to newer standards. This type of restoration is practical because it will produce a motorcycle which is nearly as good as, or better than, new at a fraction of the cost for a new bike. It also allows the owner to individualize the bike to suit his own riding habits and appearance requirements. Modifying a brand new bike in a like manner could become prohibitively expensive.

Original Paint Restoration

If the original paint is in reasonably good condition, it can be restored by "compounding" and waxing.

Start by obtaining a touch-up bottle of paint from your dealer to match the original paint. If the dealer cannot obtain the proper match, you can get aftermarket brands such as Krylon or Dupli-Color from any automotive supply store. Use the brush included with the paint and dab it on any nicks or small scratches. Larger areas should be sanded smooth and touched up with spray paint also available from the same sources as the bottle-type.

After the paint has had time to dry, rub out the entire painted areas with 3-M or Dupont rubbing compound and a dampened piece of terry cloth. Follow the directions on the can for best results.

Follow the compounding by dry buffing the painted areas with a piece of clean terry cloth. Finish off with a good brand (DuPont, Turtle-Wax, etc.) of paste wax which also contains a cleaner.

To achieve a better-than-new finish, you can also apply a coat of Armor-All or silicone glaze from Meguiars. Again, follow the manufacturer's directions to achieve the best results.

Repainting

Paint which is badly scratched or deteriorated will not be salvageable and you should start from scratch. It is possible to obtain an excellent paint job with aerosol spray cans even if you have never attempted this type of work before.

Even if you do not wish to paint the bike yourself, you can save a lot of money by removing all the parts to be painted and preparing them properly for paint. Now would be a good time for a custom paint job, so consider it while you have the chance.

Remove all pieces from the bike that will be painted one color. Various parts of this manual will tell you how. Usually this will include the gas tank, fenders, headlight housing, and side covers. You may also want to install a custom gas tank and racing seat so get them done now and have everything painted at once to save money and assure a paint match.

The original paint will probably make a good primer coat for the new paint if it is properly cleaned and sanded first. Most automotive stores carry a liquid called a "paint pre-cleaner" just for this purpose. This will remove any wax and imbedded silicones from the paint. This is essential or the new paint will develop "chicken feet" crazing marks and craters.

After the pre-cleaner, clean the entire painted parts with a solution of warm water and scouring cleanser. Be sure to rinse the paint well with clean water to remove any soapy residue. While the paint is still wet, sand the entire surface with No. 600 grit wet-and-dry sandpaper to achieve an obviously rough surface. This will give the new paint a surface with a "tooth" to hang onto. Otherwise, the old paint may be too smooth and shed the new paint. Set everything aside to dry for at least 8 hours.

After 8 hours, apply masking tape to everything which does not get painted. This includes any chrome trim which cannot be removed. On most of the models, you can remove everything including fuel petcock, trim, badges, etc., and paint the parts or take them to a paint shop.

If you paint the parts yourself, be sure to use a good quality brand such as Krylon or Dupli-Color Touch-up. Cheap paints will only cause trouble. Try to use only solid primary colors like red, blue, yellow, silver, or black. Candy colors and metalflakes are tricky and should be left to the professionals. Follow the instructions on the cans for best results and paint only on warm, dry days. Never paint on a rainy or foggy day.

If the paint comes out less than perfect, do not worry. Paint which has "orange peel" (rough and wavy) can be compounded as described under *Original Paint Restoration*. Runs can be removed by lightly sanding with No. 400 wet-and-dry sandpaper followed by compounding and waxing. Since the areas being painted are so small and separated from other painted areas, discoloration or mistakes will not appear as badly. Do not attempt any of these cures until the paint has had several days to cure.

Upholstery

There are several companies who make slipcovers that simply tie onto the bike in less than a minute. These are excellent to hide tears, rips, or discoloration and they give the bike a custom look as well. They also have the advantage of costing far less than a professional reupholstery job.

If the seat is badly damaged, consider installing a custom competition style seat or one which has additional padding for comfort. It may surprise you that a good custom seat will cost only slightly more than a restored stock seat.

Chromed Parts

One of the first areas to deteriorate on any motorcycle is the chrome. You could buy all new parts to replace the old ones but these would deteriorate quickly too and the cost would be prohibitive. Instead, remove all the plated parts and take them to a metal finisher for re-plating. There are several different grades of chrome plate so ask questions instead of just requesting chrome plating. The best type is triple-plating preceded by buffing. You may prefer to have the parts nickel-plated to resist corrosion and pitting in areas near large bodies of water.

The plater will generally give you a cost break on several parts done at the same time. If so, have any parts you want customized done at this time and save time and money later.

Chrome which has not completely corroded, or stainless steel parts, can be salvaged by cleaning with very fine steel wool and chrome cleaner. Be sure to apply wax and WD-40 or Armor-All after this treatment to retard further corrosion.

Rubber or Vinyl Parts

Any rubber parts which have ozone or age cracks should be replaced. Dealers will have most parts available or can order them, and these items are generally pretty inexpensive. However, if the parts appear serviceable, clean them with very fine steel wool and scouring powder. Apply a thin coat of Armor-All or silicone to preserve the rubber and renew its appearance. Tires can be made to look brand new this way.

Performance

The other chapters of this manual will tell how to restore the bike to its original condition mechanically. If you have problems in certain areas, this chapter will tell how to improve the bike to a contemporary level or better.

WEIGHT REDUCTION

The weight of a motorcycle is divided between sprung weight and unsprung weight. Sprung weight is the weight of most of the motorcycle and excludes the wheels and the lower working half of the suspension which is the unsprung weight (**Figure 1**).

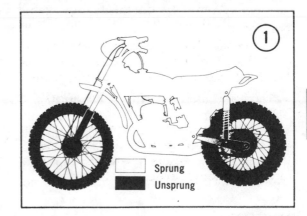

While total weight reduction will improve total performance, reduction of unsprung weight produces the greatest improvement in handling performance. A light wheel (low unsprung weight) reacts more quickly to bumps than a heavy wheel (high unsprung weight) and transmits less shock to the rest of the motorcycle. Therefore, it has less effect in altering the primary (forward) direction of the machine and contributes less to rider fatigue.

Every component of the motorcycle should be considered when trying to lower overall weight. Unfortunately, some of the lightest items can be very expensive. Most of the major items covered in this chapter are inexpensive and can be readily bought new or used. Wherever possible, use stock parts from another motorcycle to keep the cost down and to make it easier to purchase necessary items.

Rather than itemize every possible component in this section, methods for weight reduction have been included with other modification procedures. Small items are listed in each section.

Handlebars and Controls

Weight at the top of the motorcycle is more important than any other, except unsprung weight, because it has to be thrown around by the rider. In addition, a motorcycle which is light on top will be more assuring to lean over in turns. Aluminum handlebars can save as much as 1 lb. (0.5 kg) depending on the model, but are considerably more expensive than steel. Be sure to specify tube diameter when ordering.

Use Magura or K & N polycarbonate control levers and a "quick turn" twist grip for the throttle.

Gas Tank

There are basically 2 types of construction— aluminum and fiberglass. The choice of tanks should in part be determined by how low the fuel is carried since the center of gravity will be lowered. The difference will be noticed when cornering because a low-slung tank does not have that top-heavy feeling. See **Figure 2**.

Seat

Many aftermarket companies produce excellent seats in a wide array of designs. Be sure to get one which allows for plenty of movement. Ease of movement will lessen fatigue and allow

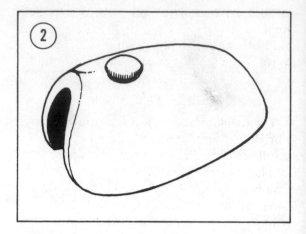

for body English to control the bike. See **Figure 3**.

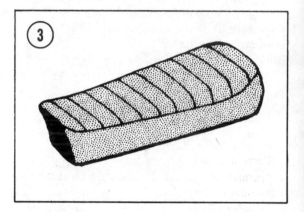

Fenders

Replace the front fender with one made of plastic. A plastic fender is strong, light, and resistant to bumps or damage. See **Figure 4**.

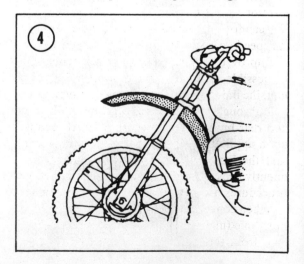

The rear fender on most models is heavy. Replace it with a plastic or fiberglass fender, but make sure the replacement is strong enough to support a taillight and license plate.

LIGHTING

The standard headlight can be replaced with a brighter quartz-iodine unit. Marchal makes an excellent unit called the Amplilux, which bolts in place without modifications. This type of light is unsurpassed for safety because it illuminates the road so much better than stock and permits greater top speeds at night without overdriving the visibility range.

CAUTION
Make sure that the light is correctly adjusted or it will blind oncoming drivers creating an unsafe condition for both of you.

This type of light may be illegal in some states because of the high-intensity. If so, you can still improve visibility with a GE Plus-25 replacement light. This unit is made for cars but there are sizes which will readily adapt.

Turn signals can be removed to improve the appearance of the bike and save 2.5 lb. (1.14 kg) but it may be illegal in some states and the lights are a safety feature at night.

WHEELS, BRAKES, AND HUBS

Efficient braking is the most critical aspect of a motorcycle regardless of its intended purpose or use. It matters little how fast it will go if it cannot be stopped in a reasonable distance. As speed goes up, braking effort should follow.

Improved braking using the stock drum units is possible with the simple substitution of a metallic lining such as the Lakewood-type available through most dealers. Machine both front and rear brake drums to ensure 100% contact upon application of the brakes. It is important that the brakes be inspected and cleaned frequently because of dirt, water, and mud. Service procedures are described in the brake chapter.

When converting from an organic lining to an inorganic (metallic) lining all traces of the lubricant from the organic lining must be removed from the brake drum. This lubricant, essential to organic linings, is incompatible with inorganic linings and will render it unserviceable if it is not removed.

If the drum is round and requires no truing, the lubricant can be removed with fine sandpaper and detergent. However, the new linings must be arced to the contour of the drum.

If the drum requires truing, the lubricant will be removed as the metal is removed. If possible, the drum should be trued while laced to the rim. The spoke tension should be checked and corrected beforehand to ensure that the drum will remain true and round when it is installed on the motorcycle. Also, the drum should be turned using the bearings that will be used when it is installed.

When the brake and wheel are installed, the brake backing plate should be centralized in the drum. This is accomplished by first tightening the axle cap bolts and the axle nut, and then tightening the brake anchor bolt with the front brake applied.

Slotting brake shoes is a popular and effective modification that can be made to drum brakes to aid them in getting rid of water that has entered the drum. The diagonal grooves in the shoes shown in **Figure 5** provide an exit path for water but only marginally reduce brake contact area. The grooves should be spaced evenly at one inch (25mm), cut to about 0.63 in. (16mm) and angled forward 45° on the backing plate side of the brake.

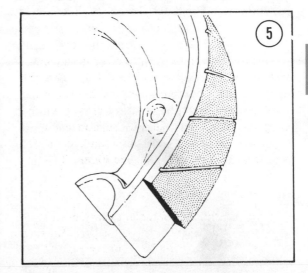

An Enduro model with a full-width front hub can be improved for off-road use with the substitution of a lightweight conical hub. The one shown in **Figure 6** is from a 1977 (or earlier) MX model and weighs only 5.8 lb. (2.8 kg). This unit is readily available, reasonably priced, and costs less than a custom hub. When used with a lightweight rim it results in a front wheel that is one of the lightest available.

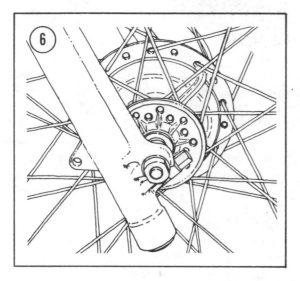

An aluminum brake torque arm and chain guide weighs 0.5 lb. (0.25 kg) compared with stock 1.5 lb. (0.7 kg). Fabricate an aluminum chain guide and torque arm from bar stock using the old guide as a pattern. Flare the edges toward the outside so the chain cannot catch the chain guide and break it.

Motocrossers should switch to lightweight aluminum alloy rims, such as D.I.D. or Akront. Do not use a flanged type rim (**Figure 7**) if the motorcycle is ridden primarily off-road or for motocross. Flanges act as mud traps and will increase unsprung weight considerably when packed with mud. Instead, use non-flanged rims.

Make certain that the replacement rim dimensions (diameter and width) are the same as the originals and that the spoke pattern matches that of the hubs. Standard gauge spokes work well on front wheels but heavy 8-gauge spokes should be used on the rear. The difference in unsprung weight between standard and heavy gauge spokes is less than 9 oz. (255 grams) while the increased strength is considerable. A

weight savings is possible by using Buchanan 70-71 T6 aluminum spoke nipples. A set of 40 weighs 6 oz. (170 grams) less than stock. Spoke holes in the rear hub must be countersunk deeper for the larger heads of the heavy-gauge spokes (**Figure 8**).

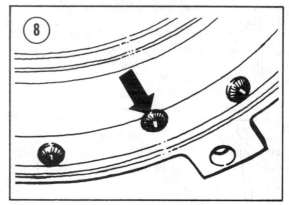

A trick used by many off-road riders is to "wire" the wheel spokes together for increased strength through triangulation. See **Figure 9**. This also prevents a broken spoke from causing further damage. One problem is that you cannot readily tell if the spokes are loose. If the spokes are wired, check their tension frequently with a spoke tightening wrench.

Avoid using clincher-type rim locks. They are unnecessarily heavy at 0.50 lb. (0.25 kg) each. Instead, use sheet metal screws to prevent the tire from slipping on the rim.

Use eight No. 10 screws on the rear wheel, four on each side, installed 90 degrees apart. See **Figure 10**. Use six No. 10 screws on the front wheel, three on each side installed 120 degrees apart. Other methods of preventing tire slippage, such as chiseling burrs along the bead

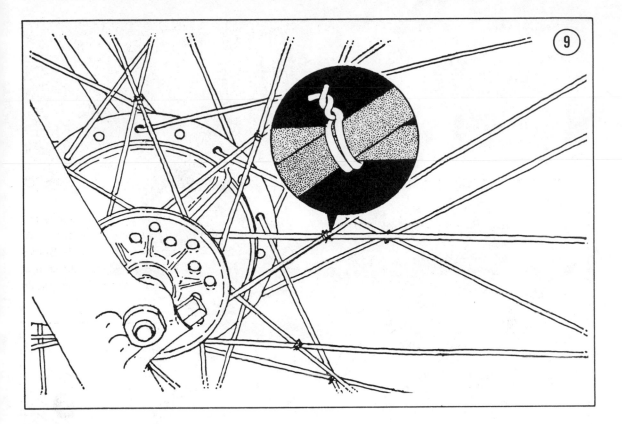

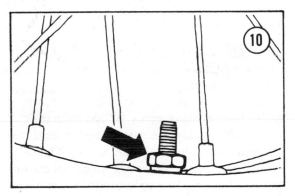

seating flange of the rim, are of little benefit and can distort the rim badly.

An additional weight savings can be made by drilling the final drive sprocket. This can amount to as much as a pound of unsprung weight saved without sacrificing the strength of the sprocket.

Figure 11 illustrates the extent to which a sprocket can be lightened. Avoid using an overlay sprocket. Instead, select an aluminum sprocket with the correct number of teeth for the gearing you desire. Refer to the *Gearing* section in this chapter for more details.

AXLES

Replace the stock axles with Rickman axles sized to fit the bearing inner diameter; they are 4 oz. (113 grams) lighter and much stronger.

The weight of the front axle can be further reduced with a tubular heat-treated chrome-moly axle with titanium spacers.

TUBES AND TIRES

Tires must sustain cornering, braking, and acceleration forces. Handling difficulties and pecularities in riding can often be traced to the characteristics of the tires. If the tires are inadequate, you cannot possibly benefit fully from other suspension or engine improvements.

Tires must be considered for traction, durability, and cost. Dunlop's K-88 is a good buy and is the lightest tire on the market. A lightweight tire is important because of unsprung weight and also because of less inertia. Extra weight of 3-4 lb. (1.5-2.0 kg) at an average distance of 10 in. (250mm) from the axle requires more power to overcome for fast acceleration.

8

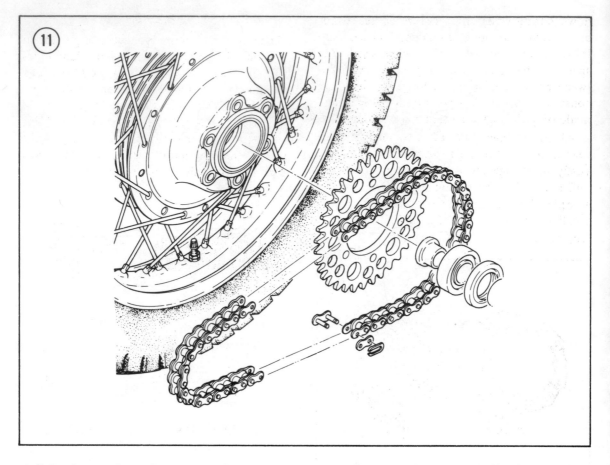

A light tire can have the same performance as chassis improvement and horsepower increases.

Tube weights can vary by as much as 1.0 lb. (0.45 kg) and there are many good brands available. For motocross, get the lightest tube possible (Dunlop normally) without worrying about brand names.

Tire pressure can make a substantial difference in how the bike handles. Too much air in the front will make it slide out in corners and transmit a lot of shock to your hands and arms. Too little pressure and it will pinch the tube causing a flat. Try 10-12 psi on the front and 14-16 psi on the rear. The rear tire does most of the work because it must power over what the front tire rolls over.

GEARING

Simply changing final gear ratios can have a tremendous effect on a bike's acceleration and top speed.

A high ratio (low numerically) has an overdrive effect and can increase top speed or sacrifice acceleration.

A low ratio (high numerically) can substantially increase acceleration by allowing the engine to rev quickly and reach optimum rpm for maximum horsepower.

The ideal gear ratio is one which allows the engine to reach optimum (not peak) rpm at the end of the longest straightaway in high gear. If the engine peaks out too soon, horsepower will fall off and speed will remain constant. Gearing which is too high never allows the engine to develop full power. However, ideal gearing, in terms of engine performance, is not always the best gearing. For instance, if the motorcycle is used extensively on the street, a slightly high ratio is desirable because it permits the engine to operate at lower speeds during long periods of constant-speed cruising. This results in greater fuel mileage and longer engine life. But, if the gearing is too high, requiring frequent downshifting when slight grades or headwinds are encountered, hoped-for added fuel economy is lost because the engine will operate at a higher speed in the lower gear. A good balance between engine performance, longevity, and fuel consumption requires a compromise that can be made only through trial-and-error testing.

Always change gear ratios by changing the rear sprocket. It may be troublesome and more costly to change the rear sprocket, but power will not be lost by having the chain bend too sharply. The risk of the chain lifting off the smaller sprocket is also eliminated. See **Figure 12**.

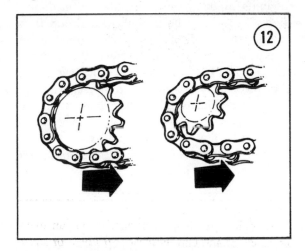

When changing ratios, you can save at least 2 lb. (0.9 kg) by using an aluminum sprocket from Circle Industries. Avoid using an overlay sprocket. Instead, select a whole sprocket with the correct number of teeth for the gearing you desire.

Drilling the final drive sprocket can save as much as a pound of unsprung weight without sacrificing strength.

CHAIN TENSIONER

A chain tensioner is an automatic, torsion spring tensioning device that eliminates chain slack. This in turn reduces the shock when applying the throttle. By lessening the shock you reduce chain stretch and shock on the transmission, increase sprocket and chain life, and help keep the chain on the sprocket to give more smooth power to the ground.

FRAME

Drilling and grinding brackets and gussets on the frame should not be attempted. Many holes drilled in an attempt to lighten the frame may look good to you but will often result in no more than a few ounces of weight removed. If you want a new lightweight frame, Red-Line (see **Figure 13**), and Boyd and Stellings make excellent chrome-moly frames. The cost may be prohibitive unless you are racing.

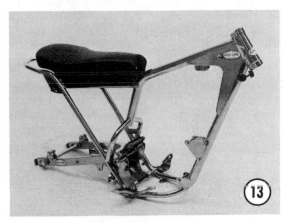

SUSPENSION AND HANDLING IMPROVEMENT

Unsprung weight reduction provides an improvement in handling, but it is not enough to stop there. The following information will further improve handling.

REAR SUSPENSION

Shock Absorbers

Shock absorbers are relatively simple devices used to slow down the reaction time of the wheels. Contrary to popular belief, the springs, not the shocks, affect the stiffness of the suspension.

Stock shock absorbers are designed for comfort not handling. Replace them with heavy-duty adjustable shocks such as Koni, Mulholland, Red Wing, or Arnaco.

Adjustable shocks have 2 advantages. First, they can be adjusted so that the damping action suits your riding style and road conditions. Second, you can progressively increase firmness as the shocks wear to maintain the same damping

8

action as new shocks. This feature alone makes the adjustables worth the extra cost.

Spring Selection

Any brand rear shock (even stock) should be fitted with chrome-silicon springs. You may want to experiment with other spring ratings for optimum performance.

With long travel rear suspension, actual spring rate does not necessarily reflect the type of ride the motorcycle will give. A better indicator of ride characteristic is the factor known as wheel rate. Wheel rate is the amount of force required to move the chassis, directly over the rear axle, down one inch (25mm). The wheel rate is the product of the force exerted by the spring through the mechanical leverage of the shock mountings times the number of springs used for suspension. Wheel rate is the controlling factor regardless of where the shocks (or monoshock) are mounted.

First, select a wheel rate from the table of suggested wheel rates according to motorcycle usage and rider ability. See **Table 3**. Then refer to the correction factors and add or subtract the appropriate amount from the original wheel rate.

To obtain a spring rate that will give the selected wheel rate you must know the mechanical leverage of the shock mounting system. This can be determined by carefully measuring your motorcycle. Put the motorcycle on a stand and remove the rear shocks so the rear wheel can be moved through its entire range of travel. Block up the rear wheel so it does not hang down lower than if the shocks were installed. See **Figure 14**. Measure from the center of the axle to the ground. Also measure the distance between the upper and lower shock mounts. Now raise the wheel up through its normal travel. Take the same measurements while the wheel is up in its full bump position. Subtract the dimension of the axle to the ground at full droop, from the dimension of the axle to the ground at full bump; this will give the amount of axle travel. See **Figure 15**. Now subtract the eye-to-eye dimension of the compressed shock, from the eye-to-eye dimension of the shock in its extended position. This will give total shock travel. You now have the total axle travel and total shock travel and are ready to compute the necessary spring rate.

Table 3 WHEEL RATES

Suggested Wheel Rates	
Mini bike	60 lbs./in.
Novice motocross racer	60 lbs./in.
Intermediate motocross racer	70 lbs./in.
Desert racer	70 lbs./in.
Trail rider	75 lbs./in.
Professional motocross racer	80 lbs./in.
Dirt track and scrambles	95 lbs./in.
Trials	100 lbs./in.
Lightweight road rider	110 lbs./in.
Correction Factors	
Very light rider	Subtract 10%
Heavy rider (200 lbs. +	Add 10%
Stand-up style	Subtract 10%
Sit-down style	Add 10%
Two passenger	Add 15%
Limited wheel travel	Add 10%
Very long travel (8 in. +)	Subtract 10%
125 Motocross	Subtract 10%

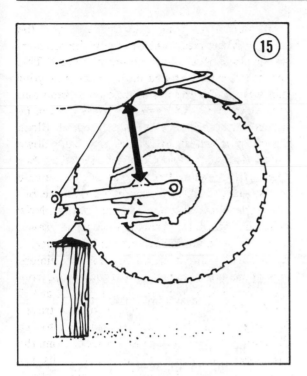

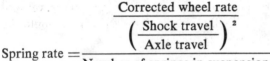
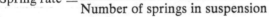

$$\text{Spring rate} = \frac{\dfrac{\text{Corrected wheel rate}}{\left(\dfrac{\text{Shock travel}}{\text{Axle travel}}\right)^2}}{\text{Number of springs in suspension}}$$

Example:

Selected wheel rate of 70 lb. minus 10% correction (70 — 7) = 63 lb./in.

Shock travel	4 in.
Axle travel	7.5 in.
Number of suspension springs	2

STEP 1. Divide axle travel (7.5 in.) into shock travel (4 in.) = 0.533

STEP 2. Square the result of Step 1. (0.533 × 0.533) = 0.284

STEP 3. Divide answer of Step 2 (0.284) into corrected wheel rate (63) = 221.83

STEP 4. Divide answer of Step 3 (221.83) by the number of springs (2) = 110.91

Now you can purchase a spring nearest the computed spring rate (in our example, 110 lb. rate springs would be correct). Remember, this formula is only a guide and rider preference is a variable that must be allowed for. S & W Engineered Products makes a wide range of springs.

Always run the lowest possible wheel rate. Lower spring rates generally require extra preload, but be sure the springs will not coil-bind when fully compressed. If the motorcycle never bottoms out, the springs are too stiff and too much of the normal ride has been sacrificed. The best compromise is to bottom-out very rarely over the roughest terrain. This applies to bikes ridden in the dirt only. If it is necessary to have the shocks topped out in order to stop bottoming, the spring rate is too low, with too much preload. It is better if the suspension sags slightly under the weight of the bike alone, that is, without a rider. This applied to bikes ridden in the dirt only.

Shock Cooler Installation

A Cycle Products West Shock Cooler will extend the life of new shocks and will keep the dampening the same for extended periods by keeping the shock oil cool. See **Figure 16**.

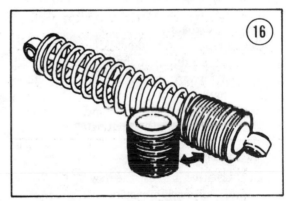

1. Use a razor blade to scrape the paint off the lower part of the shock.

2. To remove any excess paint, use a small piece of fine sandpaper or emery cloth.

3. Use a cloth dampened with lacquer thinner to wipe off any residue.

4. Try to slip on the coolers. If one or both will not slip on, then proceed to Step 5. If they do slip on, then proceed to Step 6.

5. If the shock is too big for the cooler, file down high spots.

6. Mix enough epoxy to coat both shocks. Use your finger to coat the lower body of each shock with an even layer of epoxy.

8

7. Slide the cooler over the lower body until it stops against the lower spring support and tighten the set screw.

8. Wipe off excess epoxy immediately and let dry for 2 hours.

9. Install shocks on motorcycle.

Increased Suspension Travel

Increasing rear suspension travel can substantially improve the total performance of the motorcycle by keeping the wheel in contact with the ground more often. It may look impressive to see a motorcycle flying through the air or bouncing over whoop-de-dos but the smart rider knows better. If the wheel leaves the ground, even for an instant, it cannot transmit power and maintain acceleration. The rider will also have to throttle back to keep from overreving the engine and causing damage.

Likewise, braking effort is reduced and the rider is subjected to more abuse when the suspension bottoms or tops out transmitting shock into the handlebars.

The time-honored method of increasing travel has been to use different shocks and cant them forward or forward mount the entire system as well as lengthening the swing arm. This works but it requires a lot of effort, expense, and risk. If the welding is not absolutely perfect, the suspension could collapse at a crucial moment causing serious injury.

An alternative is to use the new Skunk Works long travel suspension system with progressive linkage. This is an ingenious system which increases travel using the stock shocks, if wanted, without any major rework or welding. The system will work equally well on any model to provide up to 7.0 in. (178mm) of travel.

Figure 17 is an illustration of a typical installation. The location of the top shock mount remains unchanged while the bottom bolts onto the new suspension unit. The bottom portion of the bottom arm then mounts to the original shock mount point. The upper portion of the new unit mounts to a hole drilled in the frame gusset (a tab may have to be welded on for this to work on the F-9). If you study Figure 17 you can see that the system works using the principals of leverage and geometric progression to

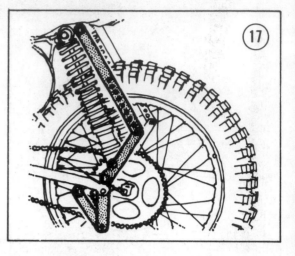

increase shock/spring effectiveness and travel respectively. The system works quite well and is very inexpensive at less than $25. You may have to adjust the spring rate depending on your riding style. We suggest 60-90, 70-100, or 80-110 lb. (25-40, 30-45, or 35-45 kg) progressive rate springs for full-size motorcycles or 75-85 lb. (30-35 kg) progressive rate springs for minicycles.

Swing Arm

The lateral play in the swing arm bushings should be checked and if any play is felt, the pivot bolt should be tightened. If play is still present, the bushings should be replaced as described in this manual.

The swing arm pivot should be disassembled, cleaned, and lubricated every 6,000 miles. Pay particular attention to the bushings and if there are any indications of wear or damage, replace them.

Major rear suspension modification is not recommended. If the fitting and welding is less than perfect there is a very real risk that the rear suspension will collapse, and almost invariably under stress when a malfunction can be disastrous.

STEERING AND FRONT SUSPENSION

Front Fork Springs

Like most manufacturers, Kawasaki uses music wire for their front springs which tend to lose their resiliency rapidly. Change to chrome-silicon wire springs, such as those manufactured by S & W, which maintain their resiliency and provide a noticeable improvement in handling. Refer to the suspension chapter for installation procedures. While the forks are apart, replace the seals and replace the stock oil with 20 wt. Torco fork oil. Try this lighter oil first and compare the results to stock. Oil which is too heavy can make the forks rigid and unyielding. Gradually increase the weight of fork oil to 40 wt. until desired damping is obtained.

The damping characteristics of standard front forks can be greatly improved with the addition of a "Trikit," available through many dealers or directly from the manufacturer, No. 1 Products. The kit sells for less than $30 and can be easily installed with the instructions that are included. In this case, the kit manufacturer's recommendation for damping oil should be followed.

Air/Oil Conversion

The Cycle Products West air/oil suspension conversion kit uses air pressure in place of the full conventional coil springs. The kit is available for most models for less than $10.

1. Support motorcycle so the front wheel is off the ground and remove handlebars. Control cables may be left on the handlebars.

2. Drain oil from fork legs.

3. Remove fork caps and springs. If you desire a more progressive front end, cut off springs by 4 in. (100.0mm) and reinstall before filling fork legs with oil. If motorcycle is not supported when removing second fork cap, the forks will collapse.

4. If your fork seals were leaking, try cleaning dirt out of the seals and wipers before reassembling. The CPW kit may cure leaky seals.

5. Refill each fork leg with a high grade fork oil or non-detergent motor oil. Fill forks to specification. See Quick Reference Data in the front of this book. If they still top out add one ounce more oil to each fork leg.

6. Remove O-rings from stock fork caps and install in groove on the air fork adaptors.

7. Install air fork adaptors in fork tubes and tighten securely.

8. Loosen triple clamp bolts one side at a time. Turn fork tube so that hole in adaptor is facing a convenient direction for filling and retighten triple clamp bolts. Repeat for other fork leg.

9. Mount handlebars in desired position.

10. Fill each fork leg with 40 psi of compressed air or dry nitrogen (30 psi if using short springs—see Step 3). Do not use oxygen or other flammable gas. With fork legs fully extended, set pressure at 35 psi (25 psi for short springs) using a tire pressure gauge. Each time you check air pressure you will lose approximately 2 lb. If forks are allowed to collapse before filling with air, they might have a tendency to stick in the collapsed position. If this happens, fill each leg with more air (you are safe to 100 psi) and pull apart by placing one foot on the axle and lifting on the handlebars. This condition will only occur when forks are allowed to collapse without air pressure or springs.

11. If, after riding, a stiffer front fork is required, add more air pressure. If a softer fork is required, let out air pressure. We recommend 2 lb. increments until desired stiffness is gained. Start high and go down. Oil viscosity controls fork dampening only. If you are satisfied with the present fork dampening stay with it.

12. After forks are filled to desired air pressure level, make a simple leak check by brushing soapy water around fork caps and seals.

Steering Dampener

Red Wing produces a device called a steering dampener which can improve the overall control of the motorcycle at high speeds, or if the front wheel should strike a small object. In effect, this is a small shock absorber which restricts sudden, sharp movement of the forks. See **Figure 18**. The unit bolts onto the forks in a matter of minutes without any special machining or welding. The kit comes with complete installation instructions.

TRANSMISSION

Inspect the transmission to ensure that all of the engagement dogs are in good condition. Bevel the transmission gears to decrease surface

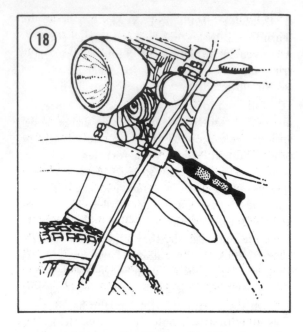

area and friction. See **Figure 19**. Then have the gears and other moving parts microplated at Microplate Co. Transmission life will be increased and friction reduced substantially for a gain in usable power.

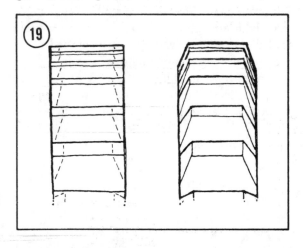

While the crankcases are apart, have them microsealed. This process removes the porosity from the castings, reducing the possibility of air leaks, and at the same time improves the heat transfer capability of the crankcase. This process should also be applied to the barrel. The work can be arranged through most dealers or directly through Microplate. Look in the Yellow Pages under the heading of Metal Finishing or consult with someone familiar with metals.

CLUTCH

Heavy-duty Barnett clutch chrome-silicon springs are necessary because the stock springs, like the stock fork springs, are made of music wire and tend to weaken quickly.

With exception of a motorcycle that is used exclusively in racing, a steel plate clutch should be used rather than an aluminum one. The steel clutch is not as sensitive to heat as the aluminum clutch and consequently requires less fussing with adjustment.

EXHAUST SYSTEM

The stock exhaust system is designed to control engine noise over a wide rpm range without seriously decreasing engine performance. Exhaust gases pass directly through relatively short pipes to matched mufflers.

The engine must have an efficient, tuned exhaust system to fully realize the potential of other modifications. Replacing the stock system with a Denco, Bassani, or similar custom exhaust system can add 10-15% more power without any other modifications except carburetor jetting and a different spark plug.

Never run the engine on the street without some sort of muffler or baffle. It may sound good to you but it only causes a loss in power and increases the risk of engine damage. Besides, it will attract unnecessary attention by the police.

CAUTION
Any exhaust system modification must be accompanied by a spark plug and jetting check as described in this chapter.

IGNITION SYSTEM

The stock ignition system consists of a battery, coil, breaker points, condenser, spark plug, and associated primary and secondary wiring. The following sections describe improvements.

There are some worthwhile and inexpensive changes that can be made to improve the stock ignition system. These include selection of a better distribution system and a spark plug in the correct heat range.

BATTERY

On street-equipped motorcycles, the battery is nearly essential for starting and lighting. But if you can live without street equipment, nearly 10 lb. (5 kg) can be eliminated by removing the battery and replacing it with a Pacifico battery eliminator or Kawasaki magneto. Instructions for installation are included with the units.

IGNITION COIL

The stock coil is barely sufficient for a stock engine, let alone one which has been modified, and should be replaced. There are several aftermarket companies who produce high-voltage coils specifically for motorcycles. One such manufacturer is Judson who produce the Cycletron brand coil. This unit is available through Webco or most dealers.

An alternative is to use a coil the same size as stock but an automotive type. Virtually any automotive coil will have a higher output so get the cheapest one possible. When using a high-output coil of any type, be sure to use an automotive ballast resistor to avoid damaging the system. A typical setup is shown in **Figure 20**. The wire from the BATT terminal on the coil should go to the battery. The wire from the points should go to the DIST terminal of the coil. The spark plug lead goes to the center of the coil.

SPARK PLUG

There is nothing wrong with a stock plug for a stock engine, but this plug may run too hot if the engine has been modified.

Spark plugs are designed to work within a specific heat range. Below 1,000°F (550°C), carbon deposits do not burn off the tip and may form a conducting track which short circuits the plug. Above 1,500°F (850°C), the plug tip gets so hot it can pre-ignite the fuel mixture like a glow plug. The spark plug operates best when the center electrode is 1,300-1,400°F (700-750°C).

Modified engines usually run hotter and require a "cold" plug that can dissipate heat rapidly. The center electrode and insulating core are made short so that there is a short conduction path to the metal body and the comparatively cool cylinder head (**Figure 21**).

A cold-running engine requires a hot plug that does not quickly dissipate heat. Thus, the central electrode stays hotter. Otherwise, the

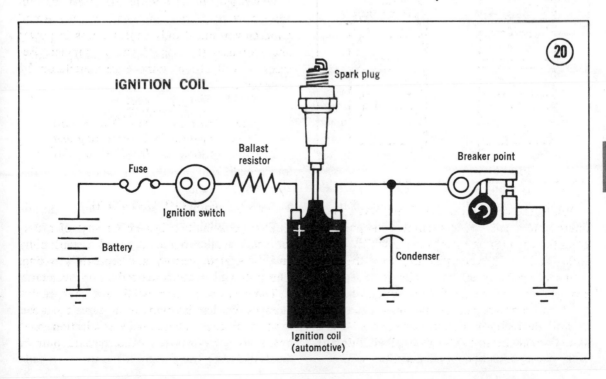

IGNITION COIL

Spark plug

Fuse

Ballast resistor

Ignition switch

Battery

Ignition coil (automotive)

Condenser

Breaker point

8

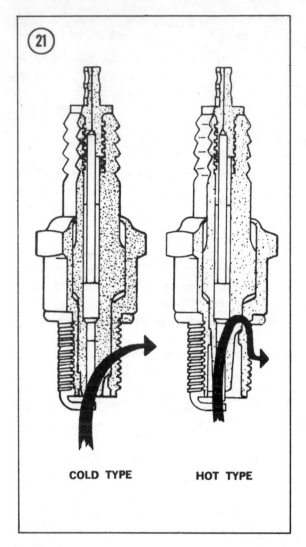

COLD TYPE   HOT TYPE

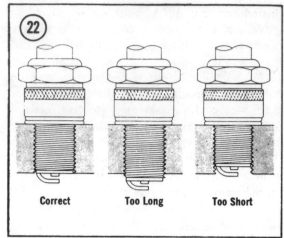

Correct   Too Long   Too Short

With the cylinder head off, torque each spark plug in place with a new washer. If the end projects no more than approximately 0.050 in. (1.27mm), grind the threaded end of the plug so that it is flush with the combustion chamber wall. If the plug extends farther than 0.050 in. (1.27mm), shim it up with spacers from Champion plugs.

CAUTION
Do not stack normal plug washers as shims or compression leaks will surely result.

Selection

To select a proper plug, conduct a plug check.

NOTE: *This test is only valid with a used plug. A new plug may give a false indication.*

1. On level ground, accelerate to top speed in fourth gear, pull in the clutch, and shut off the engine at the same time.

2. Stop the motorcycle with the brakes; do not let it stop under engine compression.

3. Remove the spark plug and compare its condition to the chart in Chapter Two. This way, you will learn the accuracy of the jetting as well as the spark plug heat range.

Also, check the color of the deposits in the exhaust pipe. Spark plug and exhaust pipe deposits are an indication of carburetor adjustment. Be sure the carburetor is properly ad-

central electrode temperature would drop below the desired range. The central electrode is made long so that the heat conduction path is long. A modified engine usually requires a plug just slightly colder than stock.

There are many products called spark intensifiers, magnifiers, multipliers, and other similar names which are useless. If your engine is properly put together, tuned normally, and working as it should, none of these "magic" devices is necessary.

Reach

To ensure proper mixture combustion, check that the spark plug does not extend into the combustion chamber. See **Figure 22**.

justed and that the deposits are light tan, not gray or black.

Spark Plug Wiring

Special ignition wire, of silicone with solid steel wire centers, are available to replace the stock wire. If the stock wire is in good condition, keep it even if it is of the resistance type. If the wire shows obvious deterioration, install a new one. Old ignition wire is often a source of mysterious misfire problems.

ELECTRONIC IGNITION SYSTEMS

There are a number of special electronic ignition systems available as aftermarket equipment. The best types are transistorized or capacitive-discharge (CDI) such as the Cycle See-Dee Unit.

Transistorized ignition systems use a transistor to switch the large primary current to the coil. The original breaker points switch a small transistor control current rather than the larger primary current to increase point life.

Capacitive-discharge ignition systems use transistors in a different way. Closing the breaker points activates a transistorized oscillator which charges a capacitor to high voltage. Opening the breaker points discharges the capacitor through the ignition coil primary and an even higher secondary voltage develops to fire the plug. When the points open again, the capacitor charges for the next spark pulse.

Electronic ignition systems can increase horsepower, acceleration, and gas mileage. They can also make cold/damp weather starting easier, increase point life, and increase spark plug life.

Plug life on a modified 2-stroke engine can be very short. For this reason, a capacitive discharge ignition (CDI) used to increase plug life can be a valuable asset.

Kawasaki has a special competition magneto and CDI unit to fit most models. There is no special part number for this item but a dealer can still special order the unit.

FUEL SYSTEM

The stock fuel system is designed to give reasonable fuel economy, good low-end torque, and fair performance over a very wide range. A number of things can be done to vastly improve performance but fuel economy and engine flexibility may suffer.

It is impossible to evaluate any fuel system changes until the stock system is working right. The first place to start is a good engine tune-up as described in Chapter Two. Do not touch the fuel system until the ignition system works perfectly.

CARBURETOR

A change in carburetion can add considerable horsepower, particularly if you also install a tuned exhaust system and change port timing.

Ram Tuned Intake Manifold (Rotary Valved Engines)

A company called Skunk Works has developed a ram tuned intake manifold specifically for the Kawasaki rotary valved engines. See **Figure 23**. This design is based on old proven racing car principles to give more power, a broader power band, and increased engine life.

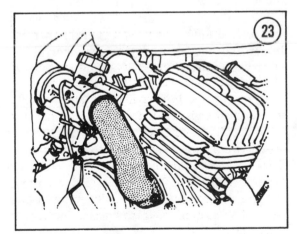

Basically, the manifold increases fuel flow through the use of sonic waves for compaction. In appearance, the manifold is a long tube on on top of which rests a much larger than stock Mikuni carburetor. The long tube permits a

8

steady flow of cool air not possible with a conventional manifold. The stock Kawasaki engine has the carburetor mounted in the engine cases where it is virtually inaccessible and exposed to engine heat and vibration. The short path between the carburetor and rotary valve does not allow the fuel to flow smoothly because the opening and closing of the valve creates negative (backward) pulses. The result is that the engine is starving for fuel at exactly those moments when it needs it the most.

The length of the tube and great distance from the heat of the engine also causes the fuel to be cooler. Cooler fuel is denser than normal thus creating a condition similar to supercharging. The cooler fuel and richer possible mixture also causes the engine to run cooler under load. This contributes to longer life and greater power potential. Since the ram-inducted engine runs cooler than stock, it stands to reason that compression, and horsepower, can be raised without causing damage.

The placement of the carburetor outside of the cases also permits a physically larger carburetor with a larger stock venturi. In the past, Kawasaki speed tuners have had to ream the stock carburetor throat with limitations of 2-3mm. The placement also allows you to remove the engine case bulge on the right-hand side to reduce weight and narrow the engine.

There are currently several manifolds available for the more popular bikes. **Table 4** lists the various models and the carburetor sizes which can be used.

Modification (Piston Port Engines)

Little can be done to improve upon the performance of the stock carburetor. The flow characteristics are well-suited to the stock engine.

Mid-range and top-end performance on a piston-port engine can be increased slightly by switching to a larger (2-4mm) Mikuni carburetor. Modification to use a G.E.M. reed valve will help took. A reed valve engine can accept a large carburetor with no fear of "drowning" the engine because it only admits needed fuel.

Jetting

Altitude and humidity have a marked effect on engine performance and must be compensated for with suitable jet sizes and needle position. Changes in port shape, the exhaust system, and displacement will also necessitate changes in jetting because they alter the engine's ability to breathe. Correct jetting and adjustment is largely a matter of experience gained through careful trial-and-error tuning.

Before making any alterations in jetting or needle position, conduct a plug check as described under *Spark Plug* in this chapter. This way, you can learn not only the condition of the jetting but also the suitability of the spark plug heat range.

Always begin jetting with a slightly larger jet than you feel you need; a too-lean mixture often results in a damaging piston seizure. Make changes in one-step increments. Do not make a

Table 4   RAM TUNED INTAKE MANIFOLD APPLICATIONS*

Engine Displacement	Stock Carburetor Size	Carburetor Size With Ram Tuned Intake Manifold
80cc	17-18mm	30-34mm
90cc	17-18mm	34-36mm
100cc	17-18mm	34-36mm
125cc	24-26mm	36-38mm
175cc	26mm	36-38mm

* Applies only to rotary-valved engines and not piston-port such as the 250cc F-11. All changes in carburetion should be accompanied with ignition and exhaust system refinements at the very least. Refer to this entire chapter for other speed tuning tips.

change of 2 sizes. Allow sufficient time to do a thorough job; time spent finding the optimum jetting and adjustments is every bit as important as other engine modifications.

As a rough guide line, add one jet size if a modified exhaust system is used. Add one jet size if port timing is changed. It is better to start rich on the jetting and adjust to suit the engine.

AIR CLEANER

The stock paper air cleaner is effective but restrictive. There are many special air cleaners made to fit the stock carburetor. One good brand is the Filtron foam type.

You should never operate the engine without an air cleaner. A clean air cleaner does not rob your engine of enough power to offset its advantages.

The incoming fuel/air charge also supplies lubrication for the lower-end bearings so clean air is a must or the engine will be damaged in less than a couple of hours. A Ken Maeley air cleaner housing with a Filtron element is a good combination. The Maeley housing has a side-mounted element that can be reached by removing a wing-nutted cover for quick replacement of the element.

ENGINE LUBRICATION

On models equipped with Superlube oil injection, remove the oil injection unit, pump, and tank for off-road use and pre-mix the gas and oil.

CAUTION
This applies only to Superlube models. Larger engines with Injectolube rely on this system for bearing lubrication.

When you put oil in the gasoline, you know it is getting into the engine if the gasoline is. You will never run out of oil while there is still gas, and you will drop 3 lb. (1.4 kg) in the process. Plug up the oiler hole in the barrel or an air leak and a blown engine will develop.

Stay away from oil additives in the crankcase or the fuel system. There is a chance they may not be compatible with the additives already in the oil. If there was a miracle ingredient which would materially benefit your engine, the oil suppliers would include it and the engine manufacturers would recommend it. Some additives such as STP or Stud, though useful in some engines, can even cause a wet-plate clutch to slip.

CYLINDER HEAD

To eliminate a frequent source of detonation and preignition, make sure there are no sharp edges or burrs in the combustion chamber. In addition, check that the spark plug does not protrude too far into the chamber.

Extensive modifications are possible and should be considered for maximum power. If you want to go "all-out" on modification, take the head to an experienced performance shop. If piston or ports have been modified, the combustion chamber may be modified to compensate for a compression ratio increase.

CAUTION
Excessively high compression will cause the engine to overheat and burn the piston or spark plug.

Cleaning and Inspection

The head must be thoroughly cleaned before any modification or measurement. Remove all carbon from the combustion chamber with a wire brush. Do not wire brush the cylinder seating surfaces. Particularly stubborn deposits can be removed by blasting with glass beads or walnut hulls. Scrape out all dirt from between the fins and wash in solvent.

CAUTION
Do not sandblast the head; sandblasting is too abrasive and can damage the sealing surfaces.

Changing Compression Ratio

Three ways to change the compression ratio are:

a. Bore

b. Stroke

c. Flycut head

Flycutting is equivalent to milling the head on a water-cooled engine. It decreases the volume of the combustion chamber.

8

Installing a big bore kit or "stroker" crankshaft will also increase the compression ratio. If you also flycut the head, you may raise the compression ratio far beyond a desirable or safe limit.

ROTARY VALVE

A rotary valve disc controls the opening and closing of ports in a manner similar to that of the piston in a piston port engine. Since the valve is a separate unit, easily accessible, changing port timing can be as simple as changing the rotary valve. In fact, many people modify several differnt rotary valves and keep them on hand for instant tuning to satisfy different needs. For example, you may want to have stock, mild and wild discs made up and kept near the bike. The simplicity and ease of changing the disc also allows the home tuner to play with different settings. The specifications in Table 1 recommend different opening and closing limits for mild or wild engines but you may vary timing either way from these recommendations. However, do not attempt to vary from stock by more than 2-3° at a time. Any change in port timing should be accompanied by changes in the fuel and exhaust system. Likewise, fuel and exhaust system changes will do little good without changes in port timing.

Modifying the rotary valve disc is extremely simple. Most modifications in the interest of more power will be toward increased duration and removal of more material than stock. However, you can obtain rotary valve discs in lightweight aluminum which are blank for cutting to any specification. To match the recommendations in Table 2, first find out what the stock number of degrees are for your engine. If the stock rating is for the valve to open a port at 125° then a protractor will help you locate TDC if the valve is not already marked as it should be. Scribe a mark for the recommended new setting using a scribe and protractor. Duplicate the shape of the original opening and cut it out using a high-speed grinder such as a Dremel or Craftsman hand-held unit. See **Figure 24**.

WARNING
Use safety glasses or goggles to reduce the risk of eye injury.

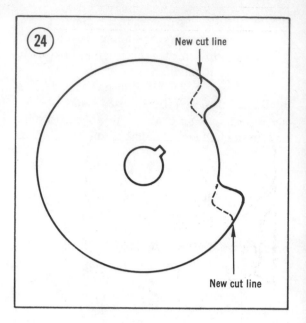

Bevel the edges of the disc so that it will not snag the port opening.

CONNECTING RODS

The oil groove in the rod should be flared to ensure more complete lubrication of the connecting rod big-end bearing. When assembling the crankshaft, refer to the engine chapter and check the alignment of the counterbalance wheels and make any corrections that are necessary.

PISTON

Stock pistons can be modified to work well enough that there is no need to change to an aftermarket type except for all-out competition. See Table 2.

A convenient way to make slight changes to port timing is to modify the top of the piston.

The area on top of the piston next to the exhaust port, or transfer ports, may be cut so that exhaust or transfer ports will open earlier and stay open longer. Do not cut the piston closer than 0.08 in. (2mm) to the ring groove. See **Figure 25**. The piston skirt may be shortened so that the intake port will open earlier and stay open longer.

When shortening the piston skirt, take care not to cut off too much. This will cause the

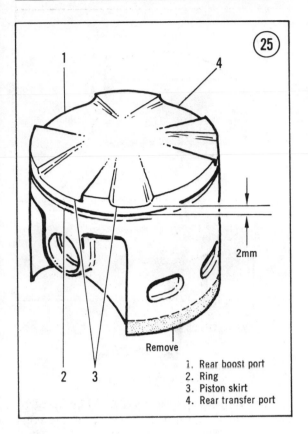

1. Rear boost port
2. Ring
3. Piston skirt
4. Rear transfer port

Remove

2mm

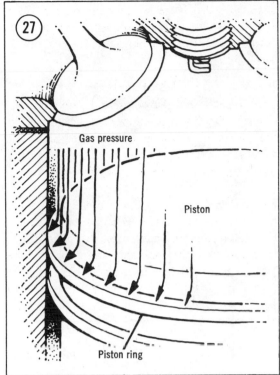

Gas pressure

Piston

Piston ring

piston to rock in the cylinder causing damage to the piston cylinder. Round off any sharp corners at the bottom edge of the skirt (**Figure 26**) to spread thrust loads over a larger area.

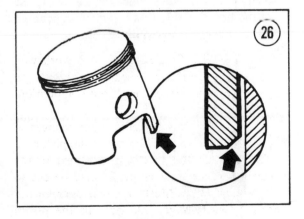

PISTON RINGS

The main purpose of piston rings is to seal gas pressure above the piston. The rings seal when gas pressure forces the rings down against the groove and outward against the cylinder wall. See **Figure 27**.

Proper side clearance between the piston groove and the ring is very critical. If clearance is too small, gas pressure does not build behind the ring and it collapses and fails to seal. Excessive clearance permits the ring to pound out the groove as it moves up and down.

Replace the standard piston rings with Poppy Super Rings. These rings are virtually unbreakable and will outlast the standard rings by several times. These rings are hard-chrome plated to reduce running friction over stock rings and consequently reduce heat. Also, they have inherently better heat transfer properties than standard rings to dissipate more heat to the cylinder and away from the piston.

Piston ring gap must be located between rear transfer port and exhaust port. Refer to **Figure 28**.

CYLINDER

A great deal of power can be created by altering port height, size, and shape but take care unless you have considerable experience with 2-stroke tuning. Modify the cylinder a little at

8

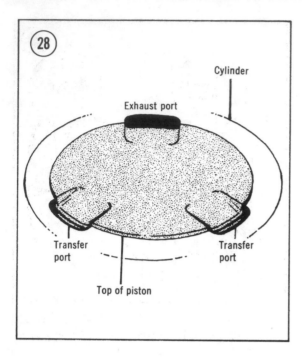

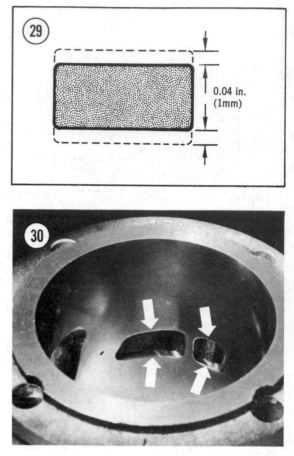

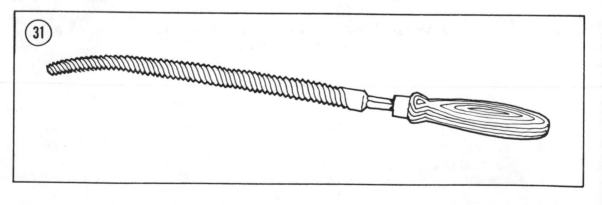

a time but make sure that each port is modified in proportion to the others. It does not do any good to modify the intake, for example, without also modifying the exhaust.

One good modification would be to add a G.E.M. reed valve kit and Mikuni carburetor.

Porting

Most piston port engines will benefit throughout the operating range by having the exhaust port widened 0.08 in. (8mm). See **Figure 29**.

In all cases with port modifications, the ports must be radiused after they have been altered to prevent the rings from snagging on the top and bottom edges (**Figure 30**). A file, heated and bent (**Figure 31**), works very well. Be sure to quench it in cold water to restore the temper.

The transfer ports should be carefully shaped and matched with the liner (**Figure 32**) to ensure the best possible flow of incoming charge. Typical conditions requiring correction are shown in **Figure 33**. A high speed grinding tool such as a Dremel or Craftsman can be used, but unless you are experienced in this work it is better to use a file and spend a little more time; a slip with a high speed grinding tool could severely damage the barrel.

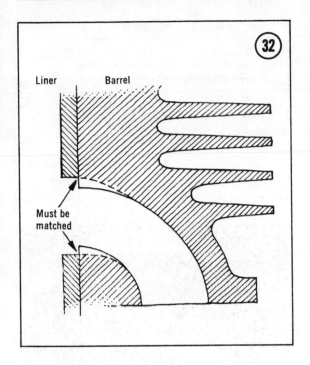

SUMMARY

The modifications described offer enough options so that it is possible to alter the Kawasaki slightly with just a few dollars and a little time to make it a generally better performer, or to construct a competitive racer.

Remember, begin by improving the handling and braking performance of the motorcycle.

These are the first steps to making a motorcycle quicker.

Be critical of the parts and services you purchase. Talk to your dealer; let him know what you are after in terms of performance and how much time and money you are prepared to spend. Dealers have a good information pipeline that includes performance bulletins and sources for components. They may be able to offer you information that was not available at the time this book was written.

8

Table 1 on the following pages lists performance parts and service supplies.

Table 1   PERFORMANCE PARTS AND SERVICE SUPPLIERS

Company	Product/Service
Accel Ignition U.S.-1 Branford, Conn. 06405	Electrical components
Akront North American P.O. Box 2307 Anaheim, Calif. 92804	Alloy wheel rims
Arnaco, Inc. 13431 Saticoy St. No. Hollywood, Calif. 91605	Tuneable shock absorbers
Azusa Engineering, Inc. (Tabloc) 1542 Industrial Park St. Covina, Calif. 91722	Sprockets
Barnett Tool and Engineering 4915 Pacific Blvd. Vernon, Calif. 90058	Clutch, cable, and clutch springs
Bassani Manufacturing 3726 E. Miraloma Anaheim, Calif. 92806	Expansion chambers
Bikoni, Ltd. (Koni) 150 Green St. Hackensack, N.J. 07601	Shock absorbers
Branch, Inc. (Flowmetrics) 2919 Gardena Ave. Long Beach, Calif. 90806	Porting and head work
Buchanan's Frame Shop 629 E. Garvey Monterey Park, Calif. 91754	Wheels, rims, and spokes
Chain Tite Fairgrounds Rd. Manlius, N.Y. 13104	Chain tensioners
Champion Spark Plug Co. 900 Upton Ave. Toledo, Ohio 43661	Spark plugs
Cir-Cycle 13000 Athens Ave. Cleveland, Ohio 44107	Engine modification components
Circle Industries 17901 Arenth Ave. City of Industry, Calif. 91748	Sprockets
Cycle Products West, Inc. 11900 W. Pico Blvd. W. Los Angeles, Calif. 90064	Shock coolers, air/oil suspension kits, head work, etc. By mail.

(continued)

Table 1   PERFORMANCE PARTS AND SERVICE SUPPLIERS (continued)

Company	Product/Service
Cycle See-Dee 7920 Sunset Blvd. Los Angeles, Calif. 90046	CDI Ignition
Daido/DID Corp. 885 Centennial Ave. Piscataway, N.J. 08854	Alloy wheel rims
DG Performance Specialists 5552 E. La Palma Anaheim, Calif. 92807	Kawasaki specialists
Electrofilm 7116 Laurel Canyon Blvd. No. Hollywood, Calif. 91605	Friction-reducing coating (similar to microplate)
Flying Machine Factory 1416 W. 259th St. Harbor City, Calif. 90710	Manufacturers of many hop-up items
Fun N Fast 18143 Napa St. Northridge, Calif. 91325	Skid plates
G.E.M. Products 496 E. St. Charles Rd. Carol Stream, Ill. 60187	Reed valve conversion kits
Hooker Headers 1032 W. Brooks St. Ontario, Calif. 91762	Exhaust systems
Joe Hunt Magneto 1724 Crenshaw Blvd. Torrance, Calif. 90501	Magneto
Impac Industries Houston 5704 Bellaire Blvd. Houston, Tex. 77081	Levers, controls
Interpart Corporation (Mulholland) 230 Rosecrans Gardena, Calif. 90248	Shocks and forks
J & R Exhaust Systems 1967 N. Glassell St. Orange, Calif. 92667	Exhaust systems
Judson Research 2239 Donnely Rd. Conshohocken, Penna. 19428	Cycletron coils
Kawasaki Parts (See your dealer)	Various stock and hop-up items

8

(continued)

Table 1   PERFORMANCE PARTS AND SERVICE SUPPLIERS (continued)

Company	Product/Service
K & N Engineering, Inc. Box 1329-561 Iowa Ave. Riverside, Calif. 92502	Filters and levers
Lakewood Cycle 7425 Fulton Ave. No. Hollywood, Calif. 91605	Metallic brake lining
Maely Enterprises Route 2, Box 758 Corona, Calif. 91720	Air cleaners
Magnaflux Corp. 7341 Ainslie St. Chicago, Ill. 60656	Magnetic inspection for flaws
Magura U.S.A. Corp. P.O. Box 1030 Lewistown, Penna. 17044	Levers and controls
Marchal American 14622 Southlawn Lane Rockville, Md. 20850	Headlights
Marubeni (Red Wing) 200 Park Ave. New York, N.Y. 10017	Shocks and forks
Maxi-Products, Inc. 1518 New Vinion Rd. Kansas City, Mo. 64118	Ignition components
Microplate 1013 W. Hillcrest Inglewood, Calif. 90301	Friction reducing coating
Mikuni American Corp. 8910 Mikuni Ave. Northridge, Calif. 91324	Carburetors
Nelson-Dykes Co., Inc. 4071 Shilling Way Dallas, Tex. 75237	Trailers
North American Imports 2325 Cerro Gordo Mohave, Calif. 93501	Alloy wheel rims
Number 1 Products, Inc. 4931 N. Encinita Ave. Temple City, Calif. 91780	Many motocross items
Pacifico, Inc. 1625 So. Hogan Rd. Gresham, Ore. 97030	Seats, electrical components

(continued)

Table 1   PERFORMANCE PARTS AND SERVICE SUPPLIERS (continued)

Company	Product/Service
Preston Petty Products 403 No. Main St. Newberg, Ore. 97132	Plastic MX tanks and fenders
Posa Enterprises 7530 E. Jackson St. Paramount, Calif. 90723	Mikuni carburetors and chain tensioners
Protopipe Exhaust Systems 100 Cristich Lane Campbell, Calif. 95008	Exhaust systems
Red Line Engineering 18257 Parthenia St. Northridge, Calif. 91324	Custom frames
Skunk Works Engineering Co. P.O. Box 203 Destin, Fla. 32541	Ram intake manifold, suspension kits, etc.
Malcolm Smith Racing Products 888 Marlborough Riverside, Calif. 91507	Various MX components
Sudco International 4653 Leston St. #710A Dallas, Tex. 75247	Mikuni carburetor kits
Sunnen Products 7910 Manchester Ave. St. Louis, Mo. 63143	Wheel rims
S & W Engineered Products 2617 W. Woodland Drive Anaheim, Calif. 92801	Springs for clutches, forks, and shocks
VDO Instruments 116 Victor Ave. Detroit, Mich. 48203	Enduro instruments
Webco, Inc. 218 Main St. Venice, Calif. 90291	Mail order sales of many items

8

APPENDIX

SPECIFICATIONS

This chapter contains major specifications for the various Kawasaki bikes covered in this manual. Since there are variations between bikes of the same engine size, be sure to consult the proper table. Specification tables are arranged in order of increasing engine size.

MODEL J1

Dimensions
Overall length	72.4 in.
Overall width	25.6 in.
Wheelbase	45.6 in.
Ground clearance	5.5 in.
Weight	167 lb.

Engine
Bore x stroke	47 x 47mm
Displacement	81.5cc
Horsepower/rpm	7.5/6,800

Transmission
Speeds	4

Ignition System
Type	Magneto

Lubrication System
Type	Superlube

Tire Size
Front	2.50-17
Rear	2.50-17

MODEL G1L

Dimensions
Overall length	72.4 in.
Overall width	29.0 in.
Wheelbase	45.7 in.
Ground clearance	5.5 in.
Weight	174 lb.

Engine
Bore x stroke	49 x 47mm
Displacement	88cc
Horsepower/rpm	8.2/6,500

Transmission
Speeds	4

Ignition System
Type	Magneto

Lubrication System
Type	Superlube

Tire Size
Front	2.50-17
Rear	2.50-17

MODEL G1M

Dimensions
Overall length	68.9 in.
Overall width	31.5 in.
Wheelbase	50.0 in.
Ground clearance	6.7 in.
Weight	165 lb.

Engine
Bore x stroke	49 x 47mm
Displacement	88cc
Horsepower/rpm	14.5/9,000

Transmission
Speeds	4

Ignition System
Type	Magneto

Lubrication System
Type	Gas/oil mixture

Tire Size
Front	2.50-18
Rear	2.75-17

MODEL G3SS-A

Dimensions
Overall length	72.1 in.
Overall width	33.0 in.
Wheelbase	45.3 in.
Ground clearance	6.7 in.
Weight	183 lb.

Engine
Bore x stroke	47.0 x 51.8mm
Displacement	89cc
Horsepower/rpm	—

Transmission
Speeds	5

Ignition System
Type	Magneto

Lubrication System
Type	Superlube

Tire Size
Front	2.75-18
Rear	2.75-18

9

MODEL G3TR

Dimensions
Overall length 72.0 in.
Overall width 33.0 in.
Wheelbase 45.2 in.
Ground clearance 6.7 in.
Weight 183 lb.

Engine
Bore x stroke 47.0 x 51.8mm
Displacement 89cc
Horsepower/rpm 10.5/8,000

Transmission
Speeds 5

Ignition System
Type Magneto

Lubrication System
Type Superlube

Tire Size
Front 2.75-18
Rear 2.75-18

MODEL GA1

Dimensions
Overall length 71.3 in.
Overall width 29.1 in.
Wheelbase 45.2 in.
Ground clearance 5.9 in.
Weight 174 lb.

Engine
Bore x stroke 47.0 x 51.8mm
Displacement 89cc
Horsepower/rpm 10.5/8,000

Transmission
Speeds 4

Ignition System
Type Magneto

Lubrication System
Type Superlube

Tire Size
Front 2.50-18
Rear 2.50-18

GA1-A

Dimensions
Overall length 71.3 in.
Overall width 29.1 in.
Wheelbase 45.3 in.
Ground clearance 5.9 in.
Weight 174 lb.

Engine
Bore x stroke 47.0 x 51.8mm
Displacement 89cc
Horsepower/rpm —

Transmission
Speeds 4

Ignition System
Type Magneto

Lubrication System
Type Superlube

Tire Size
Front 2.50-18
Rear 2.50-18

MODEL GA2

Dimensions
Overall length 71.3 in.
Overall width 29.1 in.
Wheelbase 45.2 in.
Ground clearance 5.9 in.
Weight —

Engine
Bore x stroke 47.0 x 51.8mm
Displacement 89cc
Horsepower/rpm 10.5/8,000

Transmission
Speeds 5

Ignition System
Type Magneto

Lubrication System
Type Superlube

Tire Size
Front 2.50-18
Rear 2.50-18

MODEL GA2-A

Dimensions
Overall length	71.3 in.
Overall width	29.1 in.
Wheelbase	45.3 in.
Ground clearance	5.9 in.
Weight	174 lb.

Engine
Bore x stroke	47.0 x 51.8mm
Displacement	89cc
Horsepower/rpm	—

Transmission
Speeds	5

Ignition System
Type	Magneto

Lubrication System
Type	Superlube

Tire Size
Front	2.50-18
Rear	2.50-18

MODEL MC1-A and MC1-M

Dimensions
Overall length	68.1 in.
Overall width	30.1 in.
Wheelbase	43.3 in.
Ground clearance	6.3 in.
Weight	165 lb.

Engine
Bore x stroke	47.0 x 51.8mm
Displacement	89cc
Horsepower/rpm	6.6/6,500

Transmission
Speeds	5

Ignition System
Type	Magneto

Lubrication System
Type	Superlube

Tire Size
Front	2.50-16
Rear	2.75-14

MODEL G4

Dimensions
Overall length	76.7 in.
Overall width	33.0 in.
Wheelbase	50.0 in.
Ground clearance	10.0 in.
Weight	185 lb.

Engine
Bore x stroke	49.5 x 51.8mm
Displacement	99cc
Horsepower/rpm	—

Transmission
Speeds	5

Ignition System
Type	Magneto

Lubrication System
Type	Superlube

Tire Size
Front	3.00-18
Rear	3.00-18

MODEL G5

Dimensions
Overall length	72.1 in.
Overall width	33.0 in.
Wheelbase	45.3 in.
Ground clearance	6.3 in.
Weight	183 lb.

Engine
Bore x stroke	49.5 x 51.8mm
Displacement	99cc
Horsepower/rpm	11/7,500

Transmission
Speeds	5

Ignition System
Type	Magneto

Lubrication System
Type	Superlube

Tire Size
Front	2.75-18
Rear	3.00-18

9

MODEL G31M-A

Dimensions

Overall length	76.5 in.
Overall width	33.0 in.
Wheelbase	51.0 in.
Ground clearance	10.0 in.
Weight	178 lb.

Engine

Bore x stroke	1.95 x 2.04 in.
Displacement	99cc
Horsepower/rpm	17.5/11,000

Transmission

Speeds	5

Ignition System

Type	Magneto

Lubrication System

Type	Gas/oil mix

Tire Size

Front	3.25-18
Rear	3.25-18

MODEL KE100

Dimensions

Overall length	72.1 in.
Overall width	33.0 in.
Wheelbase	45.3 in.
Ground clearance	6.3 in.
Weight	200 lb.

Engine

Bore x stroke	49.5 x 51.8mm
Displacement	99cc
Horsepower/rpm	11/7,500

Transmission

Speeds	5

Ignition System

Type	Magneto

Lubrication System

Type	Superlube

Tire Size

Front	2.75-19
Rear	3.00-18

MODEL KH100

Dimensions

Overall length	72.2 in.
Overall width	33.1 in.
Wheelbase	40.7 in.
Ground clearance	5.9 in.
Weight	187 lb.

Engine

Bore x stroke	49.5 x 51.8mm
Displacement	99cc
Horsepower/rpm	10.5/7,500

Transmission

Speeds	5

Ignition System

Type	Magneto

Lubrication System

Type	Superlube

Tire Size

Front	2.75-18
Rear	3.00-18

MODEL KV100

Dimensions

Overall length	76.7 in.
Overall width	33.0 in.
Wheelbase	50.0 in.
Ground clearance	10.0 in.
Weight	224 lb.

Engine

Bore x stroke	49.5 x 51.8mm
Displacement	99cc
Horsepower/rpm	—

Transmission

Speeds	5

Ignition System

Type	Magneto

Lubrication System

Type	Superlube

Tire Size

Front	3.00-18
Rear	3.00-18

MODEL C1D

Dimensions

Overall length	76.2 in.
Overall width	29.0 in.
Wheelbase	47.4 in.
Ground clearance	5.7 in.
Weight	210 lb.

Engine

Bore x stroke	53.0 x 53.0mm
Displacement	115cc
Horsepower/rpm	10/7,000

Transmission

Speeds	4

Ignition System

Type	Battery

Lubrication System

Type	Superlube

Tire Size

Front	2.75-17
Rear	2.75-17

MODEL C2SS

Dimensions

Overall length	72.8 in.
Overall width	29.4 in.
Wheelbase	47.6 in.
Ground clearance	7.0 in.
Weight	186 lb.

Engine

Bore x stroke	53.0 x 53.0mm
Displacement	115cc
Horsepower/rpm	11.5/7,000

Transmission

Speeds	4

Ignition System

Type	Magneto

Lubrication System

Type	Superlube

Tire Size

Front	2.75-18
Rear	3.00-18

MODEL B1L

Dimensions

Overall length	77.4 in.
Overall width	31.1 in.
Wheelbase	49.2 in.
Ground clearance	5.3 in.
Weight	255 lb.

Engine

Bore x stroke	55.0 x 52.5mm
Displacement	124cc
Horsepower/rpm	12/5,000

Transmission

Speeds	4

Ignition System

Type	Battery

Lubrication System

Type	Superlube

Tire Size

Front	3.00-16
Rear	3.00-16

MODEL B1L-A

Dimensions

Overall length	77.4 in.
Overall width	31.1 in.
Wheelbase	49.2 in.
Ground clearance	5.3 in.
Weight	257 lb.

Engine

Bore x stroke	55.0 x 52.5mm
Displacement	124cc
Horsepower/rpm	12/6,500

Transmission

Speeds	4

Ignition System

Type	Battery

Lubrication System

Type	Superlube

Tire Size

Front	3.00-16
Rear	3.00-16

9

MODEL B1M

Dimensions

Overall length	75.2 in.
Overall width	31.1 in.
Wheelbase	50.4 in.
Ground clearance	7.4 in.
Weight	220 lb.

Engine

Bore x stroke	55.0 x 52.5mm
Displacement	124cc
Horsepower/rpm	15/8,500

Transmission

Speeds	4

Ignition System

Type	Magneto

Lubrication System

Type	Gas/oil mixture

Tire Size

Front	2.75-18
Rear	3.00-18

MODEL F6

Dimensions

Overall length	78.5 in.
Overall width	33.5 in.
Wheelbase	51.1 in.
Ground clearance	9.5 in.
Weight	231 lb.

Engine

Bore x stroke	52 x 59mm
Displacement	124cc
Horsepower/rpm	15/7,500

Transmission

Speeds	5

Ignition System

Type	Magneto

Lubrication System

Type	Superlube

Tire Size

Front	3.00-18
Rear	3.25-18

MODEL KD125

Dimensions

Overall length	81.7 in.
Overall width	34.8 in.
Wheelbase	53.1 in.
Ground clearance	9.6 in.
Weight	196 lb.

Engine

Bore x stroke	56.0 x 50.6mm
Displacement	124cc
Horsepower/rpm	13/6,000

Transmission

Speeds	6

Ignition System

Type	Magneto

Lubrication System

Type	Superlube

Tire Size

Front	2.75-21
Rear	3.50-18

MODEL KE125

Dimensions

Overall length	81.7 in.
Overall width	34.4 in.
Wheelbase	53.1 in.
Ground clearance	9.8 in.
Weight	216 lb.

Engine

Bore x stroke	56.0 x 50.6mm
Displacement	124cc
Horsepower/rpm	13/6,000

Transmission

Speeds	6

Ignition System

Type	Magneto

Lubrication System

Type	Superlube

Tire Size

Front	2.75-21
Rear	3.50-18

MODEL KS125

Dimensions

Overall length	81.7 in.
Overall width	34.8 in.
Wheelbase	53.1 in.
Ground clearance	9.6 in.
Weight	214 lb.

Engine

Bore x stroke	56.0 x 50.6mm
Displacement	124cc
Horsepower/rpm	13/6,000

Transmission

Speeds	6

Ignition System

Type	Magneto

Lubrication System

Type	Superlube

Tire Size

Front	2.75-21
Rear	3.50-18

MODEL KX125

Dimensions

Overall length	79.5 in.
Overall width	34.5 in.
Wheelbase	52.8 in.
Ground clearance	7.3 in.
Weight	178.6 lb.

Engine

Bore x stroke	56.0 x 50.6mm
Displacement	124cc
Horsepower/rpm	22/9,750

Transmission

Speeds	6

Ignition System

Type	Magneto CDI

Lubrication System

Type	Gas/oil mixture

Tire Size

Front	3.00-21
Rear	4.10-18

MODEL F2

Dimensions

Overall length	77.8 in.
Overall width	33.0 in.
Wheelbase	49.4 in.
Ground clearance	5.9 in.
Weight	253 lb.

Engine

Bore x stroke	62 x 56mm
Displacement	169cc
Horsepower/rpm	18.0/7,000

Transmission

Speeds	4

Ignition System

Type	Battery

Lubrication System

Type	Superlube

Tire Size

Front	2.50-18
Rear	2.75-18

MODEL F3

Dimensions

Overall length	76.5 in.
Overall width	33.0 in.
Wheelbase	48.6 in.
Ground clearance	6.3 in.
Weight	260 lb.

Engine

Bore x stroke	62 x 56mm
Displacement	169cc
Horsepower/rpm	19.0/7,300

Transmission

Speeds	4

Ignition System

Type	Battery

Lubrication System

Type	Superlube

Tire Size

Front	3.00-19
Rear	3.50-18

9

MODEL F7

Dimensions

Overall length	80.5 in.
Overall width	33.5 in.
Wheelbase	52.0 in.
Ground clearance	9.8 in.
Weight	233 lb.

Engine

Bore x stroke	61.5 x 59mm
Displacement	174cc
Horsepower/rpm	20/7,500

Transmission

Speeds	5

Ignition System

Type	Magneto CDI

Lubrication System

Type	Superlube

Tire Size

Front	3.00-19
Rear	3.50-18

MODEL KE175

Dimensions

Overall length	82.5 in.
Overall width	33.7 in.
Wheelbase	53.9 in.
Ground clearance	9.3 in.
Weight	231 lb.

Engine

Bore x stroke	61.5 x 58.8mm
Displacement	174cc
Horsepower/rpm	16/7,000

Transmission

Speeds	5

Ignition System

Type	Magneto CDI

Lubrication System

Type	Superlube

Tire Size

Front	2.75-21
Rear	3.50-18

MODEL F4

Dimensions

Overall length	80.3 in.
Overall width	33.1 in.
Wheelbase	51.6 in.
Ground clearance	6.3 in.
Weight	265 lb.

Engine

Bore x stroke	2.75 x 2.44 in.
Displacement	238cc
Horsepower/rpm	23.0/7,500

Transmission

Speeds	4

Ignition System

Type	Magneto

Lubrication System

Type	Superlube

Tire Size

Front	3.25-19
Rear	4.88-18

MODEL F21M

Dimensions

Overall length	79.5 in.
Overall width	32.9 in.
Wheelbase	53.0 in.
Ground clearance	9.0 in.
Weight	215 lb.

Engine

Bore x stroke	70 x 62mm
Displacement	238cc
Horsepower/rpm	30.0/7,000

Transmission

Speeds	4

Ignition System

Type	Magneto

Lubrication System

Type	Gas/oil mixture

Tire Size

Front	3.50-19
Rear	4.00-18

MODEL F8

Dimensions

Overall length	82.0 in.
Overall width	32.3 in.
Wheelbase	55.0 in.
Ground clearance	8.3 in.
Weight	270 lb.

Engine

Bore x stroke	2.68 x 2.68
Displacement	246cc
Horsepower/rpm	23.5/6,800

Transmission

Speeds	5

Ignition System

Type	Magneto

Lubrication System

Type	Injectolube

Tire Size

Front	3.00 21
Rear	4.00-18

MODEL KT250

Dimensions

Overall length	79.3 in.
Overall width	32.9 in.
Wheelbase	51.4 in.
Ground clearance	12.2 in.
Weight	212 lb.

Engine

Bore x stroke	69.5 x 64.9mm
Displacement	246cc
Horsepower/rpm	16/6,500

Transmission

Speeds	5

Ignition System

Type	Magneto CDI

Lubrication System

Type	Superlube

Tire Size

Front	2.75-21
Rear	4.00-18

MODEL F81M

Dimensions

Overall length	83.0 in.
Overall width	35.0 in.
Wheelbase	55.0 in.
Ground clearance	9.0 in.
Weight	238 lb.

Engine

Bore x stroke	68 x 68mm
Displacement	247cc
Horsepower/rpm	27/6,750

Transmission

Speeds	5

Ignition System

Type	Magneto

Lubrication System

Type	Gas/oil mixture

Tire Size

Front	3.00-21
Rear	4.00-18

MODEL KX250

Dimensions

Overall length	83.0 in.
Overall width	34.5 in.
Wheelbase	55.8 in.
Ground clearance	7.7 in.
Weight	209 lb.

Engine

Bore x stroke	70. x 64.9mm
Displacement	249cc
Horsepower/rpm	34/8,000

Transmission

Speeds	5

Ignition System

Type	Magneto CDI

Lubrication System

Type	Gas/oil mixture

Tire Size

Front	3.00-21
Rear	4.60-18

9

MODEL F5

Dimensions

Overall length	82.0 in.
Overall width	32.3 in.
Wheelbase	55.0 in.
Ground clearance	9.0 in.
Weight	265 lb.

Engine

Bore x stroke	80.5 x 68.0mm
Displacement	346cc
Horsepower/rpm	33/6,500

Transmission

Speeds	5

Ignition System

Type	Magneto CDI

Lubrication System

Type	Injectolube

Tire Size

Front	3.00-21
Rear	4.00-18

MODEL F9

Dimensions

Overall length	82.0 in.
Overall width	32.3 in.
Wheelbase	55.0 in.
Ground clearance	9.0 in.
Weight	265 lb.

Engine

Bore x stroke	80.5 x 68.0mm
Displacement	346cc
Horsepower/rpm	33/6,500

Transmission

Speeds	5

Ignition System

Type	Magneto CDI

Lubrication System

Type	Injectolube

Tire Size

Front	3.00-21
Rear	4.00-18

MODEL KX400

Dimensions

Overall length	83.1 in.
Overall width	37.0 in.
Wheelbase	55.7 in.
Ground clearance	9.0 in.
Weight	234 lb.

Engine

Bore x stroke	82 x 76mm
Displacement	401cc
Horsepower/rpm	42/7,000

Transmission

Speeds	5

Ignition System

Type	Magneto CDI

Lubrication System

Type	Gas/oil mixture

Tire Size

Front	3.00-21
Rear	4.60-18

MODEL KX450

Dimensions

Overall length	81.0 in.
Overall width	34.4 in.
Wheelbase	55.5 in.
Ground clearance	7.7 in.
Weight	221 lb.

Engine

Bore x stroke	86 x 76mm
Displacement	441cc
Horsepower/rpm	38/5,500

Transmission

Speeds	5

Ignition System

Type	Magneto CDI

Lubrication System

Type	Gas/oil mixture

Tire Size

Front	3.00-21
Rear	4.60-18

INDEX

A

Air cleaner 18, 189
Axles 177

B

Battery 20, 109-111, 185
Brakes
    Adjustment 142
    Inspection 140-142
    Maintenance 22
    Performance improvement 175-177
    Troubleshooting 166
Breaker points 14

C

Cable, high voltage 104
Capacitor discharge ignition system 104-106
Carbon removal 12-14
Carburetor
    Components 130
    Description 112-114
    Disassembly, independent float
        carburetors 115-121
    Disassembly, twin float carburetors 121-126
    Float level adjustment 128
    Float mechanism 112-113
    Inspection 127-128
    Main fuel system 113-114
    Miscellaneous problems 130
    Overhaul intervals 114-115
    Performance tuning 187-189
    Pilot system 113
    Speed range adjustments 128-130
    Starter system 114
    Tune-up 19
Chain tensioner 179
Chrome restoration 173
Clutch
    Adjustment (Types 1 and 2) 51-52
    Adjustment (Type 3) 53
    Adjustment (Type 4) 53
    Adjustment (Type 5) 54-55
    Adjustment (Type 6) 55
    Adjustment, general 21
    Disassembly 46
    Inspection 46-51
    Installation 51
    Operation (Type 1) 40-41
    Operation (Types 2 and 3) 42
    Operation (Type 4) 42
    Operation (Type 5) 46
    Operation (Type 6) 46
    Performance improvement 184
    Release mechanism 42-46
    Release mechanism (Type 1) 42
    Slip or drag 165
Compression test 11-12
Condenser (models with magneto) 96-97
Connecting rods 190
Crankcase 62-65
Crankcase cover, left 34-35
Crankcase cover, right 36-40
Crankshaft
    Alignment 76-80
    Inspection 69-74
    Overhaul 75-76
    Runout 74
Cylinder/cylinder head ..30-32, 189-190, 191-192

D

Drain pump 91
Drive chain 22, 161-162

E

Electrical system
    Battery 109-111
    Capacitor discharge ignition system
        operation 104-106
    Flywheel magneto 93-96
    High voltage cable 104
    Horn 108-109
    Lights 108
    Magneto troubleshooting 96-97
    Main switch 109
    Rectifier 103
    Solid state voltage regulator 106-107
    Starter-generator 97-101
    Starter-generator troubleshooting 101-103
Electronic ignition 187
Engine
    Crankcase 62-65
    Crankcase cover, left 34-35
    Crankcase cover, right 36-40
    Crankshaft 69-80
    Cylinder and cylinder head 30-32
    Disassembly, preparation for 29
    Drain pump 91
    Engine sprocket 36
    Flywheel magneto and starter-generator ..35-36

10

Lubrication 26-28, 189
Piston, piston pin and piston rings 32-34
Piston port engines, basic principles 25-26
Removal 29-30
Rotary valve 55-57
Rotary valve engines, basic principles ...24-25
Exhaust system 159-161, 184

F

Fenders 154
Flywheel magneto
   Description 93-96
   Removal and installation 35
   Troubleshooting 96-97
Fork, front
   Description 142-143
   Oil change 22, 151
   Overhaul (early models) 145-148
   Overhaul (late models) 148-151
Frame
   Drive chain 161-162
   Exhaust pipe and muffler 159-161
   Fenders 154
   Front forks 142-151
   Fuel and oil tanks 156-158
   Handlebars 131-133
   Performance improvement 179
   Rear sprocket 156
   Seat 158
   Shock absorbers 153-154
   Stands and footrests 158-159
   Steering system 152-153
   Swinging arm 154-155
Fuel strainer 18
Fuel and oil mixture 26
Fuel and oil tanks 156-158

G

Gearing 178-179
Gearshift mechanism
   Description 57-59
   Installation 62
   Removal and inspection 59-61
General information 1-7
Generator (see Starter-generator)

H

Handlebars 131-133, 174
Headlights 108
High voltage cable 104
Horn 108-109
Hubs 135-136, 175-177

I

Idling, poor 165
Ignition coil (CDI models) 105-106, 185
Ignition coil (magneto models) 96, 185
Ignition coil (starter-generator
   models) 102-103, 185
Ignition system, performance tuning 184-187
Ignition timing
   Battery ignition models 16-18
   CDI models 18
   Magneto models 14-16
Injectolube system 27

K

Kickstarter
   Type 1 65-66
   Type 2 66-67
   Type 3 67-69
   Type 4 69
   Type 5 69

L

Lighting problems 166
Lights 108, 175
Lubrication system, engine 26-28, 189

M

Magneto, CDI 104
Magneto flywheel
   Description 93-96
   Removal and installation 35
   Troubleshooting 96-97
Main switch 109
Maintenance
   Air cleaner service 18
   Battery service 20
   Brakes 22
   Breaker points 14
   Carbon removal 12-14
   Carburetor adjustment 19
   Clutch adjustment 21
   Drive chain 22
   Electrical equipment 22
   Fork oil 22
   Fuel strainer 18
   Ignition timing (battery ignition) 16-18
   Ignition timing (CDI) 18
   Ignition timing (magneto models) 14-16
   Oil change 21
   Oil pump adjustment 19-20
   Schedule 8
   Spark plug 8-11
   Steering head bearings 22

Swinging arm 22
Wheels and tires 22
Mechanic's tips 4-6
Misfiring 165
Muffler 159-161

O

Oil and fuel mixture 26
Oil change 21
Oil pump 19-20, 27-28
Overheating 165

P

Painting 172
Performance improvement
Air cleaner 189
Axles 177
Chain tensioner 179
Clutch 184
Connecting rods 190
Cylinder 191-192
Cylinder head 189-190
Engine lubrication 189
Exhaust system 184
Frame 179
Fuel system 187-189
Gearing 178-179
General information 168-169
Ignition system 184-187
Lighting 175
Piston and rings 190-191
Restoration 169-173
Specifications 170-171
Steering and suspension, front 182-183
Suppliers 194-197
Suspension, rear 179-182
Transmission 183-184
Tubes and tires 177-178
Weight reduction 173-175
Wheels, brakes, and hubs 175-177
Piston, piston pin, and
piston rings 32-34, 165, 190-191
Primary drive gear 40

Q

Quick reference guide vii

R

Rectifier 103
Restoration 169-173
Rims 134
Rotary valve 55-57, 190
Rotary valve engines, basic operation 24-25

S

Safety hints 7
Seat 158, 174
Service hints 1, 4-6
Shock absorbers 153-154, 179-180
Shock cooler 181-182
Spark plug 8-11, 185-187
Springs 180-181, 182-183
Solid state voltage regulator 106-107
Specifications
B1L 203
B1L-A 203
B1M 204
C1D 203
C2SS 203
F2 205
F3 205
F4 206
F5 208
F6 204
F7 206
F8 207
F21M 206
F81M 207
F9 208
G1L 199
G1M 199
G3SS-A 199
G3TR 200
G4 201
G5 201
G31M-A 202
GA1 200
GA1-A 200
GA2 200
GA2-A 201
J1 199
KD125 204
KE100 202
KE125 204
KE175 206
KH100 202
KS125 205
KT250 207
KV100 202
KX125 205
KX250 207
KX400 208
KX450 208
MC1-A and MC1-M 201
Spokes 134-135
Sprocket, engine 36
Sprocket, rear 156
Stands and footrests 158-159
Starter-generator
Description 97-99
Removal and installation 35-36, 99-101
Troubleshooting 101-103

10

Starting difficulties 164
Steering system 152-153
Superlube system 26-27
Supplies, expendable 4
Suspension
   Performance improvement 179-183
   Shock absorbers 153-154
   Swinging arm 154-155
Swing arm 154-155, 182

T

Tire pressures 22
Tires 133-134, 177-178
Tools 1-4
Transmission
   Assembly 87-91
   Description 80
   Disassembly 80-84
   Inspection 84-87
   Performance improvement 183-184
Troubleshooting
   General information 163
   Operating difficulties 165-166
   Operating requirements 163-164
   Starting difficulties 164
   Troubleshooting guide 166-167
Tune-up
   Air cleaner service 18
   Battery service 20
   Breaker points 14
   Carbon removal 12-14
   Carburetor adjustment 19
   Compression test 11-12

Fuel strainer 18
Ignition timing (battery ignition) 16-18
Ignition timing (CDI) 18
Ignition timing (magneto models) 14-16
Oil pump adjustment 19-20
Spark plugs 8-11
Turn signals 108

U

Upholstery 173

V

Voltage regulator, solid state 106-107
Voltage regulator, starter-generator 98-99, 102-103

W

Weight reduction 173-175
Wheels
   Balance 135
   Bead protector 135
   Disassembly, inspection, and reassembly 139-140
   Hub, front 135
   Hub, rear 136
   Performance improvement 175-177
   Removal, front 136-138
   Removal, rear 138-139
   Rims 134
   Runout 140
   Spokes 134-135

MAINTENANCE LOG

DATE	TYPE OF SERVICE	COST	REMARKS

NOTES